Citizen Witnessing

Key Concepts in Journalism

Citizen Witnessing, Stuart Allan

Objectivity in Journalism, Steven Maras

Reinventing Professionalism, Silvio Waisbord

Citizen Witnessing

Revisioning Journalism in Times of Crisis

Stuart Allan

polity

First published in 2013 by Polity Press

Polity Press
65 Bridge Street
Cambridge CB2 1UR, UK

Polity Press
350 Main Street
Malden, MA 02148, USA

ISBN-13: 978-0-7456-5195-8
ISBN-13: 978-0-7456-5196-5(pb)

A catalogue record for this book is available from the British Library.

Typeset in 11 on 13 pt Sabon
by Servis Filmsetting Ltd, Stockport, Cheshire
Printed and bound in Great Britain by MPG Books Group

The publisher has used its best endeavours to ensure that the URLs for external websites referred to in this book are correct and active at the time of going to press. However, the publisher has no responsibility for the websites and can make no guarantee that a site will remain live or that the content is or will remain appropriate.

Every effort has been made to trace all copyright holders, but if any have been inadvertently overlooked the publisher will be pleased to include any necessary credits in any subsequent reprint or edition.

For further information on Polity, visit our website: www.politybooks.com

Contents

Acknowledgements

With the benefit of hindsight, I realise that my initial thoughts about citizen witnessing first began to take shape when preparing a chapter for an edited collection I was putting together with Barbie Zelizer at the time, *Journalism After September 11*. Our difficulty in finding someone willing and able to research and write a chapter about the online news coverage of that day's atrocities – rather few journalism scholars being focused on the internet in 2001 – meant that I ended up volunteering to try to meet the challenge myself. In the course of examining how major news sites responded to the crisis, I found myself equally intrigued by the extraordinary reportorial contributions made by ordinary citizens. Variously described as 'amateur newsies', 'instant reporters' or 'personal journalists' and the like, their first-hand, eyewitness accounts, photographs and video footage provided early evidence that a profoundly important transition was underway. Not only was journalism on the internet rapidly transfiguring into journalism of the internet, longstanding principles of news reporting – and with them familiar assumptions about who was entitled to bear witness to tragic events – were being redefined with startling implications for the brave new world of digital media.

Over the years since, my research on citizen contributions to online news slowly began to coalesce into the mode of enquiry pursued on these pages, helped along the way by many kind people. I am especially grateful to my colleagues in the Media School at Bournemouth University (a special thank-you to members of the

Acknowledgements

Centre for Journalism and Communication Research, particularly Einar Thorsen for his eleventh-hour reading of a penultimate draft), as well as to our students – their lively engagements with this book's ideas have improved them considerably. It has also been my good fortune to be a visiting professor at several universities during this period, enabling me to try out new arguments and to benefit from invigorating debate. My sincere thanks to Christine Daymon and Nigel de Bussy at Curtin University, Karin Becker at Stockholm University, Kerstin Engström at Umeå University, and Jacqui Ewart at Griffith University for their warm hospitality. I am pleased to acknowledge the support of the Arts and Humanities Research Council (UK) and the Swedish Research Council for related projects, respectively. At Polity, Andrea Drugan and her colleagues have been superb, and I am also indebted to the anonymous reviewers of both the initial book proposal and the first draft of the manuscript for their perceptive comments. Leigh Mueller's copy-editing was exemplary. And, finally, last to be acknowledged, but first in heartfelt appreciation, Cindy and Geoff.

1

'Accidental Journalism'

What does it mean to bear witness in a moment of crisis? Most journalists have been formally trained to be dispassionately impartial when documenting what they see and hear under such circumstances, recognising as they do that the truth-value of their chosen rendering of facts will be at stake. For the ordinary individual, however, any sense of journalism is likely to be far from their mind, should they find themselves unexpectedly caught-up in disturbing events rapidly unfolding around them. Nevertheless, they may well strive to engage in a form of eyewitness reportage, perhaps using their mobile telephone to capture an image, generate a video, or craft a tweet in order to record and share their personal experience of what is happening in front of them. Such spontaneous, spur-of-the-moment responses, so often motivated by a desire to connect with others, go to the heart of current debates about citizen journalism, one of the most challenging issues confronting the news media today. To help set the scene for this book's discussion, and thereby highlight several themes to be explored, we first turn to a rather intriguing example of what will be characterised as 'citizen witnessing' for our purposes on the pages ahead.

The arrival of a low-flying helicopter above Sohaib Athar's quiet suburban neighbourhood in a small town in northern Pakistan was unusual, not least because it was the middle of the night. Unusual enough to warrant a tweet, in any case, so he promptly reported 'Helicopter hovering above Abbottabad at 1AM (is a rare event)' on Twitter. Self-described on his @ReallyVirtual account as an 'IT consultant taking a break from the rat-race by hiding in the mountains with his laptops', Athar typically tweeted about his daily concerns, ranging from his family to views on technology, politics and coffee (he and his wife manage a café) in the hope that his musings would be appreciated by his 750 or so followers. On this occasion, though, he decided to share his growing irritation with the helicopter's noisy intrusion when to his astonishment a sudden explosion cut through the night. 'A huge window shaking bang here in Abbottabad Cantt. I hope its not the start of something nasty :-S', he tweeted. Before he knew it, he began processing further points of information rapidly emerging from his online network of friends in the local community.

In the tweets that followed, Athar relayed assertions – gathered primarily from friends on Facebook – that more than one helicopter was involved, they appeared to be non-Pakistani, the explosion sounded like one of them being 'shot down near the Bilal Town area' (a link to a Facebook map pinpointed the area), and a 'gunfight' had erupted that 'lasted perhaps 4–5 minutes'. Whether fact or rumour, he could not be certain. 'Report from a taxi driver: The army has cordoned off the crash area and is conducting door-to-door search in the surrounding[s]', he added, followed soon after by 'Report from a sweeper: A family also died in the crash, and one of the helicopter riders got away and is now being searched for.' Little did Athar know at the time that his efforts to offer a first-hand description of what he aptly termed in one tweet a 'complicated situation' would reverberate around the planet in the hours to come.

Elsewhere on Twitter, rumours were swirling about an impromptu White House press conference being organised, with much of the conjecture revolving around the possibility that Libyan leader Muammar Qaddafi had been captured or killed. Official confirmation that a televised statement was being prepared appeared at 9.45 p.m. when White House Communications Director Dan Pfeiffer tweeted 'POTUS to address the nation tonight at 10.30pm eastern time' (POTUS being President of the United States, Barack Obama) on Sunday, 1 May 2011. Speculation regarding possible reasons for an announcement intensified even further before Keith

Urbahn, a former political aide to ex-Defense Secretary Donald Rumsfeld, passed along a tip at 10:25 pm from an inside source, stating: 'So I'm told by a reputable person they have killed Osama Bin Laden. Hot damn.' Urbahn promptly cautioned against getting ahead of the facts, tweeting: 'Don't know if its true, but let's pray it is' and 'Ladies, gents, let's wait to see what the President says. Could be misinformation or pure rumor.' Evidently, within minutes, anonymous sources at the Pentagon and the White House began contacting major news organisations with the same information, leading the ABC, CBS and NBC television networks to interrupt their programming with the news (Stelter, 2011). When, at 11.35 p.m., more than an hour after Urbahn's unconfirmed tweet, Obama addressed his television audience, he announced 'justice has been done' in response to Osama bin Laden's responsibility for orchestrating the vicious attack of September 11, 2001. 'The death of Bin Laden marks the most significant achievement to date in our nation's effort to defeat Al Qaeda . . .', he stated; 'So his demise should be welcomed by all who believe in peace and human dignity' (Obama, 2011).

While media commentaries focused on assessing the wider implications of the US intervention for national security, questions lingered regarding how the news had come to light in the first place. Proving particularly contentious, in the eyes of some, was whether Twitter's role signalled a victory for social media networking over established media where covering breaking news was concerned. Amongst those heralding the microblogging service's 'scoop' were those enthusing about how it was transforming into the preferred medium for 'people in the know' to bypass traditional channels altogether. Others, closely scrutinising how the process proceeded so swiftly, emphasised the converging factors involved. 'Keith Urbahn wasn't the first to speculate Bin Laden's death, but he was the one who gained the most trust from the network', computer analyst Gilad Lotan (2011) pointed out; 'And with that, the perfect situation unfolded, where timing, the right social-professional networked audience, along with a critically relevant piece of information led to an explosion of public affirmation of his trustworthiness.' Here it seems likely that Urbahn's preceived credibility was due to the presumption that Rumsfeld had supplied the information in the first place, when in actuality Urbahn had been called by a 'connected network TV news producer' (as described in a later tweet) hoping to gain his insight into Rumsfeld's reaction to the raid's outcome.

Interestingly, where Sohaib Athar was concerned, he readily acknowledged that several hours had passed before he realised – courtesy of a tweet making the connection – that he had been documenting aspects of the US military's top-secret strike some 250 yards from where he lived. 'Uh oh, now I'm the guy who live-blogged the Osama raid without knowing it', he tweeted. Deluged by requests from journalists for an interview, he was modest about his achievements: 'I am JUST a tweeter, awake at the time of the crash. Not many twitter users in Abbottabad, these guys are more into facebook. That's all.'

Twitter's 'CNN moment'

Others weighing into the debate over the journalistic role of social media made a much stronger argument for its importance. 'Twitter just had its CNN moment', Matt Rosoff (2011) of *Business Insider* boldly declared in the immediate aftermath.

> Remember CNN when the Gulf War started in 1990? Before then, it was watched mostly by obsessive news followers – people in finance and government, political science professors, insomniacs. Then Saddam Hussein invaded Kuwait and suddenly CNN was everywhere. Even in bars.
>
> That's what's going to happen with Twitter after tonight's announcement that U.S. Special Forces killed Osama Bin Laden in Abbottabad, a Pakistani city about two hours from the capital Islamabad. (Rasoff, 2011)

In crediting Twitter with being 'faster, more accurate, and more entertaining than any other news source out there', Rosoff underlined how a perceived virtue in speed was redefining news priorities. Steve Myers (2011b) of The Poynter Institute appeared to concur to some extent, especially in light of how the number of Athar's followers leapt from 750 to 86,000 within twenty-four hours. This suggested to him that the reason this unwitting 'ear witness' to bin Laden's death became so influential so quickly was Twitter's capacity to facilitate bridging networks, in this instance between those with Pakistani connections, on the one hand, and those with media connections, on the other. The emergent chain of information – consisting of overlapping social circles of like-minded tweeters sharing their thoughts and observations – served to turn 'one man's offhand comments about a helicopter in the middle of the night into an internationally known work of citizen journalism', in Myers's opinion.

Writing for *SF Weekly*'s blog, Dan Mitchell (2011) begged to differ. While conceding that Athar's real-time tweets about the events may have temporarily made him a journalist 'in a small way', there was little evidence that his efforts actually mattered. 'Wondering on Twitter why there are helicopters flying around your neighborhood isn't journalism', he argued; 'The world learned that bin Laden had been assassinated after the U.S. government told several big news organizations that that would be the subject of Obama's forthcoming announcement' (Mitchell, 2011). Twitter's value is in its role as a real-time headline service, in his view, with little prospect that its use will lead to the demise of traditional news media anytime soon. Myers (2011c), writing in response to Mitchell's scepticism, stressed that Athar was a citizen journalist 'because when he came across an unusual event, he acted in a journalistic manner'. More specifically, he pointed out that not only did Athar tell others about the event concerned, he answered questions from others seeking further details, acted as a conduit for information as he gathered it, identified whether claims were rumour or linked to sources ('taxi driver', 'sweeper' and so forth), shared links to accounts from local news sources, contributed to collective efforts to determine precisely what was occurring, and offered his own analysis. 'Any one of these activities may simply amount to conversation among friends', Myers maintained; 'Taken together, it looks like journalism.' Moreover, in the days following the raid, Athar used Twitter as a 'distribution network' to post photographs of the compound, near-empty Abbottabad streets (traffic having been shut down), and the media arriving on the scene to cover the story. All aspects considered, 'Athar added to the body of knowledge. We know more about the raid, and about how people share information, because of him. That's a good thing', Myers concluded.

More than a passing dispute over semantics, then, thorny questions begin to emerge over the relative status to be granted to 'accidental journalism', as some perceive it, or the ad hoc sharing of impressions, opinions and observations of nominal significance, which others would insist citizen involvement in newsmaking recurrently represents. Still others would contend that it is a blending of the two that typically produces such remarkable forms of coverage, with those who played a pivotal part in bringing Athar's real-time dispatches to the attention of major news organisations being a case in point.

Chris Applegate (2011), self-described on his personal blog as a 'geek and wannabe polymath', was widely credited with making the connection between Athar's tweets about the helicopter above his neighbourhood and the bin Laden raid. As he later explained on his blog, Maha Rafi Atal, his journalist girlfriend, had shown him a retweet about a 'low-flying heli' in Abbottabad, which made him wonder whether anyone in Pakistan had been covering the raid as it unfolded. Using Google Realtime, he searched for tweets with the word 'Abbottabad' appearing prior to Obama's speech, almost instantly discovering Athar's reports. He promptly tweeted to his own followers: 'Wow. Turns out at least one person, @ReallyVirtual, inadvertently liveblogged the raid in Abbottabad earlier today http://bit.ly/IU5b4s', thereby playing a decisive part in breaking this dimension of the story for the world's media.

In Applegate's view, the 'whole episode shows how transformative Twitter can be', enabling someone like Athar to assume 'the role of citizen journalist, becoming a correspondent of sorts' as the news story developed:

The key thing that made Sohaib's liveblogging from earlier in the day so compelling was that it was completely unwitting, mirroring our own disbelief that Bin Laden had been quietly residing in the Pakistani equivalent of Tunbridge Wells all these years, without any of us knowing. The story chimed perfectly with our own emotions. And because the story had been unwitting, it was also candid and honest, cutting through the hype and speculation that the 24-hour news stations were resorting to. (Applegate 2011)

Self-effacingly describing himself as 'one small factor that sparked the process off', Applegate also expressed his admiration for how Athar proceeded to engage in diverse forms of journalistic activity – conducting interviews, taking photographs, reporting on the mood in the town – as 'the story matured and his fame rose'. Athar's efforts, in his view, were 'a far cry from the cynical caricature of Twitter as an echo chamber – a place where nothing new is said and everything is relentlessly retweeted' (Applegate 2011).

Interestingly, Maha Rafi Atal (2011), a New York-based freelance journalist and Forbes blogger, responded to her boyfriend Applegate's blog post. After adding a few further details about how she came to share with him the tweet that piqued his curiosity to investigate (crucial here, she points out, was how she happens to 'sit at the intersection of two networks: the network of people who follow news on Pakistan, and the network of American journalists, media critics and wonks'), she offered her own views about Athar's status as a citizen journalist. In her words:

At least for me, the power of Athar's story was as a reminder that 'war zones' are also people's homes. It brought to life the mundane details of daily life, and the poignant struggle of trying to live daily life – in Athar's case, just to have a quiet work night – in one of the most dangerous and maddening countries on earth. As Athar told me when I interviewed him for Forbes, he moved to Abbottabad a few years ago from Lahore precisely to shield his family from the violence then engulfing the city.

She continued:

What we saw in his tweets was a man who had run from the madness only to have it running after him. What we witnessed was the moment he realized it had caught up with him. That tension between what people really care about in Pakistan and the violence that prevents them from moving on with their lives, the bitter irony of life there, is something I've written on often. Yet no matter how much reporting I do, it doesn't cease to affect me emotionally. And when, after the news about bin Laden had broken, Athar realized what had happened, and began to receive an avalanche of requests from journalists, he tweeted, 'Bin Laden is dead. I didn't kill him. Please let me sleep now.' For me, that's an absolute punch to the gut. (Atal 2011)

Like Applegate, she proceeded to express her appreciation for the way Athar took on the role of citizen journalist under such trying circumstances. 'I think this is very much the ideal of how social media and citizen journalism is meant to work', she wrote; 'Not everyone can grow into their new status as a one-person-broadcast-network with such speed and grace, which is why I'm so often skeptical of how it will evolve as a model, but Athar's transformation is nothing short of a triumph' (Atal 2011).

First-person reportage

In seeking to investigate the ways in which ordinary people find themselves compelled to engage in first-person reportage, the case study above usefully illuminates a number of issues warranting close and careful elucidation. To describe those involved as 'citizen journalists' may be advantageous in certain circumstances, in part by acknowledging that their actions are recognisable as journalistic activity, but such a label brings with it certain heuristic difficulties too. As we shall see, discourses of 'citizen journalism' reveal an array of virtues in the opinion of advocates striving to transform journalism by improving its civic contribution to public life – and conceal a multitude of sins in the eyes of critics intent on preserving what they perceive to be the integrity of professional practice – in complex, occasionally contradictory ways. This book's engagement with one of its organising tenets, namely the imperative of witnessing, is intended as an intervention which is alert to the sharp pull of contrary claims and counter-claims.

Citizen journalism, for our purposes here, may be characterised as a type of first-person reportage in which ordinary individuals temporarily adopt the role of a journalist in order to participate in newsmaking, often spontaneously during a time of crisis, accident, tragedy or disaster when they happen to be present on the scene. Seen by some as an outgrowth of earlier forms of public or civic journalism, the term 'citizen journalism' gained currency in the immediate aftermath of the South Asian tsunami of December 2004, when news organisations found themselves in the awkward position of being largely dependent on 'amateur' reportage to tell the story of what had transpired on the ground. Despite its ambiguities, it was widely perceived to capture something of the countervailing ethos of the ordinary person's capacity to bear witness, thereby providing commentators with a useful label to characterise an ostensibly new genre of reporting.

In the years since the tsunami, 'citizen journalism' has secured its place in the news professional's vocabulary (for better or otherwise in the view of many news organisations), more often than not associated with relaying breaking news of significant events. It includes the provision of such diverse contributions as first-person eyewitness accounts, audio recordings, video footage, mobile or cell phone and digital camera photographs, and the like, typically shared online via email or through bulletin-boards, blogs, wikis, personal webpages and social networking sites. Described variously as 'user-generated content' as well as 'grassroots journalism', 'open source journalism', 'participatory journalism', 'hyperlocal journalism', 'distributed journalism' or 'networked journalism', amongst further alternatives, there is little doubt that it is decisively realigning traditional news reporting's communicative priorities and protocols, sometimes in profound ways.

More often than not, efforts to formulate a productive line of enquiry appeal to a discourse of witnessing – in which terms such as 'eyewitness', 'watcher', 'observer', 'bystander', 'onlooker', 'spectator' and the like, tend to figure – to characterise citizens' capacity to participate in newsmaking by sharing what they have seen, felt or heard at the scene. The intrinsic value of 'being there', on the ground, has been prized since the earliest days of crisis journalism. Viewed from the perspective of the news media, the capacity of the professional journalist to serve as a trust-worthy, reliable witness in the heat of the moment – and also, crucially, to negotiate the terms delimiting the eyewitnessing of others – underpins the discursive legitimacy of first-hand report-ing, for those who are there, as well as for those at a distance (for whom the ensuing coverage is likely to shape perceptions, possibly in a decisive manner). This is a formidable challenge, not least because eyewitnessing is as conditional as it is provisional, and, as such, fraught with difficulties. The authority of pres-ence, a situational imbrication of 'here and now', is a precarious achievement, one always at risk of coming unravelled, such are the tensions besetting human understanding, interpretation and memory. Somewhat paradoxically, however, it is this invocation of eyewitness subjectivity that throws into crisp relief the codified strictures of journalistic impartiality. The proclaimed capacity of the journalistic gaze to be impersonal, detached and dispassion-ate in its purview is a tacit, yet telling, feature of the professional ethos.

Bearing witness

Time and again, examples of reportage emerge across the media-scape that put paid to easy, ready-made distinctions between professional objectivity and amateur subjectivity. The current humanitarian emergency in Syria is a case in point, albeit for har-rowing reasons. News accounts with headlines such as 'Journalist witnesses Syrian authorities torturing activists' offer first-hand perspectives on what it means to put one's life at risk to cover a story. Arrested in a Damascus café whilst working undercover for Channel 4 News, Sean McAllister was blindfolded and driven to a prison where he was held against his will.

> I was placed on a seat in an empty room on my own. Outside I could hear beatings in a neighbouring room. People being slapped and wailing painfully as they were being whacked. . . .

If they are not satisfied with the info, you would be brought out at three in the morning into the torture chamber and whipped with the cable [. . .] It was so heavy, so awful, it must have broken bones and the howling, the noise of a human being hit with that is something that just, you know, you shiver and shake. You hear a sound that you've never heard before, I've never heard before. And I've seen people dead. And I've seen people dying. And I've seen people decapitated, but this sound, hearing a man cry, is just like, awful, there's nothing to compare it with. (cited in Channel 4 News, 2011b)

McAllister, to his credit, reveals himself to be a vulnerable human being, rather than reasserting the pretence of being a dispassionate relayer of cold, hard facts with robot-like precision. 'My biggest trauma, nightmare', he added, 'was looking at how they were treating their own people and imagining that that could be my future down there in a dark cell, indefinitely, without any idea of when you're going to be released.'

This type of first-person testimony provides the reader with distressing insights, the emotive affectivity of which being difficult, if not impossible, to convey within the time-worn conventions of scrupulously objective reporting. Journalists, when asked, will acknowledge the dangers, but typically insist that they have an obligation to bear witness, to be their audience's eyes and ears in situations where individuals less determined to seek out the truth would do well to avoid.[1] Witnessing, few would dispute, is the lynchpin of good reporting. If journalists behave most of the time like 'insatiable voyeurs', to borrow a phrase from Roger Cohen (2009b) of the *New York Times*, this is not to diminish what is a defining characteristic. 'In the 24/7 howl of partisan pontification, and the scarcely less-constant death knell din surrounding the press', he contends, 'a basic truth gets lost: that to be a journalist is to bear witness.' The rest, he adds, 'is no more than ornamentation'.

Foreign correspondent Marie Colvin's reputation for bearing witness in the world's trouble-spots earned her considerable respect amongst fellow journalists. Instantly recognisable because of the black eye patch she wore, having lost her left eye to grenade shrapnel in the Sri Lankan civil war, she was in Syria for the *Sunday Times* in February 2012. In what proved to be her final words, she wrote on a private Facebook page for journalists: 'In Baba Amr. Sickening, cannot understand how the world can stand by and I should be hardened by now. Watched a baby die today. Shrapnel, doctors could do nothing. His little tummy just heaved and heaved until he stopped. Feeling helpless. As well as cold! Will keep trying to get out the information.'

Colvin was killed alongside French photojournalist Remi Ochlik when a rocket hit the house in which they had taken refuge during an onslaught of shelling targeting civilians in Baba Amr, a suburban neighbourhood of Homs. She had been the only journalist from a British newspaper in the besieged city, having surreptitiously slipped over the border from Lebanon on a smuggler's route used to transport food and medical supplies, such was her determination to document the unfolding crisis. 'Covering a war means going to places torn by chaos, destruction and death . . . and trying to bear witness', she had said during a memorial service two years earlier; 'It means trying to find the truth in a sandstorm of propaganda when armies, tribes or terrorists clash. [. . .] Our mission is to report these horrors of war with accuracy and without prejudice' (Colvin, 2010).

In the ensuing news coverage of Colvin's death, references to the importance of bearing witness featured prominently, as signalled in the following headlines:

Marie Colvin: Foreign Correspondent Lauded for Her Courage as She Bore Witness to Wars Across the World (*The Guardian*, 23 February 2012)

Recalling a Journalist Who Died Bearing Witness to a Siege (*The New York Times*, 23 February 2012)

Colvin's Death Highlights Risk of Bearing Witness to War (*The Globe and Mail*, Canada, 24 February 2012)

The Death of a Witness (*Sydney Morning Herald*, 24 February 2012)

Evidence continues to mount that Colvin, Ochlik and the other journalists in the same building, which had been serving as a makeshift press centre, were deliberately targeted by President Bashar al-Assad's regime (Nicolas Sarkozy, the then French President, contended they were 'assassinated' in the attack) to prevent their reporting of the atrocities perpetrated on civilians. 'They are killing with impunity . . . I should stay and write what I can to expose what is happening here', Colvin had written in an email sent three days before she was killed, all too aware her life was in peril. 'Nothing seemed to deter her', John Witherow (2012), Editor of the *Sunday Times*, observed in a note circulated to colleagues informing them of her death, while Anthony Loyd (2012) of *The Times* described her as 'the foremost champion among us, a woman who was the embodiment of all that was brave and wise and good in journalism'.[2]

Possible truths

The journalist as 'people's witness', steadfastly committed to eye-witness fidelity to what he or she saw and heard, will not waver when 'bearing witness of human actuality to those who could not actually be there' (Inglis, 2002: 3). Philosophical nuances notwithstanding, principles of truth, fact and verification have long served as news reporting's guiding tenets. In highlighting the centrality of witnessing, however, it is vital not to overlook the degree of scepticism journalists routinely put into effect when processing truth-claims. Experience tells them individuals on the scene, despite their best intentions, may be offering a less than accurate recollection of what they have seen or heard. Under duress, memories can be faulty, lines of vision obscured, the significance of events misinterpreted. Ensuing testimonies may be unconsciously compromised to the point that they are of little journalistic value or, even worse, become inadvertently misleading. When truth-claims otherwise seem dependable, wary journalists nonetheless strive to double-check their veracity, mindful that there are occasions when individuals have much to gain by deliberately falsifying statements. The skills necessary to sift through eyewitness assertions to determine relative trustworthiness are a source of pride, hard-won in the face of constant pressure to ensure a news story will not come unravelled should declared facts become the subject of dispute.

Journalists utilise a number of tactics to narrativise truth-claims so as to protect their reputation, or at least minimise possible risks to their proclaimed reportorial integrity. Quotation marks around an individual's words, for example, serve as an accustomed cue or prompt to the reader that the evidential basis for a truth-claim resides with the individual cited as proffering it – in contrast with a statement that has been paraphrased. Implicitly, their use in the news account represents a distancing device, enabling journalists to differentiate their authorial voice from the speech of the source, should the words of the latter eventually prove unreliable. As such, it amounts to one of several pragmatic (even defensive) strategies codified within the strictures of impartial reporting, an epistemological anchoring of facticity that journalism shares with other genres of discourse – in particular legal discourse – where standards of verification in witness testimony feature prominently.[3] Journalism's respect for tacit rules when processing contingent evidence (including the presumed truth of imagery) ordinarily becomes visible only when they have been violated; that is to say, when witnesses are revealed to be lying, grinding an axe or spinning the apparent facts in a particular way to advance their own agenda.

More typically, the inscription of witnessing in news reporting is much more subtle, effectively blurring the journalist's capacity in this regard with that of the sources he or she has selected to give it expression. Witnessing necessarily involves a complex process of mediation, despite rhetorical claims about 'facts speaking for themselves' in journalistic parlance. Indeed, Barbie Zelizer (2007) suggests that the most salient feature of eyewitnessing – namely, 'its ability to convince publics of the distant experience or event in a seemingly unmediated style' – goes to the heart of its centrality to newsgathering (2007: 424). In tracking the evolution of 'eyewitnessing' as a keyword of journalistic practice in the US, she helpfully discerns four stages in its development as a means to validate certain preferred norms in the accounting of reality collectively recognised by members of the journalistic community to be appropriate (see also Zelizer, 2002b, 2010). In the first period, broadly aligned with journalism emerging as a recognisable craft centuries ago, the idea of the eyewitness report appears as a means to express personal experience of public events, Zelizer maintains. Typically, such reports were furnished by 'nonjournalistic individuals', whose personal accounts tended to emphasise 'romanticized, overtly subjective and stylistically elaborate features' in keeping with the highly emotive – and rather colourful – tenor of most chronicles of the time. The second period, underway by the mid-1800s, signals the expansion of this role to include a more diverse array of participants, not least journalists themselves, self-consciously acting as eyewitnesses. The style of their reports, Zelizer argues, 'became more concrete and reality-driven' – that is, more reliable in their rendering of facts in response to public scepticism about their trustworthiness.

Eyewitnessing's closer association with realism was not without its problems, but increasingly it was being regarded as connoting the mark of authenticity as a value in its own right – news photography, in particular, offering 'an alternative way of claiming eyewitness status that offset the limitations of verbal narratives' (2007: 417). The expansion of technology in the early twentieth century characterises a third period, when alternative kinds of eyewitnessing are made possible to lend credibility and authenticity to a report's assertions by virtue of the journalist's enhanced capacity to represent on-site presence. By the end of the Second World War, Zelizer maintains, 'eyewitnessing had become a default setting for good reportage', with news organisations speaking of it 'as if it had almost a mythic status' (2007: 421). And, fourthly, the contemporary period is discernible on the basis of the journalist's absence, that is, his or her frequent replacement by technological conveyance (where forms of 'unmanned' live coverage have 'moved style, subjectivity and person from eyewitnessing, leaving it seemingly unedited and disembodied'), on the one hand, or by the private citizen acting as a 'nonconventional' journalist performing the work of eyewitnessing, on the other. Concerns about issues such as reliability, accuracy, verifiability, even excessive graphicness, are not being adequately offset, in turn, by journalistic mitigation, including contextualisation, the way they were before. To the extent eyewitnessing is being 'outsourced', Zelizer fears, it risks undermining journalism's cultural authority in public life.

While there is little doubt each of these periods would reward closer critique, here they usefully accentuate the importance of attending to the evolving, socially contingent nature of the imperatives underwriting witnessing in a manner sensitive to historical specificities. Delving into these matters it soon becomes apparent that questions regarding precisely what this process of witnessing entails, especially where online journalism is concerned, invite a reconsideration of the conceptual vocabulary typically brought to bear in discussions of news reportage and its perceived influence on the perceptions of distant readers, listeners and viewers. This, in a nutshell, is our principal task at hand.

'A walking eye on the world'

To question the conception of citizenship implied in citizen witnessing is to invite a lively debate. A host of contending perspectives are likely to surface regarding how familiar notions of personal rights and duties are being recast in everyday contexts, particularly in light of what are increasingly interconnected, interdependent relations of communicative power indicative of what Manuel Castells (2009) terms the 'global network society' (see chapter 5). Rather tellingly, the news media typically elude sustained attention in otherwise relevant conceptual models, at least beyond the general recognition that the role they play in shaping how their audiences collectively recognise and respond to distant crisis events – such as accidents, disasters, conflicts or wars – warrants greater attention than it has typically received to date. Journalism's relationship to citizenship, its capacity to foster, enrich and nurture meaningful civic engagement interweaving the local and the global, seldom comes to the fore.

That said, however, popular discourses about journalism within democratic cultures recurrently throw longstanding concerns about this relationship into sharp relief. Journalists may find themselves blamed for failing to promote citizenship in the interest of furthering societal objectives, even though few of them would likely regard it as their responsibility to perform this obligation in the first place. Related criticisms holding them culpable for perpetuating a democratic deficit, whereby passive, acquiescent citizens are discouraged from taking an active interest in their own governance, will be similarly dismissed as unreasonable. Journalists tend to be uncomfortable with the idea that they should be educating audiences, preferring instead to focus on informational relay in accordance with professional norms of impartiality, fairness and balance.

Still, when set in relation to the larger political economy of the crises confronting news organisations struggling to re-profile their news provision in order to survive, let alone prosper, in a digital era, these criticisms become all the more acute. At a time when many newsrooms are under intense financial pressure to trim expenditure wherever possible, it is all too often the case that public service values are reframed on more modest terms where civic commitments are concerned. The investment vital for investigative journalism, in particular, is a luxury difficult to justify in the eyes of some managers coping with seemingly inexorable market pressures, especially when certain other types of news will be more 'cost-effective' to produce, and more likely to catch the public's wandering eye (and that of potential advertisers). As a result, the very integrity of news reporting charged with advancing citizenship in the public interest risks being compromised, many fear, when the necessary time and resources are in such short supply in so many newsrooms.

Discussions of journalism's civic commitments need to be situated within this larger political-economic context. High-quality news reporting is, in a word, expensive, leaving some news organisations buckling under the strain of supporting it. Some are collapsing altogether, while others are subjecting their employees to 'reorganisation', 'downsizing', 'layoffs', 'cutbacks' and the like. News and editorial posts are often being 'concentrated', with remaining staff members compelled to 'multi-task' as they adopt greater 'flexibility' with regard to their salary and working conditions. 'Converged' content is being 'repackaged', a polite way of saying that its quantity – and, too often, quality – is shrinking as 'efficiencies' are imposed (Allan, 2012b; Boczkowski, 2010; Bruns, 2005; Domingo and Paterson, 2011; Fenton, 2010; Friend and Singer, 2007; McChesney and Pickard, 2011; McNair, 2011; Meikle and Redden, 2011). Conventional journalist-source dynamics are similarly reforming, in part due to stop-gap measures taken to blunt the sharper edges of cutbacks where employment in the newsroom is concerned. These measures have led to the increasing reliance on PR press releases in the guise of news (aptly described by Davies (2008) as 'churnalism'), as well as to ever greater emphasis placed on the contributions to newsmaking offered by members of the public. The appropriation of the latter, typically characterised as 'user-generated content' in firm denial of its journalistic qualities, has become so systemised into bureaucratic protocols that it is an almost routine feature of newsgathering. Despite persistent difficulties with verification and authentication, processing this material is relatively affordable, and its appeal for audiences is readily apparent – factors that make it all but irresistible in the eyes of those otherwise defining the scope of their news provision on the basis of bottom-line profit maximisation.

And yet, these strategies of containment – ensuring 'the audience' knows its place and acts accordingly – consistently fail to hold fast. Diverse forms of public participation in newsmaking are flourishing as never before, neatly sidestepping the mainstream media's professional gatekeepers striving to mediate or, more to the point, regulate and monetise their contributions within preferred institutional boundaries. Pessimistic appraisals of the decline, if not outright death, of inquisitive, vigorous news reporting worthy of the name are being readily countered by bold assertions about the promise of citizen-centred reporting to usher in grassroots alternatives. Such 'random acts of journalism' (Lasica, 2003) performed by 'people formerly known as the audience' (Rosen, 2006) underscore a transformative shift journalists acknowledge yet remain reluctant to fully embrace: citizens are doing it for themselves.

'Armed with cellphones, BlackBerries or iPhones', Don Peat (2010) of the *Toronto Sun* observes, 'the average Joe is now a walking eye on the world, a citizen journalist, able to take a photo, add a caption or a short story and upload it to the Internet for all their friends, and usually everyone else, to see.' Noteworthy here is the phrase 'a walking eye on the world' for its conception of witnessing as everyday observation, as well as the emphasis placed on the compulsion to share within a social network of like-minded individuals simultaneously open to the wider webscape. Still, the relationship of equivalence posited between the ordinary citizen engaged in bearing witness ('the average Joe' or Jill 'armed' with a mobile telephone to keep an 'eye on the world') and the 'citizen journalist' is problematic. More than a question of semantics, the person inclined to self-identify as someone engaging in a journalistic role – perhaps an independent blogger, photographer or videographer – is likely to differentiate themselves from those who just happen to be nearby when a potentially newsworthy incident happens.

Having the presence of mind to raise a camera-equipped mobile to capture the scene, for example, may well be a laudable achievement under the circumstances, but this represents a different level of engagement. 'Let's face it, most of the people who capture this imagery have jobs to work, errands to run, houses to maintain and families to take care of', crowdsourcing analyst Eric Taubert (2012) maintains. 'If asked, they don't consider themselves citizen journalists', he adds, although they will often welcome the opportunity to have their imagery shared with a wider audience. 'Great content captured by smartphone-wielding citizens can die on the vine without ever being seen', he adds, 'unless that content finds its way into the hands of journalists who know how to wrap a story around it, fact-check it and place it into the distribution chain.' In other words, unless the citizen in question is prepared to assume this responsibility for themselves – which, admittedly is getting easier to do by the day via digital media – they will likely turn to a news organisation to perform it on their behalf.

Accordingly, in formulating an approach to help clarify the relative degree of personal investment in citizen journalism, our attention will focus on the varying levels or registers of witnessing at its heart. In attending to the nuances of these gradations, we shall resist the temptation – in Taubert's (2012) words – to throw the term 'citizen journalism' on 'the trash heap of inflammatory archaic jargon' in favour of narrowing its definitional remit to advantage. Here I hasten to acknowledge from the outset, however, the impracticalities associated with attempts to generate a singular, unifying framework. The desire to secure a general theory may be understandable, but is rather unlikely to produce insights of lasting value. Theory-building benefits from proceeding with a more modest set of objectives, I would suggest, in the first instance by examining ostensibly obvious, taken-for-granted features of the terrain with a view to identifying and critiquing incipient points of tension, gaps and inconsistencies. Whether such fault-lines portend to fracture the foundations of boundaries between professional and citizen witnessing or, alternatively, to realign them on more sustainable terms is a question that will guide our mode of enquiry.

This book

My choice of title, *Citizen witnessing: revisioning journalism in times of crisis*, underscores the stakes for this project as a real-world intervention. In striving to introduce and elaborate 'citizen witnessing' as a key concept in journalism, I shall engage with pressing theoretical concerns in a manner alert to exigent professional interests. Our discussion's scope is limited to a certain selection of related themes, but it is my hope that it will serve to encourage others to pursue numerous avenues equally worthy of exploration highlighted on these pages.

In taking as its principal focus the reportorial imperative of witnessing in online news coverage of crisis events, this book signals its departure from more familiar approaches to citizen journalism more generally.[4] In recent years the term 'media witnessing' has emerged as a way to describe how digital technologies are transforming this capacity to bear witness, encouraging a number of productive lines of investigation. Definitions tend to vary depending upon disciplinary priorities, but in its most general sense, as Paul Frosh and Amit Pinchevski (2009b) pointed out, the term refers to 'the witnessing performed *in*, *by*, and *through* the media. It is about the systematic and ongoing reporting of the experiences and realities of distant others to mass audiences' (2009a: 1). Here they further specify the term's remit by suggesting it strives to capture simultaneously 'the appearance of witnesses in media reports, the possibility of media themselves bearing witness, and the positioning of media audiences as witnesses to depicted events' (2009a: 1). In the case of a television news report, for example, it 'may depict witnesses to an event, bear witness to that event, and turn viewers into witnesses *all at the same time*' (2009a: 1). This tripartite distinction deserves further scrutiny for reasons I will explore below, but here we note the theoretical – and journalistic – concerns it highlights provide an impetus for research to move beyond the scope of more traditional concepts utilised in analyses of media effectivity.

My primary aim in the course of this book's discussion is to discern a conceptual basis for formulating an alternative perspective, one intended to help to facilitate efforts to recast prevailing forms of social exclusion endemic to the 'us' and 'them' dichotomies that tend to permeate Western news media reporting concerned with crisis events. More specifically, this book will offer an evaluative appraisal of diverse attempts to think through the journalistic mediation of witnessing with a view to assessing, in turn, certain wider implications for research investigating ordinary citizens' impromptu involvement and participation. In the course of this discussion, I shall elaborate the concept of 'citizen witnessing' as one possible way forward to negotiate the conceptual territory fiercely lit by clashing assertions over whether journalism will thrive or perish with ever-greater public involvement in newsmaking. While the difficulties are formidable, they are not insurmountable. I believe that journalism's public service assurances may be imagined anew in light of the capacity of citizen witnessing to enhance democratic cultures. In meeting this challenge of innovation, journalism will benefit by securing new opportunities to reconnect with its audiences in a manner at once more transparent and accountable, while at the same time encouraging a more openly inclusive news culture committed to greater dialogue, deliberation and debate.[5]

Beginning in chapter 2, the evolving nature of this increasingly challenging relationship – that is, between the journalist as professional observer and the ordinary citizen engaged in first-hand, embodied forms of truth-telling – will be examined in order to bring to light issues central to current debates about journalism's wider role within a democracy. To this end, this chapter adopts a historical perspective, in the first instance to draw out differing conceptions of the impartially objective journalist as a trustworthy eyewitness. Next, we trace the contours of an emergent debate over journalism's social responsibilities, most notably the contrary arguments put forth by journalist Walter Lippmann and philosopher John Dewey, respectively, in the 1920s. It is 'altogether unthinkable that a society like ours', Lippmann maintained, 'should remain forever dependent upon untrained accidental witnesses', a claim which Dewey – as if in anticipation of today's citizen journalist – sought to refute.

My intention from chapter 3 onwards is to reverse the emphases of scholarly studies focusing on the realm of professional news reporting by bringing to the fore 'amateur' contributions to breaking, first-to-the-scene news, paying close attention to issues of form, practice and epistemology. Following a discussion of the importance of witnessing for the very integrity of news reporting (illustrated with reference to journalists such as Anna Politkovskaya and Wilfred Burchett), two formative precedents of online citizen witnessing will be examined in detail: specifically, Abraham Zapruder's 8mm 'home movie' footage of the assassination of US President John F. Kennedy in 1963 and the 'amateur camcorder video' of Rodney King being beaten by Los Angeles police officers in 1991. The latter portion of this chapter, in turn, will pinpoint several ways in which the rise of the internet as a news platform has contributed to the redefinition of journalism – and thus who can lay claim to the social authority of journalistic witnessing where crisis reporting is concerned.

Chapter 4 engages with a set of issues which often tend to be overlooked in research studies of citizen journalism. Having briefly traced the emergence of varied conceptions of the figure of the witness over time, attention is devoted to the capacity of journalism – television news, in particular – to privilege subjunctive forms of witnessing in which the suffering of distant others risks engendering traumatic responses. Media imagery, in particular, draws us into a positionality of witnessing, where our apparent complicity in what is rendered visible in front of the camera becomes undeniable. 'We know about genocide; we know about the calculation of death in millions', John Ellis (2000) maintains. 'We know about famine and absolute poverty. We know because we have seen the images and heard the sounds which convey them', which makes it impossible for us to claim ignorance as a defence (2000: 9–10). In order to consider how social media in the hands of ordinary citizens are transforming these more familiar dynamics, the chapter examines citizen contributions to the reporting of the Mumbai attacks in November 2008. It was during this crisis that the journalistic significance of Twitter for breaking news became readily apparent, signalling the onset of new forms of citizen witnessing.

Manuel Castells's (2007, 2011) conception of 'mass self-communication' in the 'global network society' informs chapter 5's exploration of young people's use of witnessing strategies via social media to articulate protest and dissent regarding state power. Several examples – including the Greek student rebellion following the police shooting of a fifteen-year-old, the killing of Neda Agha-Solton who was protesting against government repression in Iran (mobile-telephone footage of which making it 'probably the most widely witnessed death in human history', Krista Mahr (2009) of *Time* magazine argued), the social havoc of the London riots, the Occupy Wall Street campaign and the incidents culminating in the Arab Spring – feature in the analysis. An observation made by the Al Jazeera (2011b) network regarding the latter uprisings applies to each of these incidents to varying degrees, namely that 'Many of these citizens risked their own personal safety as they recorded the events unfolding around them.'

In so doing, 'the result was often iconic images that have come to symbolise the Arab Spring, a process many analysts speculate would have taken a very different course were it not for the images that captivated the world'.

A further dimension of citizen witnessing, namely the role of the whistle-blower in investigative journalism, is brought to light in chapter 6. The controversial website WikiLeaks is centred for close examination, particularly with respect to the alternative ethos of witnessing that its founder, Julian Assange (2006), advocates: 'Everytime we witness an act that we feel to be unjust and do not act', he argues, 'we become a party to injustice.' This chapter evaluates several of WikiLeaks's reportorial interventions in this light, each of them bringing to public attention documents provided by a whistle-blower intent on advancing an efficacious form of witnessing as a progressive form of civic engagement. WikiLeaks's alternative conception of citizen-centred 'scientific' journalism will be assessed, with particular attention given to the top-secret Afghanistan war logs posted in 2010. The ensuing controversy sparked wide-ranging debate about the prescribed ideals of professional reporting, as well as its capacity to hold power to account in a manner consistent with the public interest.

Chapter 7 brings the discussion to a close, drawing together a number of themes informing the preceding chapters while, at the same time, seeking to sharpen this enquiry further by examining citizen witnessing during the Arab Spring, in general, and the conflict in Libya, in particular. With respect to the latter, the significance of graphic mobile-telephone footage of captured leader Muammar Gaddafi immediately before and after the moment of his execution is evaluated, primarily with regard to the ethical implications the use of this eyewitness imagery posed for news organisations caught in a quandary over what was appropriately newsworthy. In a 'pix or it didn't happen' era, journalistic decisions regarding the apposite mediation of grisly images risk being subjected to intense criticism, causing searching questions to be asked about the setting of normative limits over what distant audiences will be allowed to see – answers to which, I believe, will prove to be of vital importance for future initiatives in citizen newsmaking.

By its end, then, it is hoped this book will succeed in making a compelling case for the continued development of the concept of citizen witnessing for journalism research.

2

The Journalist as Professional Observer

Even the most sincere, dedicated eyewitness cannot offer a 'naïve picture of the scene' keeping apart opinion and observation, Walter Lippmann wrote in *Public opinion* (1922), a book offering an incisive critique of news reporting at the time, and one that continues to resonate today. 'Of any public event that has wide effects', he maintained, 'we see at best only a phase and an aspect.' The nature of the event in question will be necessarily transfigured in the course of relaying its apparent facts to others. 'A report is the joint product of the knower and known, in which the rôle of the observer is always selective and usually creative', Lippmann added; 'The facts we see depend on where we are placed, and the habits of our eyes' (1922: 53–4).

The 'habits of our eyes' is a telling phrase, signalling as it does our predisposition to make sense of what Lippmann calls 'the great blooming, buzzing confusion of the outer world' in particular ways shaped by our previous apprehension of the familiar and the strange. 'For the most part we do not first see, and then define, we define first and then see', he writes, thereby succinctly pinpointing the epistemological challenge confronting impartial, objective news reporting, namely the inescapability of personal bias. And yet journalism regarded as a profession in its own right recurrently upholds the conviction that the dispassionate reporter possesses a unique capacity to separate facts from values, a defining characteristic widely held to distinguish the true professional from the amateur pretender.

Of course, simply to ask whether journalism is a profession in the first place is to tempt controversy. Responses will vary depending on circumstance, but even those quick to offer a resounding 'yes, of course' will likely add a caveat that it is a profession in crisis – one threatening to come asunder in the brave new world of digital media. Several reasons for this apparent transformation are being hotly contested, but none more so than the rise of the 'citizen journalist' threatening to storm the ramparts of what was once regarded as the exclusive domain of the skilled reporter. Adopting a historical perspective, though, it is worth considering how – and why – the language of professionalism secured its purchase on journalists' collective sense of membership, respecting certain rules of inclusion and, equally significant, rules of exclusion. Looking across a number of national contexts, it seems fair to suggest that over the course of the last century, varied conceptions of journalism as an art, craft, trade, vocation or occupation have been gradually, albeit unevenly, displaced in favour of a proclaimed professional status, one to be differentiated at all costs from that projected onto the non-professional, inexpert citizenry. Indeed, in considering this question of status, it is revealing to observe how frequently the importance of impartial witnessing on behalf of distant publics underpins preferred definitions of what counts as journalism.

This chapter, in seeking to provide a contextual backdrop to this book's exploration of citizen witnessing, will proceed to examine certain guiding tenets of journalism's evolving relationships with its publics. In aiming to draw out some of the fissures and corresponding silences engendered by competing definitions of journalistic identity in this regard – where professionalism is typically counterpoised against amateurism – attention will turn to a series of issues considered central to its modern formation at the start of the twentieth century. Next, this chapter turns to consider Walter Lippmann's thinking about the nature of these relationships, paying particular attention to his writings in the 1920s. Read from a contemporary vantage point, the essays and books he published in this period represent a significant intervention, remarkable in its own right but also for the debating stance it provoked for one of his most perceptive critics, the philosopher John Dewey. In taking several points of contention as its thematic focus, this chapter endeavours to address this book's larger objective of contributing to efforts to reinvigorate ongoing discussion about the enduring value of witnessing underpinning journalism's proclaimed authority in democratic culture.

The fidelity of the eye

In undertaking an enquiry into the importance of the citizen witness for journalism, we recall our earlier discussion of the gradual evolution of the eyewitness as a distinctive figure. Delving deeper, before the emergence of modern journalism, historical accounts have sought to trace varied inflections of witnessing and their diverse connotations. Close scrutiny of *The Oxford English dictionary*'s principal definition – 'The action of bearing witness or giving testimony (in witnessing of, as a witness to; to bear witnessing, to bear witness)' – reveals aspects of how its etymological lineage interweaves religious, literary and juridical conceptions over the span of centuries.

Scholars have long noted the tensions implied between connotations of vision – seeing with one's own eyes – and testifying to what cannot be observed first-hand, namely bearing witness on the basis of faith to that which eludes personal recognition (Oliver, 2001; Weine, 2006). In terms of its inflection within a wider visual culture, Peter Burke (2001) describes the emergence of the eyewitness principle in painting from the ancient Greeks onwards: in effect the rule exhorting artists to 'represent what – and only what – an eyewitness could have seen from a particular point at a particular moment' (2001: 14; see also Azoulay, 2008; Gombrich, 1982). Paintings striving to achieve this stylistic commitment by looking as truthful as possible would often encourage the impression that the artist was concerned to provide accurate testimony, Burke suggests, yet their evidential status in this regard remained a matter of interpretation. Related histories of visual culture recurrently privilege the ways in which codified rules of authentication and verification give shape to testimonies of witnessing within what Foucault (1980) termed 'regimes of truth' within a given society. Nicholas Mirzoeff's (2011) alternative history, for example, poses searching questions regarding the ways in which diverse modes of visuality have contributed to the normalisation of power relations underpinning state authority over what can be seen, where, when and by whom – constituting, in effect, a contest between visuality and countervisuality. 'The right to look claims autonomy from this authority, refuses to be segregated, and spontaneously invents new forms', he writes (2011: 4). In other words, the right to look is 'the claim to a right to the real', which necessarily places witnessing on the terrain of human rights, and, as such, makes it a site of political struggle.

Numerous other historical studies of related aspects of witnessing document its varied inflection as a concept, some of the most significant detailing the 'first-hand seeing' of the atrocities of the Holocaust. Issues of attestation and testimony, when set in relation to unspeakable evil, reveal why the need to elaborate witnessing further in conceptual terms has proven essential for purposes of remembrance, despite intrinsic difficulties. Differing registers of witnessing can be interwoven, such as when photographs make real horrors for distant others across time, space and place. In *On photography*, Susan Sontag (1977) recalls her childhood encounter ('a negative epiphany') with images of the Bergen-Belsen and Dachau concentration camps, which she happened across by chance in a bookshop. In her words:

> Nothing I have seen – in photographs or in real life – ever cut me as sharply, deeply, instantaneously. Indeed, it seems plausible to me to divide my life into two parts, before I saw those photographs (I was twelve) and after, though it was several years before I understood fully what they were about. What good was served by seeing them? They were only photographs – of an event I had scarcely heard of and could do nothing to affect, of suffering I could hardly imagine and could do nothing to relieve. When I looked at those photographs, something broke. Some limit had been reached, and not only that of horror; I felt irrevocably grieved, wounded, but a part of my feelings started to tighten; something went dead; something is still crying. (1977: 20)

In distinguishing between suffering and 'living with the photo-graphed images of suffering', she points out that the latter 'does not necessarily strengthen conscience and the ability to be compassionate'. Indeed, she adds, both conscience and compassion can be corrupted. 'Images transfix. Images anesthetize', she writes; 'An event known through photographs certainly becomes more real than it would have been if one had never seen the photographs ... But after repeated exposure to images it also becomes less real' (1977: 20). Revisiting this position some twenty-five years later, however, Sontag (2003) is not so certain. 'What is the evidence', she asks, 'that photographs have a diminishing impact, that our culture of spectatorship neutralizes the moral force of photographs of atrocities?' (2003: 94). It is revealing that she suggests the question now turns on television news, with its capacity to drain images of their force by subjecting them to select usages, and incessantly, repetitiously so. She points to 'the instability of attention that television is organized to arouse and to satiate by its surfeit of images', contending that this 'image-glut' works to keep 'attention light, mobile, relatively indifferent to content' – and thereby, in so doing, contributes to 'the deadening of feeling' (2003: 94, 95).[1]

The status of the journalist as witness – or 'those professional, specialized tourists known as journalists', to use Sontag's phrase – thus comes to the fore. More specifically, in considering how journalism's proclaimed fourth estate role is being transformed within this 'culture of spectatorship', one promptly encounters a series of metaphors revolving around verbal articulation – the voice of public opinion must be heard – privileged over and above those of sight. In what to my mind is a fascinating study, Jeffrey Edward Green (2010) examines democracy in 'an age of spectatorship' with a view to rendering problematic conventional emphases placed on the doctrine of *vox populi* – the voice of the people – in the modern tradition of democratic thought. The problem of voice proves contentious because of what it overshadows; democracy, when perceived as hinging upon an empowerment of the People's voice (e.g. with respect to voting at elections, opinion polls, single-issue protests and the like), risks being too narrow in its focus, thereby calling into question its relevance. Political power under-stood strictly in terms of voice, Green suggests, is likely to be 'out of touch with the way politics is experienced by most people most of the time and by the People itself (the mass of everyday, non-office-holding citizens in their *collective* capacity) all of the time' (2010: 3–4).

Rhetorical appeals to a Habermasian public sphere notwith-standing, most of us are much more inclined to be watching and listening to others engaged in 'rational-critical debate' and decision-making than to be directly involved ourselves (Habermas, 1989). Spectatorship, Green argues, is inscribed in the very nature of political action conceived in these terms; rather than relating to politics with our voices, more often than not we are spectators who relate to politics with our eyes. The implications for sustain-ing democratic ideals are profound. 'In bringing politics before the eyes of the People to an unprecedented degree', he writes, 'the mass media has also normalized a set of political practices – the photo-op, the sound bite, the press leak, and, more gener-ally, the issueless politics of personality – that have undermined the rationality of public discourse.' The result of this amounts to 'further alienating everyday citizens from the sense that they are a party to genuine political decision making and the reasoning on which it is based' (2010: 4–5). In re-considering democracy from an ocular rather than vocal perspective, it follows, this question of spectatorship invites fresh thinking about longstanding concerns.

The citizen-spectator

Efforts to extend and elaborate the interests of ordinary individu-als are certain to encounter familiar discourses of active citizenship versus passive spectatorship. Typical in this regard is the assump-tion that 'the eyes are outside of power', Green maintains – that is, 'spectatorship, if it signifies anything, indicates domination (the subordination of the many who watch to the few who are watched on the public stage) and that, accordingly, empowerment occurs only through taking up speech, action, and decision – which of course is precisely what the spectator does not do' (2010: 8). To move beyond this conceptual impasse, it is vital to recognise that the spectator is not powerless, but rather possesses a capacity for vision with transformative potential through inspection, observance and surveillance of those in positions of authority.[2]

Green introduces the notion of the 'popular gaze' as an empowered form of looking – based on, in his terms, an 'ocular model of popular empowerment' rooted in plebiscitary democracy – whereby leaders cease to be able to manage fully the conditions of their own publicity. Still, due to 'unprecedented technological and organizational resources', it remains the case that leaders and their political machines can control public appearances to the point that they are prepackaged, scripted, and even micromanaged to the smallest detail, including the angle of the camera shot, the background scenery, and, increasingly, the reactions of an allegedly independent assembled audience' (2010: 14). Candour, then, becomes an important principle, one to be pursued in the critique – and reform – of democratic imagery. This is not to deny that the popular gaze depends, in part, on nonocular sources (not least elections, changes in legislation, the possibility of legal action, and so forth), but rather to suggest that 'a politics of candor possesses an egalitarian value, insofar as it imposes special risks and obligations on political elites as a form of compensation for their disproportionate, never fully legitimate hierarchical authority' (2010: 17). It is in the interweaving of ocular and vocal models of popular empowerment that the capacity for enriched deliberative exchanges will be engendered in the name of greater transparency.

In everyday contexts within a modern, representative democracy, the need to clarify the nature of the citizen as spectator becomes a pressing concern. Here a continuum of sorts is envisaged by Green, which we can briefly sketch. Situated at one end is the participatory citizen, labelled 'citizen-governor', associated with direct democracy. He or she 'discusses, acts, joins, protests, takes a stand, legislates, and above all *decides* – the figure at the center of the most eloquent testimonials to the modern democratic tradition as it has been presented by Rousseau, Jefferson, J. S. Mill, Tocqueville, Dewey, down to the contemporary deliberative theorists of today' (2010: 32–3). Residing at the other end of the continuum is the 'apolitical citizen', whose status as a citizen, with due legal rights and social entitlements, is conferred in a juridical sense. This citizen 'takes little interest in public affairs, lacks knowledge about government, has no sense of being an efficacious political actor, and either does not vote or votes without a clear sense of what is being selected' (2010: 33). Effectively denied by both conceptions, Green points out, is a distinctive form of citizenship indicative of present-day democracies, namely the 'citizen-spectator'.

In occupying an intermediate place between the first two positions, this third position – the citizen-spectator – signals a meaningful psychological involvement in current affairs, but not one that translates into active participation in political life. Spectatorship, it follows, defines this citizen's mainly vicarious political experience. In other words, the citizen-spectator may be thought of as a 'citizen-being-ruled', someone who perceives a sharp distinction between his or her own political life and the realm of official politics (unless, of course, a particular issue galvanises their concern). Since the appearance of the first daily newspaper, Green writes, 'the steady development of mass communication technologies – telegraph, radio, film, television, internet – has only magnified the exposure to government of the governed by delocalizing the political spectator from the site of actual political decision making' (2010: 39). Exceptions to this general rule tend to be minor, such as leadership debates, press conferences or public inquiries into the conduct of leaders and high officials, suggesting to Green that opportunities for most citizens to subject those in power to 'compulsory visibility' (a notion he borrows from Foucault (1977)) are few and far between. Nevertheless, it is in the pursuit of candour as a critical ideal that the value of citizens' shared, collective interests is recognised, providing them with 'a sense of solidarity with other ordinary citizens also consigned to experience politics passively in a spectating capacity' (2010: 28). Herein lies the hope, he believes, for a revitalised definition of the People as an ocular rather than vocal being.

This line of enquiry, it seems to me, promises to be a productive one for our priorities here. Considered in relation to what I am calling 'citizen witnessing', it provides a useful counterpoint to the usual – that is to say paternalistic, if not pejorative – treatment of individuals refusing to uphold or inhabit textbook-like definitions of citizenship. Much work remains to be done, however, to bring to light the importance of witnessing for the citizen-spectator, which is not a feature of Green's otherwise very helpful account (nor does he pause to consider citizens' engagement with the media beyond the consumption of content, which is a rather vital dimension of our enquiry here). Beginning in the next section, we initiate a turn to address the role of journalism in a democracy more squarely, in the first instance by considering the rise of the impartially objective journalist as a trustworthy eyewitness.

Objective communicators

From the vantage point of today, it would seem that the factors which gave rise to the ideal of objectivity in journalism committed to eyewitnessing were readily discernible in the United States before other Western countries for a number of reasons. James W. Carey (1969), in a historical survey of the 'communications revolution' underway there by the 1890s, made a number of observations that together serve as a useful starting point.

In describing the 'contradictory tendencies' within this revolution, Carey pinpointed three particularly salient dimensions. The first such dimension concerns the rise of mass media of communication at a national level, encompassing the modern newspaper and national magazine as well as the ascendancy of the press services and nascent forms of electronic communication. Second was the development of specialised or minority media situated within 'special interest' – defined in relation to ethnic, occupational, class, regional or religious identifications, for example – segments of society. Important here were the ways in which these minority media intermediated to link local milieus (formerly dependent upon face-to-face contact) to the larger social structure, thereby creating national communities of interest. And, third, the emergence of a new social role around this time, namely that of the professional communicator, who 'mediates between two parties by use of a skill at manipulating symbols to translate the language, values, interests, ideas, and purposes from the idiom of one group into an idiom acceptable to a differentiated speech community' (1969: 132). It is this last dimension that is of particular relevance for our purposes.[3]

The role of the professional communicator as a 'broker of symbols', Carey suggested, finds its place in a wide range of occupations, including advertising, public relations, science communication and journalism, amongst others. In each instance, albeit in different ways, these occupations were being transformed in the 1890s by the development of new forms of training (through universities and colleges, in the main) as well as by the growth of collective associations. Professional codes of conduct were gradually being set down, conferring with them a relatively distinctive role identity and elements of a vocational ideology. Where journalism had been typically regarded as a literary genre, it was rapidly becoming a form of technical writing defined, to a considerable extent, by this task of translation. In Carey's words: 'Journalism was not characterized merely as reporting that put the words and actions of others into simpler language, but as a fluid interpretation of action and actors, an effort to create a semantic reality that invested the ordinary with significance. Journalists traditionally induced their audiences to come to terms with old realities in new ways' (Carey, 1969: 137). A crucial factor implicated in this transformation was the growing commitment to 'objective reporting'. Journalists in the US by the end of the nineteenth century were experiencing a 'conversion downwards', he argued, whereby their role was effectively being 'de-intellectualized' and 'technicalized' simultaneously. No longer were journalists independent interpreters of events; their status as professional communicators meant that they were increasingly inclined to become proficient in technical skill at writing, rather than 'intellectual skill as critics, interpreters, and contemporary historians.' Valued here was 'a capacity to translate the specialized language and purposes of government, science, art, medicine, finance into an idiom that can be understood by broader, more amorphous, less educated audiences' (1969: 137).

This 'fetish' of objectivity, previously circumscribed by the commercial advantages to be accrued by non-partisan reporting, was promptly becoming 'rationalized into a canon of professional competence and ideology of professional responsibility', according to Carey; 'It rested on the dubious assumption that the highest standard of professional performance occurred when the reporter presented the reader with all sides of an issue (though there were usually only two), presented all the "facts," and allowed the reader to decide what these facts meant' (1969: 137–8). Traditional roles of advocacy and criticism were soon eclipsed, he maintained, being largely relegated to a subordinate status in light of these new norms, procedures and conventions. The journalist as professional communicator was encouraged to assume a passive stance where reporting the claims of sources was concerned. To the extent that journalists found themselves dependent on these sources for information, and thereby inclined to internalise their attitudes and expectations, the creative work of reporting – to say nothing of its independence – was severely compromised (see also Carey, 2011). At the same time, however, longstanding anxieties about what should constitute the proper identity of the journalist were gradually becoming reconciled to the institutional dictates of professional communication.

The research literature concerned with the ascendancy of various discourses of professionalism in journalism is vast, with the formative influence of diverse institutions (such as press clubs, trade unions, as well as editor and publisher associations) in the latter half of the nineteenth century receiving due recognition. The reporter, in effect, was a social invention of the 1880s and 1890s, Michael Schudson's (1978) research suggests, signalling the onset of what might be termed the 'Age of the Reporter', to use one newspaper editor's turn of phrase. Where early newspapers tended to revolve around a single person performing a number of different roles (printer, advertising agent, editor and reporter), this period sees a growing degree of specialisation made possible, in the main, by the commercialisation of the press. The emergence of the reporter as a relatively distinct occupation is a gradual achievement, which takes shape in varied ways, due, in part, to differing ideals defining good practice.

Differences between the ideals of factuality (an 'information' model, emphasising the truth value of news) and of entertainment (a 'story' model, stressing an aesthetic or enjoyable 'consummatory value') in the writing of news, Schudson maintains, hinged on whether the prime purpose was to gather facts or to get a story. 'Rightly or wrongly', he observes, 'the informational ideal in journalism is associated with fairness, objectivity, scrupulous dispassion', and as such tends to be held in higher regard than the arguably less reliable, trustworthy or responsible story ideal (1978: 90). Few journalists in the latter portion of the nineteenth century and first two decades of the twentieth perceived a sharp divide between 'objective' facts and 'subjective' values, however; the influence of personal predisposition on perception was seldom questioned, being regarded as firmly based on the self-evident 'reality' of the everyday world. This 'naïve empiricism', as Schudson describes it, would not prove impervious to challenge. In the years following World War I, it gave way to the point that it was largely displaced by the more sophisticated ideal of 'objectivity' – or the 'habit of disinterested realism' as we shall see it termed in the writings of Walter Lippmann below – as a response to the widespread public scepticism of the times. Far from being 'the final expression of a belief in facts', Schudson writes, objectivity represented 'the assertion of a method designed for a world in which even facts could not be trusted' (1978: 122).

Social responsibilities

In what proves to be a complementary line of enquiry, Géraldine Mulhmann (2008, 2010) discerns the emergence of the journalist as 'witness-ambassador', the key figure in the modern, 'unifying' journalism that eventually assumes dominance in Western democracies. The sense of 'unifying' pertains to the 'desire to bring people together', which is most apparent in journalism's concern to provide readers with the 'truth' ('something that is acceptable to all, beyond differences of opinion'), increasingly apparent from the end of the nineteenth century, she maintains (2008: 6). This attitude revolves around the journalist's personal presence as a reporter on the scene, serving as an on-the-spot witness rather than a commentator from afar: 'This valorization of tangible experience appears as a guarantee of the "truth" of whatever is recounted, and by this fact a guarantee that the implicit mandate entered into with the public – the mandate to provide it with an account acceptable to all, the account that anyone could have given if they had been put in the position of witness – will be respected' (2010: 34). Indeed, Mulhmann contends, it 'is because they are *witnesses* that they can be good *ambassadors*; and because they are *ambassadors* and must honour this mandate, that they must be *witnesses*' (2010: 34). Journalists, in adopting this role on behalf of their public, signal a marked shift of emphasis from reporting that expresses a personal opinion (the 'I' of first-person narrative) in favour of positioning themselves as representatives of the 'we'. The ensuing bond forged with the readership brings with it certain social responsibilities, which would continue to complicate journalists' self-conceptions of their proper role for some time yet.

The inscription of the journalist as independent eyewitness within conceptions of fact-based journalism proves to be an uneven, contingent process of negotiation. In contrast with the legal or medical professions, which adopted strict procedures of entry, licensed codes of ethics, and formal methods of self-regulation, no such measures were thought to be consistent with the practice of journalism envisaged by graduates of the various educational institutions devoted to training journalists that were emerging in the late nineteenth and early twentieth centuries. Where the Columbia School in New York was concerned, however, it had been its benefactor Joseph Pulitzer's steadfast belief that journalism's status – that is to say, its elevation in the eyes of readers, as well as for journalists themselves – nonetheless deserved equal recognition with these other professions. Professionalism, in every sense of the term, was to provide the guiding ethos to which all journalists should properly aspire. The factors shaping identity formation were to revolve around a declared commitment to the virtues of public-spiritedness.

Precisely what the attendant 'standard of civic righteousness' envisaged by Pulitzer would entail defied easy elucidation, finding only a broad definition in relation to the 'character' necessary to advance the 'public good' instead. Moral courage, so vital for public service, would have to be taught – an aptitude for its principles, and with it the determination to behave responsibly, was not inborn. Here it is Pulitzer's (1904) distinction between 'real journalists' and 'men [and women] who do a kind of newspaper work that requires neither knowledge nor conviction' that underscored the difference between the personal qualities to be engendered by journalism education and those derived from 'mere business training' (1904: 19). To be cultivated, at all costs, was a 'pride in the profession', for the journalist alone 'has the privilege of molding the opinion, touching the hearts and appealing to the reason of hundreds of thousands every day'. Every day, he added, 'opens new doors for the journalist who holds the confidence of the community and has the capacity to address it' (1904: 12).

Shortly after the close of the conflict that became known as World War I, the German sociologist Max Weber (1919) published one of his most important essays, 'Politics as a vocation', which brought these issues to the fore. Whilst primarily concerned with redefining the nature of the state and the legitimate use of force, as well as different classifications of political leadership, he nevertheless offered a basis for an alternative perspective. Drawing a contrast with journalism in Britain, he noted that the journalist on the European Continent lacked a fixed social classification, which helped to explain why the importance of their representative status was not accorded sufficient recognition. Indeed, he went further, arguing that the journalist belongs to 'a kind of pariah caste that in the eyes of "society" is always judged socially by its lowest representatives from the point of view of morality' (1919: 55).

It was regrettable, Weber felt, that the 'strangest ideas' about journalists and their work were in circulation, leading him to suggest:

Not everyone realizes that to write a really *good* piece of journalism is at least as demanding intellectually as the achievement of any scholar. This is particularly true when we recollect that it has to be written on the spot, to order, and that it must create an immediate *effect*, even though it is produced under completely different conditions from that of scholarly research. It is generally overlooked that a journalist's actual responsibility is far greater than the scholar's, and that on average every reputable journalist's *sense* of responsibility is by no means inferior, as indeed we saw during the war. It is overlooked because in the nature of the case it is the *irresponsible* pieces of journalism that tend to remain in the memory because of their often terrible effects. (1919: 55; emphasis in original)

Despite his personal conviction that the discretion of the able journalist was deserving of praise, however, he pointed out that members of the public had come to 'regard the press with a mixture of disdain and abject cowardice'. Rather than ascertaining the factors giving rise to these conditions, he stressed that the journalist's public responsibility was at odds with 'sensation-seeking', regardless of how popular the latter may be with newspaper readers. At a time when his or her duties were becoming ever more intensive, not least because of increasing pressures to be up to date, 'particularly onerous inner challenges' had to be faced. Weber added:

It is no small thing to consort with the powerful people of this earth in their drawing rooms, apparently on a basis of equality, to be flattered because you are feared, while all the time knowing that no sooner has the door closed behind you than your host may have to defend himself to his guests for having invited the 'scoundrels from the press' (1919: 57)

Equally daunting was the need to negotiate the demands of the 'market' without, at the same time, 'succumbing to absolute superficiality' in one's reporting.

Not everyone was prepared to wax lyrical about the scholarly advantages of journalism education, however, even among journalists themselves. Critical assessments published around this time tended to dwell on a number of common themes (see Angell, 1922;

Hayword and Langdon-Davies, 1919; Sinclair, 1920). Particularly salient in this regard were concerns expressed regarding the extent to which popular disillusionment with wartime propaganda campaigns created a wariness of 'official' channels of information, a problem perceived by some commentators to be seriously compounded by 'press agents' and 'publicity' or 'promotion experts' (Allen, 1922; *The New York Times*, 1920). For those journalists alert to the danger of equating facts with officially sanctioned definitions of truth, the need for more 'scientific' methods of processing information accurately was increasingly recognised.[4] Here it is the contribution of Walter Lippmann to debates about journalism and its publics which proved remarkably influential at the time and, for reasons we shall see, continues to shape pertinent debates today.

'Untrained accidental witnesses'

'Merely to talk about the reporter in terms of his [or her] real importance to civilization will make newspaper men laugh', Walter Lippmann wrote in *Liberty and the news* (1920); 'Yet reporting is a post of peculiar honor. Observation must precede every other activity, and the public observer (that is, the reporter) is a man [or woman] of critical value' (1920: 79–80). At stake in this process is nothing less than the very health of democratic society itself, he believed. The 'objective information' required for governing institutions to operate effectively necessitates that the press supply 'trustworthy news', a role demanding that the 'newspaper enterprise' be transformed from 'a haphazard trade into a disciplined profession'. And, it follows from this premise, this explains the reason why the relationship between journalism and its public warrants rigorous assessment and critique.

It is 'altogether unthinkable that a society like ours should remain forever dependent upon untrained accidental witnesses', Lippmann contends in the book that amounts to his first sustained engagement with what he chose to call the 'modern news problem'. Writing with remarkable flair and conviction, he makes clear his belief that 'the present crisis of western democracy' is also, at the same time, 'a crisis in journalism'. He stresses the intrinsic value of facts, maintaining that they must be made available to members of the public so as to facilitate their efforts to engage with the pressing questions of the day. The reason people everywhere feel baffled and misled, he contends, is because they do not possess sufficient confidence in what they are being told. Journalism in its modern state, he is convinced, is complicit in this situation. Several underlying causes are briefly rehearsed – such as the corruption of those who exercise 'moneyed control' over the 'so-called free press', their self-interested pettiness, and their tendency to make light of serious matters – before Lippmann offers his alternative explanation. Edification, he believes, is being privileged over and above veracity (a veiled criticism of the likes of Adolf Ochs in New York or Lord Northcliffe in London). 'The current theory of American newspaperdom is that an abstraction like the truth and a grace like fairness must be sacrificed whenever anyone thinks the necessities of civilization require the sacrifice' (1920: 8), he added with customary panache.

Reporters, it follows, have effectively assumed for themselves the work of 'preachers, revivalists, prophets and agitators'. In so doing, their 'idea of what is patriotic' is actually serving to temper the 'curiosity of their readers'. For Lippmann, the implications are dire:

> Just as the most poisonous form of disorder is the mob incited from high places, the most immoral act the immorality of a government, so the most destructive form of untruth is sophistry and propaganda by those whose profession it is to report the news. The news columns are common carriers. When those who control them arrogate to themselves the right to determine by their own consciences what shall be reported and for what purpose, democracy is unworkable. Public opinion is blockaded. (1920: 10–11)

To the extent that the press fails to deliver factual information, offering in its place little more than the whims of personal opinion, the basis of government will be decisively undermined. He writes: 'All that the sharpest critics of democracy have alleged is true, if there is no supply of trustworthy and relevant news. Incompetence and aimlessness, corruption and disloyalty, panic and ultimate disaster, must come to any people which is denied an assured access to the facts. No one can manage anything on pap. Neither can a people' (1920: 11). The very future of popular government by consent is at risk, Lippmann warns, if standing in its place are news organisations busily 'manufacturing consent' to suit their own self-interested purposes. The reporting of daily news must be wrested away from 'untrained and biased hands', and realigned with new standards of independence and integrity that signal a renewed commitment to 'reporting the facts'. It is on this note that *Liberty and the news* comes to a close, its final sentence neatly underscoring the basis for Lippmann's reformist agenda. 'We shall advance', he writes, 'when we have learned humility; when we have learned to seek the truth, to reveal it and publish it; when we care more for that than for the privilege of arguing about ideas in a fog of uncertainty' (1920: 104).[5]

In a modern world so complicated that it defies citizens' powers of understanding, it follows that the journalist will similarly struggle when trying to interpret the significance of events for their benefit. Lippmann's next book, *Public opinion* (1922), further elaborates upon this dilemma, boldly challenging the foundational ideals of democracy. Representative government can be criticised for its apparent reliance on an unworkable fiction, he writes, namely that 'each of us must acquire a competent opinion about all public affairs' (1922: 19). An impossible demand, it should be abandoned for being untenable in practical terms. The idealised conception of community prefigured by such a doctrine bears little resemblance to life in modern society. Moreover, it would be unreasonable to expect the press to succeed in the task of furnishing the omnicompetent citizen with sufficient information to maintain this fiction in any case. The press may be the 'chief means of contact with the unseen environment', Lippmann argues, but it is incapable of assuming responsibility for presenting citizens with 'a true picture of all the outer world' to an adequate extent. The newspapers, it follows, are 'defective' in their organisation of public opinion (1922: 19).

In striving to reverse certain 'ancient beliefs' about truth and democracy, Lippmann contends that public opinion must be organised for the press, and not the other way around. 'We expect the newspaper to serve us with truth however unprofitable the truth may be', he observes; 'For this difficult and often danger-ous service, which we recognize as fundamental, we expected to pay until recently the smallest coin turned out by the mint' (1922: 203). The burden placed upon the press to fulfil its obligations thus stands in sharp contrast with the commitment – or, more to the point, lack thereof – displayed by the fickle citizen consumer to it in return. 'Somebody has said quite aptly', Lippmann remarks, 'that the newspaper editor has to be re-elected every day' (1922: 203). In effect, the attention of the reader – as a member of the 'buying public' – becomes a commodity, the sale of which by the newspaper to the advertiser underwrites its viability. The point of view judged to be representative of the buying public, it follows, cannot be safely ignored. 'A newspaper which angers those whom it pays best to reach through advertisements is a bad medium for an advertiser', Lippmann states; 'And since no one ever claimed that advertising was philanthropy, advertisers buy space in those publications which are fairly certain to reach their future custom-ers' (1922: 205). At the same time, those readers with the most money to spend are likely to have their opinions recognised to a greater extent.

It is telling that Lippmann chooses to sidestep questions about the class politics giving shape to this notion of a 'buying public', or even the emergent tensions between competing conceptions of the reader – that is, as citizen or consumer – which might have been expected to follow in this line of critique. Instead, he emphasises the typical newspaper's struggle to turn what is a 'medley of catch-as-catch-can news stand buyers' into that most elusive of quarry, namely 'a devoted band of constant readers'. Given that no newspaper can depend on the unwavering support of its readers, every effort must be made to maintain their loyalty from one day to the next. 'A newspaper can flout an advertiser, it can attack a powerful banking or traction interest, but if it alienates the buying public, it loses the one indispensable asset of its existence',

Lippmann remarks (1922: 205). And yet, to understand why the reader engages with the newspaper in the first place, it follows, the nature of news itself must be reconsidered.

Departures from the ordinary

News is not a mirror of social conditions, Lippmann argues, nor is it a simple collection of obvious facts spontaneously taking shape in knowable form. Contrary to a certain mythology, it is only in exceptional circumstances that news offers a first-hand report of 'raw material' gathered by the journalist; rather, he or she is much more likely to encounter such material only once it has been 'stylized' by someone else (not least 'the publicity man') beforehand. 'All the reporters in the world working all the hours of the day could not witness all the happenings in the world', Lippmann remarks; 'Reporters are not clairvoyant, they do not gaze into a crystal ball and see the world at will, they are not assisted by thought-transference' (1922: 214). Certain everyday routines enable the reporter to watch over a small number of places – such as City Hall, Police Headquarters, the Coroner's office, or the White House for that matter – where occurrences likely to prove worthy of coverage can be assumed to be transpiring. Especially valued are those occurrences which represent overt departures from the ordinary, something specific that has 'obtruded itself' from the norm so as provide the reporter, in turn, with a peg for the ensuing story. In other words, unusual happenings which can be 'fixed, objectified, measured, and named' are much more likely to be considered newsworthy. 'The course of events must assume a certain definable shape', Lippmann writes, 'and until it is in a phase where some aspect is an accomplished fact, news does not separate itself from the ocean of possible truth' (1922: 215).

Proceeding from his relatively imprecise formulation of this relationship in *Liberty and the news*, he proposes that a more realistic way forward is to appreciate better the constraints under which reporters operate. 'It is possible and necessary for journalists to bring home to people the uncertain character of the truth on which their opinions are founded', he believes. More than that, however, the press can also direct 'criticism and agitation' in a manner which will prod both social scientists and state officials into establishing 'more visible institutions' to formulate usable social facts. In waging this fight for 'the extension of reportable truth', the press can help to ensure that these institutions – as opposed to newspapers alone – will adequately equip citizens with the information they require in a democratic society. The press, Lippmann writes, 'is too frail to carry the whole burden of popular sovereignty, to supply spontaneously the truth which democrats hoped was inborn. And when we expect it to supply such a body of truth we employ a misleading standard of judgment' (1922: 228). The entire democratic theory of public opinion needs to be reconsidered, he argues, because of its failure to understand the limited nature of news, the illimitable complexities of society, and the relative competence (including the presumed 'appetite for uninteresting truths') of ordinary citizens.

On this basis, Lippmann declares his break from the prescriptive role envisaged for the press as a vital organ of direct democracy. It is deemed an impractical alternative to those institutions that should rightly assume responsibility for making public life sufficiently intelligible for popular decisions. While the press may be likened to the beam of a searchlight that 'moves restlessly about, bringing one episode and then another out of darkness into vision', it is impossible for individuals to do 'the work of the world by this light alone. They cannot govern society by episodes, incidents, and eruptions. [Rather, they require] a steady light of their own' (1922: 229). Lippmann's recommendations for change are forthright. In suggesting that the trouble lies at a deeper level than the press, he points to a myriad of contributory factors which can be traced to a common source: 'the failure of self-governing people to transcend their casual experience and their prejudice, by inventing, creating, and organizing a machinery of knowledge' (1922: 229–30). Herein can be identified the remedy, namely that a 'system of intelligence' be set in motion to provide the means of analysis necessary to ensure the coordination of decision-making (and, in so doing, act as a check upon a wayward press). Until governments – and newspapers – have a 'reliable picture of the world' on which to act, little headway will be made 'against the more obvious failings of democracy, against violent prejudice, apathy, preference for the curious trivial as against the dull important, and the hunger for sideshows and three legged calves' (1922: 230).

While Lippmann does not dwell on how this 'system of intelligence' will be operationalised, he is convinced that real progress will be achieved once the theory of the 'omnicompetent citizen' is safely discarded. Citizens need not be presented with expert opinion on all social questions before them, he argues, for it is too great a burden to bear. The responsible administrator is better equipped to act on their behalf, making effective use of the intelligence system to assist representative government and administration (both in politics and in industry) from one day to the next. 'Only by insisting that problems shall not come up to him [or her] until they have passed through a procedure', Lippmann writes, 'can the busy citizen of a modern state hope to deal with them in a form that is intelligible' (1922: 252).

Chasing phantoms

Public opinion made a considerable splash. Looking across a range of reviews printed at the time of its publication, it soon becomes apparent that Lippmann's advocacy for an enhanced role for a 'system of intelligence' based on social science in public life attracted particular attention.[6] Comments proffered by John Dewey (1922) in his review for the *New Republic* were especially noteworthy. One of the most eminent philosophers of the day, Dewey brought to bear in his engagement with the young journalist's writings a hard-won experience of progressive politics. His review of *Public opinion* would prove to be an important step toward formalising his own counter-position in the years to come.

Dewey begins his assessment by revelling in the pleasures of the text. He finds inspiration in Lippmann's willingness to challenge those analysts who simply take the force of public opinion for granted, seeing much to admire in the way he goes about rendering problematic their most basic assumptions. Of particular import in this respect, Dewey points out, is the doctrine of 'the omnicompetent individual' demanded by democratic theory, and with it the idealised conception of public opinion arising in spontaneous fashion as a matter of political instinct. Broadly concurring with Lippmann's insights into the ways in which this 'problem of knowledge' impacts on journalism, Dewey turns to the possible remedies on offer. It is here where the two part company from one another.

Specifically, Dewey takes issue with Lippmann's reluctance to envisage newspapers as being capable of ever performing the role of enlightening and directing public opinion, as well as with his proposals regarding the organisation of expert intelligence. In his words:

> Mr. Lippmann seems to surrender the case for press too readily – to assume too easily that what the press is it must continue to be. It is true that news must deal with events rather than with conditions and forces. It is true that the latter, *taken by themselves,* are too remote and abstract to make an appeal. Their record will be too dull and unsensational to reach the mass of readers. But there remains the possibility of treating news events in the light of a continuing study and record of underlying conditions. The union of social science, access to facts, and the art of literary presentation is not an easy thing to achieve. But its attainment seems to me the only genuine solution of the problem of an intelligent direction of social life. (Dewey, 1922: 288; emphasis in original)

A competent treatment of the day's events, he maintains, can be positively 'sensational' to the degree it reveals the underlying forces shaping events that otherwise appear to be 'casual and disjointed'. It is vital that the reporting of news sets facts in relation to one another so as to create, in turn, 'a picture of situations on which men [and women] can act intelligently'. Journalism, he is convinced, can be transformed so as to offer an objective record of the news, just as the types of expert organisations Lippmann envisages can be endorsed as long as they are closely aligned with the concerns of ordinary people. 'The enlightenment of public opinion still seems to me to have priority over the enlightenment of officials and directors', he contends. Democracy, it follows, requires a 'thoroughgoing education' for each and every one of its citizens – and not just the privileged elite who meet with Lippmann's approval.

Dewey's passionate appeal to democratic theory thus appears to be almost romantic in its sentiments when counterpoised against Lippmann's scepticism, a contrast which became even starker following the publication of the latter's *The phantom public* in 1925. From the opening paragraphs of its first chapter, titled 'The disenchanted man', Lippmann provides a bleak appraisal of 'direct democracy's' apparent shortcomings:

> The private citizen today has come to feel rather like a deaf spectator in the back row, who ought to keep his mind on the mystery off there, but cannot quite manage to stay awake. He knows he is somehow affected by what is going on. Rules and regulations continually, taxes annually and wars occasionally remind him that he is being swept along by great drifts of circumstance. (Lippmann, 1925: 3–4)

The failure of newspapers to report on the social environment in a way that will enable citizens to grasp it fully is painfully apparent, he argues. This 'disenchanted man' – and woman   has become painfully aware that their 'sovereignty is a fiction' – that is, they know that, while they reign in theory, they do not govern in practice. Lippmann contends that this is perfectly understandable because the part they play in public affairs appears to be inconsequential to them, despite its celebrated status within democratic rhetoric. The accepted ideal of the omnicompetent citizen is as familiar as it is unattainable. In other words, the belief that there exists a public capable of directing the course of events is profoundly misguided, in his view, for such a public is an abstraction – 'a mere phantom' – that is being falsely exalted.

Lippmann's stature ensured that *The phantom public* elicited a range of responses in the press. Once again, though, it is John Dewey's (1925) review that discerns an especially insightful line of critique. In contrast to those anxious to dismiss Lippmann's criticisms out of hand, he sees in them a 'statement of faith in a pruned and temperate democratic theory', one that will improve matters by refining claims made about the public and its powers. He concurs with Lippmann's plea for the 'ethical improvement' of the press so that it may better service, in turn, the scientific organisations Lippmann envisions guiding publicity in relation to the public. This, to Dewey's way of thinking, is a technical question ('discovering, recording and interpreting' the conduct of insiders having a public bearing) as well as an aesthetic one (ensuring that the results of such enquiries are sufficiently interesting and weighty). 'I do not suppose that most persons buy sugar because of belief in its nutritive value; they buy from habit and to please the palate', he writes; 'And so it must be with buying facts which would prepare various publics in particular and the wider public in general to see private activities in their public bearings and to deal with them on the basis of the public interest' (1925: 54).

'The public' versus 'publics'

Dewey's conception of 'the public', as this last point suggests, placed him at odds with Lippmann's pluralised notion of 'publics', albeit in a manner which he found richly suggestive. Inspired to prepare a methodical assessment of its implications (to the extent it represented a 'debate', it was somewhat one-sided), he published *The public and its problems* two years later. At the heart of this book is Dewey's (1927) attempt to formulate an alternative trajectory, namely by marshalling sufficient evidence to support a defence of democratic ideals in the face of Lippmann's pessimism. While much could be gained from the latter's critique – Dewey appears to be in broad agreement with Lippmann's diagnosis of the modern condition – his own analysis produces sharply divergent conclusions.[7]

'Optimism about democracy is to-day under a cloud', Dewey observes as a starting point for his discussion of what he terms the 'eclipse' of the public. While a considerable portion of *The public and its problems* is devoted to more abstract philosophical matters, there is little doubt in Dewey's mind that the current form of political democracy 'calls for adverse criticism in abundance'. Critics are confounded over what has become of 'the Public', he points out. It 'seems to be lost', existing in effect as a figure of language imputed by officials in justification of their behaviour. 'If a public exists', he writes, 'it is surely as uncertain about its own whereabouts as philosophers since Hume have been about the residence and make-up of the self' (1927: 117). At a time when electoral statistics indicate that the number of voters exercising their 'majestic right' is steadily decreasing (the 'ratio of actual to eligible voters is now about one-half', he observes), difficult questions arise regarding the continued viability of democratic institutions in practical terms. The social idea of democracy will be 'barren and empty' unless it is 'incarnated in human relationships' that make it meaningful. These relationships encompass the state, but also extend beyond into the realms of family, school, industry and the like – indeed 'all modes of human association' indicative of everyday communities. Indeed, he adds, democracy is in essence 'the idea of community life itself' (1927: 148).

This reappraisal of democracy casts journalism in a different light. The news media are to be regarded as intermediaries between a divisive political system – the very legitimacy of which is increasingly open to dispute by competing interests – and its distrustful citizens. Pressing social problems demand nothing less than an alternative form of journalism, namely one capable of ensuring that it contributes to the formation of a socially alert and informed public. Pausing to clarify his conception of news, Dewey writes:

> 'News' signifies something which has just happened, and which is new just because it deviates from the old and regular. But its *meaning* depends upon relation to what it imports, to what its social consequences are. This import cannot be determined unless the new is placed in relation to the old, to what has happened and been integrated into the course of events. Without coordination and consecutiveness, events are not events, but mere occurrences, intrusions; an event implies that out of which a happening proceeds. Hence even if we discount the influence of private interests in procuring suppression,

secrecy and misinterpretation, we have here an explanation of the triviality and 'sensational' quality of so much of what passes as news. (Dewey, 1927: 179–80)

The event-centred priorities of news, together with a corresponding fascination with newness virtually for its own sake (so as to supply 'the element of shock' required), thus combine to isolate the 'catastrophic' – such as crime, accidents, personal conflicts and so forth – from its connections to the social world. That is to say, in recognising the extent to which news represents the exceptional, the 'breaches of continuity', Dewey is suggesting that the unexceptional warrants greater attention than it would typically receive. Journalism must become more rigorous in its analyses and, at the same time, more compelling in its presentation of facts.

It is in thinking through the social consequences engendered by news reporting that Dewey reaffirms Lippmann's espousal of social science's contribution to public life. To reinvigorate the press along more scientific principles, such that social science is seen to give shape to its priorities to a much greater extent, is to instil in its daily reporting a new set of moral values. Precisely what should constitute a news event, it follows, needs to be reconsidered. In a more speculative turn, he prophesies that 'the assembling and reporting of news would be a very different thing if the genuine interests of reporters were permitted to work freely' (1927: 182). Although he does not elaborate on this point, it is apparent that Dewey is discerning in the press a capacity for social reform that Lippmann steadfastly refused to grant it. The journalist, like the social scientist, is charged with the responsibility of providing the information about pressing issues of the day – as well as interpretations of its significance – so as to enable members of the public to arrive at sound judgements. In grappling with what he perceives to be essentially an 'intellectual problem' rather than one of public policy, it seems apparent to Dewey that democracy must become more democratic – that is, more firmly rooted in everyday communities of interaction. To the extent that the journalist contributes to the organisation of the public – not least by facilitating lay participation in the rough and tumble of decision-making – the citizenry will be equipped to recognise, even challenge, the authority exercised by powerful interests.

Dewey's conviction that the Great Society can be transformed into the Great Community rests, crucially, on his belief in the rationality of ordinary people to bring to life democratic ideals when provided with the opportunity to do so. 'Until secrecy, prejudice, bias, misrepresentation, and propaganda as well as sheer ignorance are replaced by inquiry and publicity', Dewey explains, 'we have no way of telling how apt for judgement of social policies the existing intelligence of the masses may be' (1927: 209). This appeal to the citizenry's 'embodied knowledge' effectively underscores the basis for his opposition to the elitism of Lippmann's stance. 'A class of experts', Dewey contends, 'is inevitably so removed from common interests as to become a class with private interests and private knowledge, which in social matters is not knowledge at all' (1927: 207). While he concedes that Lippmann is rightly critical of certain instances of foolishness engendered by majority rule, it is vital to recognise that it is the means by which a majority is established in the first place that is of paramount importance. The very process by which minorities contest one another with a view to becoming a majority must be preserved at all costs. 'No government by experts in which the masses do not have the chance to inform the experts as to their needs can be anything but an oligarchy managed in the interests of the few', Dewey maintains (1927: 208).

It goes almost without saying, of course, that it is rather unlikely that the expert – or 'administrative specialist' – will take account of the needs of ordinary citizens by his or her own volition; rather, he or she will have to be compelled to act in this way. Although he acknowledges the necessarily conflictual nature of this dynamic, Dewey is reluctant to dwell on the social divisions permeating democratic politics. Like Lippmann, he does not engage with the issues raised by the women's movement (the right to vote having been finally achieved in the 1920s), or comment on civil rights concerns, in a sustained way. Nor does he choose to elaborate on how journalism – alongside the arts and social sciences – might empower citizens to 'break through the crust of conventionalized and routine consciousness' (1927: 183). Nevertheless, he makes plain his personal alignment with 'the masses' in opposition to 'leaders and authorities', pointing out that the world has suffered more from the latter than from the former. 'The essential need', he writes, 'is the improvement of the methods and conditions of debate, discussion and persuasion. That is *the* problem of the public' (1927: 208). How best to realise this agenda in strategic terms, however, would be left for others to determine.

Divergent visions

Various attempts have been made over the years to characterise Lippmann and Dewey as feisty opponents waging an impassioned, even acrimonious dispute. These efforts make for interesting reading, especially to the degree that legitimate points of contention are highlighted, but risk overstating the nature and intensity of their engagement. With the exception of an occasional footnote or citation, or possible veiled reference, there is little concrete evidence to indicate that either deliberately formulated their position in the hope of sparking a formal debate.[8] From the vantage point of today, it is apparent that they shared a considerable amount of common ground, yet their differences remain intriguing.

Lippmann's pessimistic appraisal of journalism's possibilities in an era when 'manufactured consent' passes for representative democracy may seem cold and distant compared with Dewey's heartfelt beliefs about participatory communication, yet it equally behoves the latter to make good the courage of his convictions and outline a radical form of alternative critique. Uniting the projects of both writers is a desire to effect social change, to contribute to efforts to improve upon the existing machinery of democracy, as long as it remains a question of reform. Neither of them advocated a structural transformation of the economic, political or cultural logics underpinning the inequalities endemic to public life at the time. Democracy and capitalism were effectively conflated in their respective interventions (although, in fairness, Dewey underscored the engendered tensions), making it virtually impossible to call for the recasting of the former without being seen to be reaffirming the preservation of the latter.

What may have seemed to be simply an interesting exploration of abstract ideals in its own right, albeit one effectively contained within narrow ideological parameters, looks acutely relevant in light of the changes confronting news organisations today. A good many of the issues considered above will be shown to assume an exigent quality in the chapters ahead, not least with regard to the impact of the protracted financial crisis on the resources made available for newsgathering, but also in terms of the ways in which digital convergences set in motion by the internet and social media are forcing news organisations to refashion their relationship with their publics. Where Lippmann's ideas once seemed to hold sway – his 'untrained accidental witnesses' resonating with the cynicism of elitist disdain for the amateur – now it is Dewey's conception of participatory initiatives rooted in everyday, social networks of communal interaction that chimes with the ethos of citizen-led media. These varied inflections, as we shall see, help us to think through the complex, uneven interplay of journalistic and citizen witnessing.

3

Bearing Witness, Making News

Journalists frequently emphasise the importance of witnessing for sustaining the integrity of their craft, particularly where gaining access to see, hear, even feel what is happening has proven arduous, or worse. Occasions available to reflect on their personal experiences, especially where they have proven traumatic, are few and far between, however. Personal blogs – and, for a select few, op-ed features, memoirs and autobiographies in the fullness of time – may prove important in this regard, affording space to share details of occurrences that would otherwise be left safely outside the boundaries of the impartial news report. For most, however, a stiff-upper-lip mentality prevails, such is the tacit discipline of professionalism. Meanwhile, every year, organisations such as the Committee to Protect Journalists, the Independent Press Institute (IPI), Reporters Without Borders and Amnesty International, amongst others, release reports counting the number of journalists killed in the course of reporting on human tragedies unfolding in crises around the world. 'We mourn the loss of the 103 journalists who were killed this year', Alison Bethel McKenzie of IPI stated with respect to 2011; 'To get the story you need to go to dangerous places, whether that is the frontline in a war zone or the top of a crumbling building or the bottom of the ocean, and we salute our colleagues who take those risks for us every day' (cited in IPI, 2012). Needless to say, the price paid for being there, for courageously putting themselves in harm's way in pursuit of a news story that matters, fails to register in statistics alone. Time and again, closer scrutiny of the circumstances involved reveals that it is the journalist's commitment to bearing witness that has placed their life in peril.

'I am a pariah', wrote Russian investigative journalist Anna Politkovskaya (2006) shortly before she was murdered, 'the main result of my journalism throughout the years of the second Chechen war, and of publishing abroad a number of books about life in Russia and the Chechen war.' Despite numerous death threats, she persevered in documenting abuses of civilians' human rights, constantly aware of the grave personal risks she was taking in covering atrocities publicly denied by the authorities. Privately, top officials in the Kremlin were willing to speak to her in order to advance their personal agendas, typically insisting on clandestine meeting places where they could be certain interviews would not be observed. These contacts were maintained despite her 'pariah' status, as she called it, with officials convinced she was 'not one of us', and, as such, 'not on our side'. In her words:

> So what is the crime that has earned me this label of not being 'one of us'? I have merely reported what I have witnessed, no more than that. I have written and, less frequently, I have spoken. I am even reluctant to comment, because it reminds me too much of the imposed opinions of my Soviet childhood and youth. It seems to me our readers are capable of interpreting what they read for themselves. That is why my principal genre is reportage, sometimes, admittedly, with my own interjections. I am not an investigating magistrate, but somebody who describes the life around us for those who cannot see it for themselves, because what is shown on television and written about in the overwhelming majority of newspapers is emasculated and doused with ideology. People know very little about life in other parts of their own country, and sometimes even in their own region. (Politkovskaya, 2006)

To 'merely' report what she 'witnessed, no more than that', proved to be a death sentence. All too aware that certain members of the Russian authorities regarded journalists as a problem that needed to be 'cleansed' from the political arena, she foretold her own assassination in an unpublished article, with the chilling words: 'So they are trying to cleanse it of me and others like me.'

On 7 October 2006, Politkovskaya's body was discovered in the lift of her apartment block in Central Moscow, with a pistol and four cartridges nearby. Earlier that day she had been preparing a report accusing pro-Moscow Chechen security forces of torture. Widely heralded as 'Russia's bravest reporter' in the ensuing news coverage, tributes celebrating her fearless, campaigning journalism were published around the globe. Speculation was rife that her killer had been contracted in order to exact revenge for her work, one of several possible scenarios rehearsed by commentators, but to this day the crime remains unsolved. This had not been the first attempt on Politkovskaya's life, yet she had remained steadfast in her refusal to be intimidated. Having described herself as 'fanatically dedicated to this profession of reporting the world around us', she had readily acknowledged that life could 'be difficult, more often humiliating. I am not, after all, so young at 47 to keep encountering rejection and having my own pariah status rubbed in my face, but I can live with it.' What mattered most, she believed, was to get on with her job, 'to describe the life I see, to receive visitors every day in our editorial office who have nowhere else to bring their troubles, because the Kremlin finds their stories off-message, so that the only place they can be aired is in our newspaper, *Novaya Gazeta*'.

The journalist's belief in the intrinsic value of witnessing – 'to describe the life I see' – represents a guiding tenet of investigative practice, one which is recurrently upheld in normative terms, not least in editorial guidelines, stylebooks, training manuals, textbooks and the like (see also Fowler-Watt, forthcoming; Markhourn, 2011; Matheson, 2003; Wallace, 2009). More often than not, its significance is deemed consistent with a broader historical trajectory, where figures such as Anna Politkovskaya may be rightly acknowledged for extending a tradition of professional resilience and determination. While some accounts may romanticise the intrepid nature of various achievements, even to the point of inviting a certain mythologising of milestones (Watergate being one example), this is not to deny that a commitment to witnessing is a vital dimension of journalism's collective identity – that is, its projection as an 'imagined community' (Anderson, 1983) unevenly sustained in time, space and place. Still, whilst recognising its

importance when journalism is seen to be fulfilling its social obligations, the challenges of bearing witness effectively ensure it will
fall short of these proclaimed ideals. Such will be the case with the
best of intentions, let alone when ad hoc compromises complicate
matters. What happens, we might ask, when journalism fails to
respond appropriately, such as when complicity in reproducing as
fact an official version of events is accepted as the price to be paid
for exclusive access, when self-censorship feels like patriotism in
the national interest, or even when being forced to cede responsibility over telling a news story to a citizen witness needs to be
concealed for fear of reputational risk or embarrassment? These
concerns, amongst a myriad of related ones, begin to show how
fraught the mediation of witnessing can prove to be.

This chapter develops our line of enquiry by considering in
the first instance a remarkable example of journalistic witnessing
under extreme conditions. To my mind, the reportage of Wilfred
Burchett for the London *Daily Express* in the ruins of Hiroshima
decimated by an atomic bomb in 1945 exemplifies the status of the
journalist as professional observer, not least because his commitment to witnessing called into question the proclaimed rationality
of officially sanctioned truth-claims about the non-existence of
'radiation sickness'. Of particular importance here, I shall argue,
was the extent to which his reporting bore witness to the experiences of the *hibakusha* (literally, 'explosion-affected persons')
struggling to stay alive in the shattered city. Next, in moving from
the professional journalist to consider citizen witnessing, this
chapter reverses the logic of most studies of citizen journalism in
a way that may seem counter-intuitive at first. Where such studies
tend to exhibit a tendency to conflate its emergence with the rise
of the participatory culture of the internet, we shall examine
two noteworthy precedents of form, practice and epistemology.
Specifically, Abraham Zapruder's 8-mm 'home movie' footage of
the assassination of US President John F. Kennedy in 1963 will
be considered in depth, together with George Holliday's 'amateur
camcorder video' of Rodney King being beaten by Los Angeles
police officers in 1991. Finally, the latter portion of the chapter
will explore the rise of citizen-led reporting on the internet prior

to the arrival of 'citizen journalism' as a phenomenon, showing how these early examples contributed to changing perceptions of journalism's capacity for witnessing – and with it who could lay claim to the title 'journalist' – in the digital age.

'The Atomic Plague'

The headline of the *New York Times* on 7 August, 1945 spanning the width of the front-page, declared:

> First Atomic Bomb Dropped on Japan;
> Missile is Equal to 20,000 Tons of TNT;
> Truman Warns Foe of a 'Rain of Ruin'

Beneath several subtitles, the news item – filed by Sidney Shalett (1945) and datelined Washington, 6 August – began with the lead:

> The White House and War Department announced today that an atomic bomb, possessing more power than 20,000 tons of TNT, a destructive force equal to the load of 2,000 B-29's and more than 2,000 times the blast power of what previously was the world's most devastating bomb, had been dropped on Japan.
>
> The announcement, first given to the world in utmost solemnity by President Truman, made it plain that one of the scientific landmarks of the century had been passed, and that the 'age of atomic energy', which can be a tremendous force for the advancement of civilisation as well as for destruction, was at hand. (Shalett, 1945)

No details regarding the bombing's effects were presented in the account. 'What happened at Hiroshima is not yet known', Shalett noted, before quoting an unnamed source from the War Department as saying that it 'as yet was unable to make an accurate report' because 'an impenetrable cloud of dust and smoke' had 'masked the target area'. In the absence of information about Hiroshima, the news item turned to the first test of the atomic bomb in New Mexico, three weeks earlier, to describe 'this terrible new weapon'.

In the following days, Hiroshima promptly receded from newspaper headlines. Indeed, the *New York Times* reporting of the 'atom bomb loosed on Nagasaki' on 9 August was overshadowed by the Soviet Union's declaration of war on Japan, which received far more extensive coverage. While press attention to the atomic bombings waned, occasional details emerged via press releases from the War Department. Typically these items focused on such matters as the history of the Manhattan Project, the design and manufacture of the bombs, and the biographical details of those closely involved. Much was also made of the possible industrial applications of 'the basic power of the universe', with news items heralding the 'new era of power' to be ushered in by atomic (or 'cosmic' in some accounts) energy. For military officials anxious to sustain what was evidently overwhelming public approval for the atomic bombings, the question of how best to manage news reports about the horrific aftermath of the attacks risked disrupting otherwise suitably patriotic coverage. Given that in all likelihood it would be just a matter of time before Western journalists attempted to visit the devastated cities, a decision was taken to organise a carefully screened group who could be trusted to reproduce faithfully official definitions of the realities they would confront.

On 3 September, this authorised delegation of four journalists (along with an official censor) was flown into Hiroshima from Washington. Those included were from the *New York Herald Tribune*, the *New York Times*, the Associated Press (AP) and United Press, respectively, along with photographers from the US Strategic Bomb Survey. Manhattan Project deputy-commander, Brigadier-General Thomas D. Farrell, together with a group of its physicists, were on hand to explain the scientific principles involved in the atomic bomb technology. The Pentagon ensured that members of the team would be accompanied at all times by military spokespeople and press officers, who determined what the reporters were able to see and provided them with an array of carefully prepared background papers. Most lacked experience as war correspondents, arguably making the task of ensuring their co-operation that much easier to achieve. In any case, little effort was made to resist the controlling influence of the officials shepherding them around the ruins of Hiroshima, not least because the promise of their guaranteed 'scoop' hung in the balance.

The 'official line' on Hiroshima from Washington revolved around the perceived necessity of restricting reportage to the technological achievement of the atomic bomb itself, especially with regard to its tremendous destructive power on the urban infrastructure. Each member of the authorised delegation of reporters had been brought to Hiroshima in order to 'report on the devastating power of America's new war-winning weapon', a task which they appeared prepared to fulfil. Certainly, this appeared to have been the case with W. H. Lawrence of the *New York Times*. His first report, 'Visit to Hiroshima Proves It World's Most-Damaged City', appeared in the 5 September edition of the newspaper. It described, at times vividly, the terrible scale of the destruction in the 'flattened, rubble-strewn' city. It is Lawrence's second report, datelined Tokyo, 12 September 1945, that is more telling, however:

No Radioactivity in Hiroshima Ruin

Army Investigators Also Report Absence
Of Ground Fusing – 68,000 Buildings Damaged

By W. H. Lawrence (By Wireless to The *New York Times*)

Brig. Gen T. F. Farrell, chief of the War Department's atomic bomb mission, reported tonight after a survey of blasted Hiroshima that the explosive power of the secret weapon was greater even than its inventors envisaged, but he denied categorically that it produced a dangerous, lingering radioactivity in the ruins of the town or caused a form of poison gas at the moment of explosion . . .

He said his group of scientists found no evidence of continuing radioactivity in the blasted area on Sept. 9 when they began their investigations, and said it was his opinion that there was no danger to be encountered by living in the area at present . . .

'The physical destruction in the target area was practically complete', he reported. 'The scene was one of utter devastation. The total number of destroyed and damaged buildings was 68,000, or somewhere between 80 and 90 per cent of all buildings in the city. (Lawrence, 1945)

Radioactivity, Lawrence reports Farrell as stating, had occurred only 'in a limited area whose geographical extent he would not estimate', and 'this exclusively at the moment of the explosion'. Farrell's insistence that there was 'no evidence of continuing radioactivity in the blasted area', like his assertion that there was no danger for those living in the area, passed unchallenged by Lawrence.[1]

Also arriving in Hiroshima on 3 September, however, was Wilfred Burchett, an Australian journalist in the employ of London's *Daily Express* newspaper. Self-described as a 'maverick' who regarded the activities of the 'select party of housetrained reporters' with some contempt, Burchett intended to file a report from the epicentre below where the bomb exploded. To do so, he knew all too well, was openly to defy official restrictions. His dispatch, published by the *Daily Express* two days later, took up most of the front page and a large portion of a page within. It began as follows:

The Atomic Plague

In Hiroshima, thirty days after the first atomic bomb destroyed the city and shook the world, people are still dying, mysteriously and horribly – people who were uninjured in the cataclysm – from an unknown something which I can only describe as the atomic plague.

Hiroshima does not look like a bombed city. It looks as if a monster steamroller has passed over it and squashed it out of existence. I write these facts as dispassionately as I can in the hope that they will act as a warning to the world.

In this first testing ground of the atomic bomb I have seen the most terrible and frightening desolation in four years of war. It makes a blitzed Pacific island seem like an Eden. The damage is far greater than photographs can show.

When you arrive in Hiroshima you can look around for twenty-five and perhaps thirty square miles and you can see hardly a building. It gives you an empty feeling in the stomach to see such man-made destruction. (Burchett, 1945)

The newspaper account continued with a description of the damage in the remains of the city. Burchett relayed how the police chief of Hiroshima took him, along with the local manager of the Japanese news agency Domei, to visit those hospitals still able to treat survivors of the attack:

> In these hospitals I found people who, when the bomb fell suffered absolutely no injuries, but now are dying from the uncanny after-effects.
>
> For no apparent reasons their health began to fail. They lost appetite. Their hair fell out. Bluish spots appeared on their bodies. And then bleeding began from the ears, nose and mouth.
>
> At first, the doctors told me, they thought these were the symptoms of general debility. They gave their patients Vitamin A injections. The results were horrible. The flesh started rotting away from the hole caused by the injection of the needle. And in every case the victim died.
>
> That is one of the after-effects of the first atomic bomb man ever dropped and I do not want to see any more examples of it . . .
>
> The counted dead number 53,000. Another 30,000 are missing which means certainly dead. In the day I have stayed in Hiroshima, 100 people have died from its effects. They were some of the 13,000 seriously injured by the explosion. They have been dying at the rate of 100 a day. And they will probably all die. Another 40,000 were slightly injured. (Burchett, 1945)

These figures, as Burchett (1983) later acknowledged in his book *Shadows of Hiroshima,* were provisional, based on information from the police at the time that would later be revised to upwards of 130,000. 'At the time', he pointed out, 'there was obviously no way of estimating how many victims lay under the ashes nor how many would die soon after from the effects of radiation' (1983: 121). Consequently, he stated that he 'reported what I had seen and heard, while [Lawrence] sent back a prefabricated report reflecting the "official line"' (1983: 17).

Crossing boundaries

Truth-claims presented in the reportage of the members of the authorised press delegation demonstrated to Burchett just how far his own reporting had strayed from the approved position. Indeed, as he wrote, 'I was forced to recognize the existence of an official policy to suppress accurate reportage of the terrible after-effects of nuclear war' (1983: 9). Certainly the realities of life in Hiroshima after the atomic attack, as he witnessed them, bore little resemblance to the depictions presented elsewhere in the newspaper press. Meanwhile, anger and resentment directed at his presence by officials and rival reporters ensured that he was refused transport back to Tokyo with the US Air Force charter aircraft. Similarly, his request that a copy of his report be passed on to his *Daily Express* colleague at press headquarters in Tokyo was also denied by an official. Little did he know, moreover, that further steps would be taken to block his efforts to file follow-up reports on what he had experienced first-hand in Hiroshima. As Burchett (1983: 16) later observed, 'I had no inkling that in writing what I did, I was taking on the US military and political establishment.'

The US military's reaction to Burchett's exclusive had far-reaching repercussions. Burchett attributed the delay of nine days in the *New York Times*'s publication of Lawrence's account from Hiroshima to how 'the nuclear chiefs and their public relations men fumbled with their gears, eventually deciding to mount a counter-offensive to disprove the existence of radiation sickness or any causes of death other than blast and burns' (1983: 44). The official denial of the report's claims (dismissed as 'Japanese propaganda') was quickly followed by a declaration making Hiroshima off-limits to journalists. Back in Tokyo, Burchett was taken to a US Army hospital for tests, where it was found that his white corpuscle count was down, attributed erroneously by the hospital authorities to the antibiotics he had used to treat a knee infection. A drop in white corpuscles, he later learned, 'is a typical phenomenon of radiation sickness' (1983: 23). Burchett speculated that the real reason he was taken to a military hospital so promptly was to ensure that he was isolated from other journalists who might have reported his descriptions of the 'atomic plague' as he had witnessed it. In any case, when he was discharged from the hospital, he discovered that his camera with its full roll of photographs taken in Hiroshima had been stolen. To make matters worse, he was then informed that US General MacArthur had withdrawn his press accreditation and issued an order for his immediate expulsion from Japan (an action which Burchett was later able to have rescinded).

Shortly thereafter, new restrictions were placed on all Allied journalists, including a revised press code that imposed prior censorship on any item concerned with the human aftermath of the atomic attacks. Evidently, this prohibition curtailed the publication of reports discussing how to treat survivors suffering from atomic-bomb-related symptoms. It also served to halt news about the *hibakusha* emerging from Nagasaki. George Weller of the *Chicago Daily News* had slipped away from his military escort on a guided tour in northern Japan in order to board a train to the city to see for himself what had happened (like Burchett, he later expressed his dismay with the other reporters – 'the conformists in my own profession' – covering only officially approved stories (Weller, 2006: 5)). The only Western reporter in the scorched city, he filed a series of lengthy news accounts, including observations made in hospitals about the dead and dying (taking due care to avoid, in his words, 'all horror angles'). One dispatch, typed at 1.0 a.m. on the morning of 9 September, began:

> The atomic bomb's peculiar 'disease', uncured because it is untreated and untreated because it is undiagnosed, is still snatching away lives here. Men, women and children with no outward marks of injury are dying daily in hospitals, some after having walked around for three or four weeks thinking they escaped. The doctors here have every modern medicament, but candidly confessed in talking to the writer – the first Allied observer to reach Nagasaki since the surrender – that the answer to the malady is beyond them. Their patients, though their skins are whole, are simply passing away under their eyes. (Weller, 2006: 43)

This and his other reports, duly forwarded to MacArthur's press headquarters in Tokyo for clearance and transmission, were never released for publication in the press. Years later, Weller argued that the official curtailment of criticism, compounded by 'sycophants, especially newsmen who gave up the fight against censorship', meant the lessons to be learned regarding the human consequences of radiation were not adequately understood by members of the public. 'What the United States badly needs', he wrote, 'is a long cold bath of reality' (2006: 276).

In attempting to draw the world's attention to the atomic survivors' plight, Burchett and Weller had endeavoured to place a human face on official statistics regarding the atomic obliteration of the two cities.[2] Still, the broad parameters marking the normative limits of public debate about the atomic attacks and their aftermath had largely taken shape by 1946. A particularly salient feature of popular perceptions, as discerned impressionistically by various opinion surveys, was the near-absence of publicly expressed remorse. Time and time again, these surveys claimed to show that the vast majority of American citizens considered the invention and use of the atomic bomb to have been a welcome development, hailing its use as a means to save the lives of Allied soldiers (see Hogan, 1996; Lifton and Mitchell, 1995). Examinations of media coverage during this period find little evidence of sustained critiques being presented, and where voices of dissent were advanced (even in such limited form as 'letters to the editor' in newspapers) they often engendered extraordinarily hostile reactions (see Bird and Lifschultz, 1998; Boyer, 1985; Hammond, 1997; Weart, 1988). Such challenges to the emergent imperatives of what was rapidly evolving into a 'nuclear consensus' amongst military, political, economic and scientific – as well as journalistic – elites were typically branded as being disloyal and unpatriotic, if not downright immoral, in their opposition. By the end of the year, the organising tenets of what would evolve into a fully fledged doctrine of 'nuclear deterrence' were being consolidated in ideological terms, not least on the front pages of the world's newspapers.

Our attention in the next section turns from the lone journalist committed to bearing witness at great personal cost to consider the actions of an avid 'home movie' enthusiast, Abraham Zapruder. His attempt to record a memento of his President's visit to his city would become synonymous with witnessing of a different order. The 8-mm film's visual evidence exacerbated a deepening crisis in state power that lingers to this day, the impact of which on news reporting continues to be felt. 'Its voyage onto the pages of *Life*, and later into public archives and across the Internet', one commentator recently observed, 'foretold a world in which citizen video, incentivized with Flip cams, high-speed internet, cash rewards, and Youtube hits, would become an increasingly central part of journalism' (Pasternack, 2010).

A 'home movie' of Kennedy's assassination

Long before the term 'citizen journalism' entered journalism's vocabulary, Abraham Zapruder's home-movie recording of the assassination of US President John F. Kennedy on 22 November 1963 in Dallas, Texas, was being heralded by some commentators for its role in the birth of amateur news reporting. Painfully apparent to many of those first encountering frames selected from the footage reproduced on the pages of *Life* magazine was the extraordinary perspective they offered of one of the most tragic moments in the country's history. Later described by his office receptionist, Marilyn Sitzman, as 'one of hundreds' taking photographs of the presidential motorcade that day, Zapruder had accidentally managed to capture the murder of the President in what various journalists described as a 'scratched', 'juddery', 'jerky', 'soundless' and – most significantly – 'devastating' film. In the words of one writer in the *New York Times* years later, the 'assassination may be the first event of international importance to have fused with one representation, so much so that Kennedy's death is virtually unimaginable without Zapruder's film' (Woodward, 2003).

Zapruder, the part-owner and manager of a factory making women's dresses, had walked from his office to Elm Street to film the President's visit to the city. Having left his camera at home that morning, he was encouraged by work colleagues to return to collect it so that he might shoot a film of interest to his grandchildren. The movie camera in question was a Bell & Howell 8-mm Director Series model, equipped with a telescopic lens and loaded with colour Kodachrome II safety film. Moving his way through the crowds gathered along the motorcade's route, he decided to climb atop a concrete abutment for a better view across Dealey Plaza. Suffering from vertigo, however, he required the help of Sitzman to keep him steady. As the motorcycles leading the motorcade approached, he began filming, but soon stopped when he realised the president's car was some distance behind. Shortly after, he began to film again – the pause later proving controversial in light of what continuous filming might have recorded (an additional rifle shot or shots ostensibly heard by other witnesses) – not realising at first the horrific nature of what was transpiring before his telephoto lens. The pertinent footage, shot in colour at 18.3 frames per second, is 26 seconds in duration (486 frames in total). 'Movie Amateur Filmed Attack' was the headline of a *New York Times* article published the next day, which described Zapruder as an 'amateur movie camera enthusiast' (Johnston, 1963). Several other amateur films were shot that day, although none managed to capture the grisly moment in question.

No news organisation succeeded either, which is the principal reason why Zapruder's footage came to occupy such a contested place in the emergent media ecology of the early 1960s, especially when set against the dramatic rise of television news occurring. 'The rapidity with which news of the assassination of President Kennedy reached virtually every adult in the United States is an impressive demonstration of the influence of the modern news media', observed Bradley S. Greenberg in his study of how news of the shooting was diffused throughout the general public (1964: 225). An unexpected event of this magnitude focused all 'channels of communication' (i.e., both the media and person-to-person channels) at the same time, with nearly one-half of the respondents surveyed saying they first heard of the announcement of the shooting within fifteen minutes (more than 70 per cent were informed within thirty minutes). When asked how they initially found out what had happened, most cited television and radio – the latter being particularly important for people at work at the time – or word-of-mouth contact from other people relaying the news. Much depended on where an individual happened to be, of course, but the relative significance of personal communication proved far more critical than previous research would have indicated, Greenberg argued, suggesting to him that only those physically isolated from their community would have avoided learning what had happened within approximately three hours. Further, this study indicated that those individuals who were better informed about what had happened were more inclined to be active in sharing details with others. The uneven flow of information within or across social networks during a crisis situation thus comes to the fore, with these findings indicating that an individual's position or status, as well as his or her interpersonal ties within the transmission process, shapes the relative amount of information they receive and the speed at which it arrives.

Considered in light of the attention devoted to the role of digital media in social networking today, this early study of news diffusion underscores the necessity of attending to the ways in which individuals relate to diverse forms of news and informational relay (echoes here of breaking news of the raid on Osama bin Laden's compound described at the outset of this book). Even more remarkable is the length of time before the film in question was made available for members of the public to view – twelve years would pass before it would be broadcast on national television for the first time. The morning after Kennedy died, its ownership had been secured by regional editor Richard B. Stolley (1998) on behalf of *Life* magazine. 'Seventeen hours after John F. Kennedy was assassinated in Dallas, I watched him die again – in Abraham Zapruder's shocking home movie', he later recalled. Meeting with Zapruder in the hope of buying the film for his publisher, he knew he had to agree terms quickly before it went to a rival news organisation. 'I was the first journalist to see the film, and before the morning was over, I had persuaded Zapruder to sell it to LIFE', he added; 'We paid a total of $150,000 for all rights.' The arrangement appeared to hinge on a promise made to ensure the footage would never be used in a crude or tasteless way, evidently a serious concern Zapruder expressed. In Stolley's words:

> During our negotiations, Zapruder said again and again how worried he was about possible exploitation of his 26 seconds of film. He told

me about a dream he'd had the night before: He was walking through Times Square and came upon a barker urging tourists to step inside a sleazy theater to watch the President die on the big screen. The scene was so vivid it made Zapruder heartsick. Later, while testifying before the Warren Commission, which was investigating the assassination, he wept as the film was shown. 'The thing would come every night', he said of the dream. 'I wake up and see this.' (Stolley, 1998)

Determined to protect its exclusive rights to the film, especially as conspiracy theories regarding who really killed the President began to swirl (official insistence that Lee Harvey Oswald was solely responsible engendering widespread scepticism), *Time* remained steadfast in its refusal to provide public access to the footage. Instead, a selection of thirty individual frames were published in a black-and-white four-page spread in the 29 November issue, followed by a colour feature in a 'John F. Kennedy Memorial Edition' on 6 December of that year. 'We decided not to authorize the film's use on television, partly for competitive reasons, partly because the head wound in motion is far more ghastly than in print', Stolley explained. On 6 March 1975, however, ABC Television decided to risk a lawsuit by broadcasting a 'bootleg version' on Geraldo Rivera's late-night talk show *Good Night America*, thereby finally placing the film squarely in the public domain. In July 1998, a digitally remastered version of the in-camera original was released on video (the VHS cassette sold for $19.95), enabling members of the public finally to have their first personal access to this form of visual evidence of the crime.

Truth through the viewfinder

Contrasting assessments regarding how effectively journalists reported on the events have proven contentious over the years, not least with respect to the difficulties news organisations experienced in their struggle to convey the moment of death. Barbie Zelizer (1992), in a trenchant analysis, observes that news reporting on the day was 'fraught with problems', namely that 'journalists did not see Kennedy shot, filed reports on the basis of hearsay and rumor, lacked access to recognizable and authoritative sources, and provided faulty information' (1992: 38). Despite there being about fifty journalists in the motorcade, she points out, the most detailed eyewitness testimony, as well as the most revealing photographic documentation, was provided by ordinary bystanders ('local merchants, housewives, and businesspeople'). In her assessment, these and related factors amounted to a 'situation of journalistic failure', one perceived by journalists themselves as threatening to call into question the very legitimacy of their cultural authority as storytellers. In the aftermath of the crisis, they therefore sought to rehearse certain rhetorical strategies regarding these actions with the intention of counterbalancing criticisms of their problematic performance.

This outcome was achieved, Zelizer argues, by concerted efforts to tell the assassination story through one larger narrative that revolved around two pivotal events: the murder of Lee Harvey Oswald two days later in front of television cameras broadcasting live, and Kennedy's funeral, held the following day in Washington, DC. Coverage of these two events, in sharp contrast with the assassination, was widely deemed to be highly successful in journalistic terms. Oswald's death transpired before millions of television viewers, while network reporting of the President's funeral was credited with helping to heal a wounded nation. 'Within all of these circumstances', she writes, 'the fact that the media had missed the actual shooting of the president was transformed from an independent mishap that cast serious doubts on their professionalism into an incidental part of a larger journalistic triumph' (1992: 39). Synecdochic retellings typically blurred 'professional' and 'amateur' contributions to the reporting, accomplished in part through personalisation, whereby emphases were placed on journalists' recollections of their own experiences, as well as through omission, such as *Life*'s decision to leave out any reference to Zapruder in the report accompanying the images taken from the film he shot (Barnhurst and Nerone, 1999; Zelizer, 1992: 68). Contrary to customary rules of acknowledgement, it read: 'On these and the following two pages is a remarkable and exclusive series of pictures which show, for the first time and in tragic detail, the fate which befell our President' (*Life*, 1963). In effect, Zelizer contends, journalists striving to reinstate their authority resorted to questionable tactics to downplay, if not conceal outright, their status as second-hand witnesses.

Disputes over who was responsible for Kennedy's assassination continue to divide commentators, with some questioning journalism's capacity to get to the facts of the matter once and for all. The Warren Commission's 1964 report insisting that Oswald had acted alone did little to placate those convinced that a conspiracy was being covered-up, Zapruder's film representing evidence, in their eyes, of inconsistencies in the official version of events (see Vågnes, 2011; Wrone, 2003). Every year since, in commemoration of the anniversary, news and documentary broadcasts have recurrently performed a public ritual of remembrance, in some years amounting to 'a virtual blizzard of assassination anniversary narratives' (Vande Berg, 1995). Talk of conspiracy has remained a consistent feature, occasionally coming to particular prominence, such as when Oliver Stone's 1991 film *JFK* rehearsed alternative explanations. Stone had reportedly paid the Zapruder family $85,000 for the right to use the footage in his film, which once again ignited public discussion about its evidential value.

In June 1998, the sale of the Zapruder film's exclusive rights similarly proved newsworthy. 'On the surface, it is a transparent record of 26 seconds during a Dallas motorcade', a *New York Times* editorial (1998) commenting on the negotiations observed; 'In fact, it is more opaque than that. A viewer learns to see it, to identify the gestures and motions, one horrible instant after the next. To the cost of that learning each person must attest on his [or her] own.' Time and again, news reports returned to the theme that the historical value of the footage was immeasurable, its iconic status making the assassination virtually impossible to envisage beyond its purview. In the view of arts critic Richard B. Woodward (2003), the Zapruder film has 'wormed itself so deeply into the culture that many of the pathways it opened are no longer visible'. Nevertheless, he continued, 'enough traces of its legacy can be seen – from rampant paranoia about government and disgust with the news media to a loss of faith in photographic truth and the acceptance of graphic violence as part of the movie experience – that recognition of its legacy is in order 40 years later'. More recently, Stolley, in an interview, recalled his good fortune in being in the right place at the right time to secure his exclusive. 'The stringer got word from another reporter, who got word from a cop fourth-hand, and I happened to be in the Adolphus Hotel', he stated. 'It was luck . . . I mean one lucky thing . . . a little bit of skill.' Reflecting on its historical status, he continued: 'Right then it was an astonishing piece of film on a tragic murder, and since then it's become probably the most famous home movie of all time' (cited in Denmon, 2011).

In assessing the relative importance of Zapruder's film as an instance of citizen journalism, much depends on the definitional criteria employed, both at the time and in retrospect. In the view of some, it simply represents 'accidental evidence' (Chalfen, 2002), which is valuable in its own right without making further claims about the intentions of the individual generating it. For others, however, Zapruder's apparent desire to document the event for purposes of a personal record, to be shared with family and friends, represents journalistic activity, accidental or otherwise. Helen Boaden (2008), Director of BBC News, points out that 'accidental journalism is nothing new', so it matters little that Zapruder 'had no idea he would capture the most iconic example of citizen journalism'. Vital to its categorisation in this regard, in the opinion of others, is the transference of his imagery from the private realm to the public sphere. Its appropriation by a news organisation, they argue, conferred upon it journalistic status, namely by virtue of professional judgements made about intrinsic news value.

Still others, such as Dan Gillmor (2006), contend that such considerations cease to be relevant where citizen media are concerned. 'In Dealey Plaza that day', he writes, 'one man happened to capture a motion picture – somewhat blurred but utterly gruesome nonetheless – of those terrible events. Zapruder's work, by any standard we can imagine, was an act of citizen journalism.'

For Gillmor, what matters most in such situations is 'the utter authenticity of the image, made so by the fact that the man was there at the right time with the right media-creation gear'. Indeed, in thinking about how mobile technology affords opportunities for witnessing, he encourages us to consider how today's recording devices might have been pressed into service back in 1963. 'Dozens or hundreds of people in Dealey Plaza would have been capturing high-definition videos of the assassination, most likely via their camera-equipped mobile phones as well as devices designed to be cameras and little else', he imagines; 'They'd have been capturing those images from multiple perspectives. And – this is key – all of those devices would have been attached to digital networks.' Public viewing of the film sequence, which as noted above took twelve years to reach national television, would presumably have occurred almost instantly as videos were posted online. 'Professional news organizations, which would also have had their own videos, would have been competing with a blizzard of other material almost from the start', Gillmor adds. Given the gruesome nature of the images, he further envisages that the online accounts might well have been a primary source for viewers, rather than broadcast media.

We can only speculate, of course, what Zapruder himself would have made of efforts to credit him with playing a formative role in developing citizen journalism with his contribution of home-movie reportage. Described in reports at the time as wanting to do the right thing by the President, including giving the first copy of the film to the FBI, there was little doubt he was deeply upset by his unexpected role as an eyewitness. 'He obviously loved the president', recalled one of the reporters called to the scene, Darwin Payne, who found Zapruder in tears. Standing together in an office they watched a news anchor report that the President had been shot and wounded, possibly severely. 'No, he's dead', Zapruder told Payne. 'I was watching through my viewfinder and his head exploded like a firecracker' (cited in Hennessy-Fiske, 2011). Perhaps the traumatic nature of the experience explains why Zapruder, who died in August 1970, reportedly refused to pick up a film camera ever again.

Videoing the beating of Rodney King

By the early 1990s, home-movie cameras were waning in popularity, mainly because video cameras or 'camcorders' were being priced at a level that made them affordable for middle-class families for the first time. Their 'point-and-shoot' capabilities rendered them relatively easy to use, and they were sufficiently portable and lightweight to hold steady for short periods. Most enthusiasts were content to share the results with family and friends, but for others an emergent genre of 'reality television' programmes – such as *America's Funniest Home Videos* from January 1990 – offered a weekly selection of video clips submitted by viewers, most of which featured humorous mishaps from everyday domestic life. Television newscasts made infrequent use of material sent in from 'amateur videographers', unless compelled to do so by the undeniable news value of what had been caught on tape. Footage shot by eyewitnesses on the scene of a breaking news event were prized over all others, but worthwhile examples of 'folk journalism' – as some 'professional shooters' called it – were few and far between.

One exception to the rule would spark an extraordinary controversy that continues to be referenced as a pivotal moment in the rise of citizen journalism today. George Holliday, thirty-one, a plumbing supply manager, was awoken in his Los Angeles apartment by the sound of sirens in the early hours of Sunday, 3 March 1991. Peering out at what he soon realised was some sort of disturbance involving the Los Angeles Police Department (LAPD), he promptly picked up his new Sony Handycam and stepped onto his second-floor balcony. From this vantage point he shot eight minutes' worth of footage, bearing witness to several white police officers violently beating a black driver ordered from his car, Rodney King, aged twenty-five (it later emerged that King was on parole for a robbery conviction, and his car had been pulled over following what police alleged was a high-speed chase). In response to what officers claimed was King's resistance to arrest, they twice fired an electric Taser gun into his back before proceeding to kick and club him repeatedly as he lay on the ground, desperately pleading 'Please stop! Please stop!' Several other officers arriving on the scene stood by and watched as King suffered more than fifty baton blows, leaving him with a fractured cheek and eye socket, a broken ankle, damaged kidneys, five teeth missing, and multiple bruises and lacerations. Holliday could not believe what he was witnessing. 'I was thinking, "What did the guy do to deserve this beating?"', he later recalled in an interview; 'I came from a different culture [in Argentina], where people would get disappeared with no due process. Police would pick people up on suspicion. I didn't expect this in the US' (cited in Goldstein, 2006).

In the morning, Holliday contacted the police department, asking for an explanation about what had transpired. He was rebuffed. He next telephoned CNN, but evidently no one would take his call, leading him to Los Angeles independent station KTLA-TV. In a handshake agreement, the station agreed to pay him $500 for first-run broadcast rights. Its affiliate agreement with CNN to share news footage enabled the latter to broadcast the video early Tuesday morning, followed later in the day by the three (ABC, CBS and NBC) national networks. Allegations of police brutality, particularly from within Los Angeles's ethnic minority communities, seldom featured in news reporting for reasons typically to do with prejudice and discrimination (unintentional and otherwise), but also because they simply occurred too frequently. Despite Police Chief Daryl Gates claiming the beating was 'an aberration', and news reports describing it as 'shocking', several newspapers noted that civil rights leaders were pointing out that it was only the latest incident indicative of a wider pattern of police violence. King himself was quoted in some accounts shortly before his release from police custody three days later:

> I'm glad I'm not dead. I'm lucky they didn't kill me. [. . .] They handcuffed me and tied me and they shocked me with some kind of device they use [. . .] I was scared, I was scared for my life . . . The guns were pointed right at me . . . I wondered, 'Why are they drawing down on me like this?' [. . .] After they hit me with a shocker, they got a kick out of that . . . because how long they left it in me. It was like they had a little toy and wanted to see how it worked. (cited in AP, 1991)

The same account noted several witnesses insisting that they had not seen King resist, flatly contradicting the LAPD's version of what happened. Viewed in this context, Holliday's videotape could be credited with making an all-too-routine dimension of life in certain parts of the city – virtually invisible in newsworthy terms – visible in brutal detail, and thus into a news story of immediate national – and, soon after, international – significance. 'It's a picture medium', Steve Friedman, Executive Producer of NBC's nightly news, told reporter Deborah Hastings (1991a); 'If you have a fire and you have no pictures of the fire and no one got killed, you don't mention it. If you have great pictures of flames leaping out, you use it.' CNN spokesperson Steve Haworth concurred: 'Even a verbal account does not carry the drama of a picture. It's hard to tell whether this story would have run without pictures' (see also Hastings, 1991b).

A guest appearance by George Holliday on CNN's half-hour programme *Crossfire*, three days later saw him subjected to close interrogation over his video recording. Presenter Mike Kinsley introduced the programme, which focused exclusively on the controversy, by calling the truth-value of the videotape into question:

> Good evening. Welcome to Crossfire. What you're watching is not Kuwait City, it's Los Angeles, and those men with the sticks are not Saddam Hussein's elite Republican Guard, they're the L.A. Police Department. Our guest George Holliday happened to have his camera nearby when this scene took place outside his apartment window early Sunday morning. The victim Rodney King is black. The cops pulled him over after a high speed chase. The tape shows him being kicked repeatedly and hit more than 40 times with night sticks while lying helpless on the pavement, but does the tape show everything? The officers involved say that King resisted arrest and charged them twice before he was subdued. Witness[es] say King offered no resistance. One says that afterwards the officers, quote 'were all laughing and chuckling like they had just had a party.' Los Angeles is in an uproar. Police Chief Darryl Gates says this is an isolated incident. (CNN transcript, 1991)

When questioned about what he had witnessed, Holliday confirmed he was unable to say for certain what had sparked the incident. Identified by CNN simply as 'Amateur Photographer', he explained:

> I was sleeping at the time. I was woken up by the sound and when I looked out of my window I saw the suspect leaning against his car. At that time I decided to go and get the camera and film this and in that meantime I wasn't watching what was happening and when I got out there with the camera he was already being hit so I don't know really what happened. (CNN transcript, 1991)

When asked why he had decided to tape what was happening, Holliday replied:

> Well, I had just bought the camera a couple of weeks ago and you're trigger happy when you've got a new camera and it's the first thing that occurred to me. When I first looked out of my window, there wasn't any action going on or any beating or anything like that and I just wanted to get some footage on my camera and by the time – (CNN transcript, 1991)

Interrupted before he could complete his point, he was then questioned about how the police responded to his telephone call to them the morning after the attack (no response, as noted above, was forthcoming). In the days to follow the *Crossfire* broadcast, media interest in Holliday became increasingly intense, to the point that he felt forced to go into hiding to avoid reporters staked outside his home. Despite complaining about being besieged by the press, however, he did agree to further television interviews, including on *Geraldo* and *Good Morning America*, and spoke at the Los Angeles Press Club. Rumours began to circulate that he was actively considering offers from Hollywood for a movie version of his life story.

In the months to follow, Holliday's efforts to secure financial compensation from news organisations for broadcasting his video encountered stiff resistance, with most insisting its airing fell under 'fair use' principles. 'George Holliday was concerned about the world seeing what happened', Warren Cereghino of Tribune Broadcasting told the *Washington Post* in June of that year; 'He's a nice guy who happened to be in the right place at the right time. He shot this piece of tape that set the world on fire, and he's basically been forgotten' (cited in Kurtz, 1991). Felony assault charges brought against four of the ten police officers involved, together with deepening public pressure on police chief Gates to resign, ensured news reports returned time and again to the video footage in the weeks leading up to the trial. References to other examples of police violence recorded by citizens further illustrated press discussion, with headlines such as 'Videotaped Beating Puts Nation's Police in Spotlight' (AP, 25 March 1991) exploring its prevalence. At the same time, the growing affordability of consumer video cameras became a newsworthy topic in its own right, with concerns raised about topics such as surveillance, privacy and even whether citizens using cameras in this way were safeguarded within the limits of shield laws intended to protect journalists.

Breaking the frame

'And that's the way it is these days', Sylvia Rubin (1991) observed in the *San Francisco Chronicle*; 'In the past few months, those grainy, shaky images shot by amateurs have been all over the news, ranging from the benign – snow falling in the Hayward hills – to the chilling – the beating of Rodney Glenn King by Los Angeles policemen.' She proceeded to suggest that the LAPD tape exemplified 'the merging of TV news with home videos, the latest trend in prime-time newscasts'. Supporting her point were quotations from local news editors. 'It's almost a standard thing now to run home videos on the news', Al Corral of KPIX stated; 'News consultants like us to use the stuff, the audience loves it – it's the next big wave.' Rubin's further interviews revealed similar reflections, with most saying their stations were now using two or three videos on average – labelled 'home videos' on screen – per month. Costs varied, but evidently most contributors were paid about $100, the same amount a stringer might expect to earn for a tape using professional equipment. 'I think they are a positive thing, but it hasn't made a huge difference in TV news', Fred Zehnder,

News Director at KTVU, is quoted saying; 'We would never buy or accept home videos on a controversial issue.' If certain dimensions to a story were best covered by the professional, examples of when the 'amateur news hound' contributed remarkable footage from a unique perspective came readily to mind. The parameters of a news story, it seemed, were being enlarged by video images. The 'L.A. beating video worked because ... just when you thought it was over, they started in on him again. It was ceaseless', Peter Howe of *Life* added; 'One frame of that never would have worked by itself.'

Further descriptions of 'the camcorder boom' discernible in news coverage at the time similarly warrant a close reading for the insights they provide into the relative extent 'amateur footage' or 'homemade tapes' were perceived to be transforming journalism. 'Video Boom has Spawned a New Breed of Citizen Newshounds' read the headline of a pertinent report in the *Atlanta Journal and Constitution* by Bo Emerson (1991). Here 'intrepid professionals' are counterpoised against 'video-camera-toting-amateurs', with the latter's capturing of news stories credited with 'changing the face of television, and the way we look at each other'. In addition to 'newshounds' and 'amateur cameramen', further terms used to label those involved included 'hobbyists', 'home videographers', 'videophiles', 'video vigilantes', 'eyewitness newsfinders' and even 'citizen reporters' on occasion, amongst others.

Debates over whether or not amateurs with cameras deserved similar recognition to professionals took on an added urgency following the acquittal of the four police officers in a court trial that had been relocated to Simi Valley, a conservative and predominantly white suburb. The repeated showing of Holliday's videotape making it impossible for the police officers involved to deny the use of force, their attorneys concentrated on persuading the jury that it did not tell the whole story. Missing was the larger context, they argued, namely King's alleged act of defiance. Further, they proceeded to subject the videotape to a frame-by-frame analysis in order to demonstrate why the officers' actions constituted reasonable self-defence. Viewed in this way, it seemed, police actions could be made to fit a narrative whereby they were responsive to a threat posed by King, who was characterised as being in control of the situation (and therefore 'asking for it', in the words of one juror quoted in the press). The jury, which did not include a black member, had taken seven days to find the officers innocent in a verdict announced on 29 April that stunned onlookers. 'Today, the jury told the world that what we all saw with our own eyes was not a crime', the city's Mayor, Tom Bradley (1992), declared at a press conference. Ted Koppel of ABC News stated 'This is one of those cases in which the first reaction is one of slack-jawed amazement', before posing the question that was already reverberating across the airwaves: 'How could that jury, if they looked at the same videotaped beating that we've all seen a dozen times or more on television, how could they look at that and then vote for acquittal?' (cited in Jacobs, 2000: 115).

Emergent, still inchoate, discourses of citizen witnessing, centred on the evidence of the videotape, were suddenly unravelling. Within two hours of the verdict's announcement, the city erupted in flames, with riots spreading through impoverished neighbour-hoods, mainly in South Central Los Angeles, where racial divisions were bitterly entrenched. As the rioting continued to spiral out of control over subsequent days, the National Guard, and soon after the US Army, were mobilised to restore public order. King himself appealed for the violence to end, asking 'Can we all just get along?' In the aftermath of the 'LA Riots', as they were being called, it became apparent that over 50 deaths were left in their wake, with hundreds of people injured, and over 1,000 buildings destroyed (estimated property costs were at the $1 billion mark). More than 7,000 people were arrested, the police making every effort to secure photographs and videotapes from journalists and city residents alike to use as evidence for mounting prosecutions.

In common with Zapruder's film footage for the Kennedy assassination, anniversary journalism has helped to ensure Holliday's videotape continues to be recognised as part of public memory, representing a milestone – if not tipping point of sorts – in journalism's histories. At the time of the ten-year anniversary, appraisals in the press tended to focus on its wider significance for policing. 'It was 10 years ago Saturday that Rodney King was beaten in

what became an enduring symbol of police brutality and a flash-
point for racial tensions', Linda Deutsch (2001) of AP reported;
'Mere mention of the 1991 beating causes those in power to cringe
as they recall the morning the city awoke to a chilling video of the
black motorist being clubbed and kicked over and over by four
white police officers as he writhed in agony on the ground.' The
impact of 'amateur video' on journalism featured in some reports
that year, such as CNN correspondent Ann McDermott's (2001)
voice-over commenting on a segment of the tape: 'These were the
camera shots seen round the world, the videotaped beating of
Rodney King. And suddenly, video meant power. It could turn a
man into a symbol of police oppression and it could help touch off
a riot.' She went on to add: 'Every day it seems new outrages are
captured by amateur camera people.' In an interview with the *Los
Angeles Times* marking fifteen years after the incident, Holliday
expressed his misgivings about the news media. 'I don't watch the
news or read the papers anymore', he told the reporter, who in
turn observed that he 'may have pioneered "citizen journalism,"
but he feels that he was swallowed up and spit out by CNN and
the like, which, he said, gave him little credit and no compensation for his contribution to history'. Holliday recalled how some
people blamed him for being 'the guy who caused the riots', but
nonetheless added 'every time a policeman has recognized me,
they tell me I did the right thing' (cited in Goldstein, 2006; see also
Myers, 2011a).

On the twentieth anniversary, Eric Deggans (2011) observed in
a commentary for CNN that 'Holliday became the leading edge
in a revolution of technology and social attitude that has made
amateur reporters of us all.' He proceeds to point out:

> Of course, when Holliday captured police delivering more than
> 50 blows to King on March 3, 1991, the technological times were
> different.
>
> The internet was barely more than a curiosity at colleges, largely a
> text-based message service with no icons or attractive graphics.
>
> Cell phones were the size of concrete bricks, and nearly as heavy.
> Video-sharing websites, portable telephones with cameras and digital
> video were still mostly dreams in science fiction stories.

But more than that, the idea that anyone could capture news on their own wasn't yet part of the culture. News was what [national television newscasters] Dan Rather and Tom Brokaw told us it was. (Deggans, 2011)

The incident signalled journalism's growing transformation from craft to an act, he argued, whereby 'every person with web access and a cell phone is a media outlet, capable of committing an act of journalism the moment a news event comes near'. On a fitting tributary note, Deggans concludes by expressing his gratitude:

Thanks, George Holliday. Not just for saving a hapless man's life and putting the question of police methods in poor minority communities on the front burner, but for providing our first peek at a world where the ultimate passion of journalism – to document impactful events as completely as possible and let others experience them quickly – has been passed along to everyone. (Deggans, 2011)

Further anniversary observations that year included Dan Gillmor's (2011) essay crediting Holliday for his act of citizen journalism: 'When people saw that video, they realized a number of things, not least of which was the possibility that average citizens could hold powerful people – the police in this instance – somewhat more accountable for wrongdoing they committed in public places.' And here he adds a vital point, in my view: 'Witnessing was being transformed into action, we all understood.'

'Amateur newsies'

Studies of citizen journalism frequently cite Zapruder's film of Kennedy's assassination and Holliday's video of the Rodney King beating as formative examples of precedents of form and practice without pausing to explore them in depth. My rather brief mention of them in my earlier book, *Online news*, was prompted because I noticed how frequently one or the other figured in journalists' assessments of how amateurs were increasingly challenging them when it came to being first on the scene to document breaking news. At the same time, I was aware that both were telling examples of occasions when ordinary citizens generated personal reportage that contributed to holding the powerful to account – albeit with mixed results. 'Of all the witnesses to the tragedy, the only unimpeachable one is the eight-millimetre movie camera of Abraham Zapruder', an editor of *Life* said at the time, which proved rather optimistic, to say the least (cited in Woodward, 2003). In the view of many commentators, Holliday's video deserved credit for precipitating the resignation of LAPD chief Daryl Gates, and the start of a thorough reorganisation of the police force, by documenting in such graphic detail what institutional racism looks like up close. Further examples from the pre-digital age warrant similar scholarly treatment, in my view, lest we fall into the habit of aligning the rise of citizen journalism with the internet.

There is little doubt, however, that these issues have swirled with ever greater intensity as citizen journalism has succeeded in shaking – some say shattering – the foundations of journalism as a profession in online contexts. Typical treatment in this regard is meted out by Andrew Keen (2007) in his book *The cult of the amateur*, in which he contends that the distinction between expert and amateur has been blurred to a dangerous degree. In the course of a larger critique of how the 'Web 2.0 revolution' is transforming 'culture into a cacophony', he zeroes in on citizen journalists to shoulder their fair share of the blame. In marked contrast with the educated, experienced professional in possession of a craft, he argues, 'citizen journalists have no formal training or expertise, yet they routinely offer up opinion as fact, rumor as reportage, and innuendo as information' (2007: 47). Moreover, they 'revel in their amateurism with all the moral self-righteousness of religious warriors', he adds; 'They flaunt their lack of training and formal qualifications as evidence of their calling, their passion, and their selfless pursuit of the truth, claiming that their amateur status allows them to give us a less-biased, less-filtered picture of the world than we get from traditional news' (2007: 48). And so on and so forth. Still, while it is tempting simply to dismiss such cartoonish caricatures out of hand, this type of hyperbole continues to resonate within journalism's inner circles.[3] The BBC's Andrew Marr, an otherwise astute political journalist (and author of the thoughtful book *My trade: A short history of British journalism*), echoed this line of attack. 'Most citizen journalism strikes me as nothing to do with journalism at all', he told his audience at a literary festival; 'A lot of bloggers seem to be socially inadequate, pimpled, single, slightly seedy, bald, cauliflower-nosed, young men sitting in their mother's basements and ranting. They are very angry people.' In chastising 'so-called citizen journalism' for its 'spewings and rantings', he nevertheless conceded that it is 'fantastic at times' before quickly qualifying his scant words of praise by insisting that 'it is not going to replace journalism' (cited in the *Telegraph*, 10 October 2010).

There is no shortage of such criticisms, of course, some of which are closer to the mark than others. Read with a charitable eye, they usefully underscore the extent to which the phrase 'citizen journalism' has become stretched, almost to breaking point at times. In some hands, it is fair to say, the phrase is so all-encompassing it offers little by way of explanatory power, being employed at the expense of a more nuanced vocabulary necessary to attend to what is a diverse ecology of journalistic activity with adequate analytical precision. Typically overlooked in the more sweeping of claims being made are those citizens generating informed, rigorously investigated reportage – usually intended to supplement the work of professional journalists – in favour of rhetorical fictions about imaginary figures determined to supplant the efforts of their professional rivals at all costs. Much of the vituperative directed at bloggers, in particular, revolves around the perception that they are guilty of offering nothing more than biased opinions in keeping with their own sharply partisan agendas, rather than devoting themselves to legitimate aspirations, namely producing original, impartial reporting deserving of being labelled 'journalism'. It is relatively rare for the individuals under scrutiny actually to self-identify as citizen journalists, but this is a moot point, one which risks complicating efforts to position them as an 'other' threatening to weaken, if not decisively undermine journalism's proclaimed integrity.

This politics of othering, whereby the citizen journalist risks becoming a modern folk-devil of sorts, will be examined further at various points in this book's discussion. In rounding out this chapter, it is worth briefly highlighting some of the ways in which discourses of witnessing percolated beneath debates underway before the term 'citizen journalism' claimed its conceptual purchase.

In focusing on certain formative incidents – or at least ones deemed as such in retrospect – examples include 'The first Internet war' (as it was widely dubbed by journalists and press commentators) being waged over the reporting of Kosovo in 1999. Deserving of particular attention in journalistic terms was the way new forms of reporting afforded members of the public in distant places an unprecedented degree of access and immediacy to breaking news in the war zone. Journalists welcoming the arrival of digital technologies – the internet, but also satellite dishes, laptops, cell or mobile telephones, digital audio and video recorders, and the like – encountered the reservations of critics, many of whom were sceptical about the relative advantages to be gained by 'cyber-journalism' where improving war reporting was concerned. In retracing the contours of this debate today, it is remarkable to observe how novel the idea that the internet could be used as an alternative platform for the eyewitness accounts of ordinary citizens seemed to be. Time and again, press reports acknowledged how the inclusion of first-person accounts of those caught up in the conflict – including those of a 'cyber-monk' offering eyewitness reports from a twelfth-century monastery, a young Albanian teenager's emails describing daily life sent to her 'electronic pen pal' in the United States (who shared them with news organisations), as well as bulletin-board postings relaying, in graphic detail, what NATO's definition of 'collateral damage' following a bombing raid looked like up close – shaped public perceptions of what was actually happening on the ground (see also Bell, 1997; Matheson and Allan, 2009). In so doing, this 'underground', 'populist' or 'amateur' journalism (as it was variously labelled in the press), performed by ordinary citizens using the web, fostered a heightened sense of personal engagement for 'us' with the distant suffering of 'them'.

In July 2000, an Air France Concorde jet on its way to New York crashed shortly after taking off from Charles de Gaulle airport in Paris, killing 109 people onboard, and 4 more on the ground. News organisations were reliant on citizen witnesses for descriptions of what they had seen and heard, as well as for any imagery they were able to contribute. 'The sight of Concorde, the world's fastest passenger aircraft, making its doomed ascent into French skies trailing a plume of fire seconds before exploding in a ball of flame, is certain to be one of the defining news images of the 21st century', journalist Valerie Darroch (2000) wrote at the time. The image in question, which she suggested was likely to be 'indelibly etched on the collective memory', had been taken by an amateur photographer. Hungarian engineering student Andras Kisgergely had been near the scene with his friend Szabolcs Szalmasi, where they were enjoying their hobby of plane-spotting. Reuters purchased the rights to the image, relaying it around the world in time for it to feature prominently on front pages the next day. A Japanese businessperson, waiting to board a flight, also happened to shoot a newsworthy image, capturing the instant the engine burst into flames. Rights for its use were secured by a British picture agency, Buzz Pictures, which in turn negotiated exclusive terms with a London newspaper, the *Mirror* (Rees, 2000).

'Now, everyone is a potential cameraman', Jonathan Duffy (2000) reported for BBC News Online. Crediting amateurs with capturing revelatory images of the crash, he described what proved to be 'the most dramatic evidence of all', namely a video shot by the wife of a Spanish lorry driver – her name was kept anonymous – as the two drove past the perimeter of the airport. 'The grainy, 15-second piece of footage, in which the flames appear to have engulfed the rear of the jet', Duffy observed, 'is a reminder of how everyday technology has brought a chilling reality to television news.' Evidently the couple were paid a 'generous' amount by a Madrid television station, Antenna 3, which in turn negotiated the global rights with the Associated Press Television News agency for a substantial sum. 'The amount paid for the Concorde film is by no means the highest paid for amateur video footage', Julian Lee (2000) remarked in *The Times*, 'but it underlines the increasingly important role that members of the public are playing in news-gathering.'

This role was a particularly poignant one in much of the citizen reporting during the September 11, 2001 attacks and their immediate aftermath. Less than ten minutes after the first passenger jet struck the World Trade Center, eyewitness accounts began to appear on the web, followed shortly thereafter by an astonishing array of images and video footage documenting the unfolding crisis. 'The eyes were everywhere', visual editor David Friend (2007) later recalled; 'Witnesses were observing, and photographing, the deadliest terrorist strike in American history even before they realized it . . . As the moments elapsed, and people took to the streets, Manhattan seemed alive with cameras' (2007: xiii).[4] The contributions of 'amateur newsies' to 'personal journalism', otherwise described as 'DIY [Do-It-Yourself] reporting' or 'citizen-produced coverage', appeared from diverse locations, so diverse as to make judgements about their relative accuracy difficult, if not impossible. 'Anyone who had access to a digital camera and a Web site suddenly was a guerrilla journalist posting these things', said one graphic-designer-turned-photojournalist at the time; 'When you're viewing an experience through a view finder, you become bolder' (cited in Hu, 2001).

Comparing and contrasting differing perspectives proved vital in this regard, encouraging expansive definitions of what counted as a 'news' site. Staff working at Scripting.com for example, a site ordinarily devoted to technical discussions of web programming, moved swiftly to post eyewitness accounts and images. One of the site's writers later commented: 'The Web has a lot more people to cover a story. We, collectively, got on it very quickly once it was clear that the news sites were choked with flow and didn't have very much info . . . There's power in the new communication and development medium we're mastering. Far from being dead, the Web is just getting started' (cited in Kahney, 2001). Sharing this first-person reportage of harrowing experiences, presumably served as a coping strategy for some, possibly engendering a cathartic effect for others. In any case, the contrast between the contributions made via this burgeoning, collaborative newsgathering network and mainstream news reporting was stark. These eyewitness accounts, images and survivor stories, in the words of *New York Times* reporter Pamela LiCalzi O'Connell (2001), were 'social history in its rawest, tear-stained form' (see also Allan 2002, 2006; Gillmor 2006; Sontag, 2003; Sturken, 2007; Zelizer, 2002a, 2005; Zelizer and Allan, 2011).

Fears of terrorism found expression in the immediate news bulletins responding to the *Columbia* space shuttle's disintegration over Texas and Louisiana on 1 February 2003, before speculation gave way to reporting. For 'a country teetering on the brink of war', journalist Ros Davidson (2003) observed, 'the news of Columbia's crash rolled through America's time zones and the vast nation awoke to another scarcely believable tragedy [–] it was a bit like September 11, 2001, all over again'. Television newscasts had interrupted regular programming, suspending it for hours as component elements of the story gradually came into focus. Parallels were promptly drawn with space shuttle *Challenger*'s explosion shortly after lift-off seventeen years earlier, video footage of which helped to supplement the rolling coverage.

'In purely visual terms', Joanne Ostrow (2003) of the *Denver Post* noted, the 'space shuttle tragedy was an elusive news story'. She continued:

> The imagery was difficult to comprehend, whereas the Challenger disaster was telegraphed wordlessly.
>
> In 1986, the Challenger explosion was witnessed at close range, replayed ad nauseam and seared into memory. It served as the visual touchstone for a generation.
>
> The Columbia disaster was not so immediately accessible to the cameras.
>
> Amateur video captured some of the details but from far away, the view obstructed by a telephone pole. Another angle offered a small gleaming star falling through the skies, strangely accompanied by another, and then another cluster of light.
>
> Ultimately, television's images of Columbia's smoking debris – pieces of charred metal and torn insulation wafting in the wind on a brown field – could only convey the aftermath. (Ostrow, 2003)

The absence of a 'single indelible image' meant television news-casts turned to computer-animated illustrations to try to explain what had transpired, as well as to earlier visual material (much of it featuring the seven crew members who perished that day) and interviews with family members to convey the disaster in human terms.[5] As the day wore on, however, more and more citizen imagery came to light. The *Boston Globe*'s Mark Jurkowitz (2003) observed that 'as often happens in today's interconnected, high-tech universe, much of the reporting was done not by jour-nalists, but by ordinary citizens: witnesses, video camera owners, and law-enforcement officials' (he cites a CBS interview featuring a video camera 'hobbyist' who captured the shuttle's break-up, described as 'an unbelievable fireball'). Indeed, imagery solicited from members of the public – amateur astronomers and space flight enthusiasts, in particular – would become vital pieces of evidence for NASA's efforts to pinpoint the source of the calamity as well as to locate debris. 'No other aviation accident has been witnessed by as many people as this one . . . certainly thousands of people across six states, and quite a few of those were pointing all sorts of cameras', technology editor Craig Covault commented at the time (cited in Bostwick, 2003).

These and related examples of citizen witnessing figure to varying degrees in histories of citizen journalism, even though the latter term – as noted above – did not secure its place in the pro-fessional lexicon until the aftermath of the South Asian tsunami in December 2004. By then, it was becoming readily apparent that what counted as journalism in the 'network society' (Castells, 2000) was in a state of flux, with familiar reportorial principles being recast anew by competing imperatives of *convergence* in the mainstream media – and of *divergence* being played out in the margins by 'the people formerly known as the audience', to use academic blogger Jay Rosen's (2006) apt turn of phrase.

4

Witnessing Crises in a Digital Era

Current debates over what should count as 'citizen journalism' continue to prove contentious, even acrimonious at times, for reasons shaped by the perspective, interests and motivation of the individual or group advancing their preferred definition. While there is little danger that consensus is about to emerge any time soon, it is worth bearing in mind that deliberations over the status of the 'amateur' in relation to that of the 'professional' are discernible from the earliest days of something recognisable as 'journalism' in the first place. Indeed, the very notion of the journalist prefigures, to varying degrees depending on its inflection, the non-journalist engaged in related, yet distinctive forms of activity.

Important to recognise for our purposes here is how frequently competing conceptions of citizen journalism revolve around crisis reporting. In considering how its place in the journalistic lexicon was secured, commentators will point to the gradual unfolding of an over-arching narrative that began to consolidate in the immediate aftermath of the South Asian tsunami of December 2004. This was the decisive moment, as noted in chapter 1, when citizen journalism became a prominent feature on the mediascape. The remarkable range of first-person accounts, camcorder video footage, mobile or cell phone and digital camera snapshots – many of which were posted online through blogs and personal webpages – being generated by ordinary citizens on the scene (holidaymakers, in many instances) was widely prized for making a unique contribution to mainstream journalism's coverage. One newspaper headline after the next declared citizen journalism to be yet another startling upheaval, if not an outright revolution, being ushered in by internet technology. News organisations, it was readily conceded, were in the awkward position of being dependent on amateur material in order to tell the story of what was transpiring on the ground. 'Never before has there been a major international story where television news crews have been so emphatically trounced in their coverage by amateurs wielding their own cameras', observed one British newspaper; 'Producers and professional news cameramen often found themselves being sent not to the scenes of disaster to capture footage of its after-math, but to the airports where holiday-makers were returning home with footage of the catastrophe as it happened' (*The Independent*, 2005; see also Allan, 2006; Beckett, 2008; Riegert et al., 2010).[1]

The significance of bottom-up, inside-out contributions from ordinary individuals in relation to the top-down, outside-in imperatives of professional news reporting was being increasingly regarded as indicative of a broader 'citizen journalism movement' throughout 2005 (Schechter, 2005). The summer of that year, in particular, saw two crises unfold that appeared to consolidate its imperatives, effectively dispensing with claims that it was a passing 'fad' or 'gimmick' for all but its fiercest critics (Allan, 2006). The immediate aftermath of the bombs that exploded in London on 7 July destroying three underground trains and a bus, leaving 56 people dead and over 700 injured, was thoroughly recorded by citizens making use of digital technologies. Mobile-telephone cameras captured the scene of fellow commuters trapped under-ground, with many of the resultant images resonating with what some aptly described as an eerie, even claustrophobic, quality. Video clips taken with cameras were judged to be all the more compelling because they were dim, grainy and shaky, and – even more important – because they were documenting an angle on an event as it was actually happening (see also Reading, 2009; Sambrook, 2009).

Similarly, citizens reporting of the devastation wreaked by Hurricane Katrina the following month augmented professional news coverage in important ways. 'I think Katrina was the highest profile story in which news sites were able to fill in the gaps where government wasn't able to provide information, where people were unable to communicate with each other', observed Manuel Perez, Supervising Producer of CNN.com; 'A lot of the most compelling info we got was from citizen journalism' (cited in Online News Association, 28 October 2005). Michael Tippett, founder of NowPublic.com, concurred. In underscoring the extent to which journalism was being effectively democratised, he contended that perceptions of the journalist as an impersonal, detached observer were being swept away. 'This is the real reality news', Tippett insisted; 'People are uploading videos and publishing blog entries, saying, "Let me tell you about my husband who just died." It's a very powerful thing to have that emotional depth and first-hand experience, rather than the formulaic, distancing approach of the mainstream media' (cited in Lasica, 2005; see also Robinson, 2009; Vis, 2009).

In the years since, there has been no shortage of crisis events that have similarly figured in appraisals of the changing nature of the relationship between professional journalism and its amateur, citizen-led alternatives.[2] For those welcoming citizen journalism and its scope for recasting longstanding reportorial principles, a paradigm shift appears to be underway. Traditional news coverage, with its 'he said, she said' formulaic appeals to objectivity, over-reliance on official sources, and dry, distancing, lecture-like mode of address, is looking increasingly anachronistic. Too often it is bland, its notions of fairness and balance contrived, even off-putting in its preoccupation with the esoteric world of elites. Citizen journalism, in marked contrast, inspires a language of democratisation. Journalism by the people for the people is to be heralded for its alternative norms, values and priorities. It is raw, immediate, independent and unapologetically subjective, making the most of the resources of web-based initiatives – collective intelligence, crowdsourcing, wiki collaboration and the like, within and across diverse, evolving virtual communities – to connect, interact and share first-hand, unauthorised forms of journalistic activity promising fresh perspectives. For critics, however, citizen journalism's dangers outweigh whatever merits might temporarily catch the eye, with news organisations at serious risk of losing credibility in their rush to embrace forms of reporting they cannot always independently confirm or verify as accurate. Citizen journalism may be cheap and popular, hence its not inconsiderable appeal for cash-strapped newsrooms, but in a world where facts matter, ethical codes warrant respect, and audience trust is paramount, it continues to spark intense debate about how best to negotiate its benefits and hazards alike.

In keeping with this book's mode of enquiry, this chapter will further extend our elucidation of witnessing, a somewhat taken-for-granted concept in much of the related commentary on citizen journalism. Familiar notions of witnessing, many of which were initially inflected in religious, legal and literary contexts, can easily acquire an abstract, even ethereal quality, seldom set against the hard grind of experience. Next, our attention turns to consider how television news reports of distant atrocities, viewed from the relative safety of Western households, lay claim to a form of witnessing where journalists strive to represent the suffering of strangers in order to 'make it real' on our behalf. This process is beset with difficulties, not least when the journalist as witness is transformed into 'reporter as rescuer', a phrase used by broadcaster Jon Snow below. Reversing these logics is citizen witnessing, with its capacity to re-write the rules of reportorial imperatives. To illustrate the issues at stake, we then turn to examine the news reporting of the Mumbai attacks in November 2008. Citizens using social networking, not least Twitter, demonstrated its potential for informational relay in a manner that astonished many journalists at the time – and continues to resonate, as we shall see, in pertinent debates today.

The figure of the witness

Recurrently overlooked in discussions of witnessing is the historical specificity of what may otherwise seem a timeless, immaterial philosophical ideal. Several of the most influential analytical approaches, Andrea Frisch (2004) argues, 'are predicated on the conceptual abstraction of the eyewitness as a quasi-Cartesian first person, an abstraction that simply ignores the web of social relationships in which witness and testimony have historically been implicated' (2004: 14). In devoting her efforts to tracing the gradual emergence of what she characterises as the figure of the modern eyewitness, she dispenses with a language of universal principles in order to highlight the interweaving of historically contingent factors.

Vital in this regard is the need to distinguish how these factors coalesced to bring about the slow, unsystematic displacement of pre-modern conceptions of eyewitnessing. In other words, the invention of the eyewitness as it tends to be understood today did not take place at a single, revolutionary juncture; rather, Frisch suggests, it arose through an uneven process of searching for more effective ways to establish and maintain the credibility of testimony under the pressure of cultural constraints. Statements made by eyewitnesses, when viewed from this perspective, cease to be regarded as 'privileged sources of an epistemic truth independent of any particular social context' (2004: 13). It is in attending to these changing contexts, it follows, that the ways in which literary, legal, religious and technological influences subtly shaped the changing rhetoric of witnessing will come to the fore.

In order to clarify further the distinctive features of the modern eyewitness, Frisch proceeds to examine first-hand accounts of travel, beginning with the writings of Marco Polo and John Mandeville, as well as the satiric novels of François Rabelais. Discernible here are earlier manifestations of what she terms 'ethical' witnessing characteristic of medieval European folklaw, whereby the evaluation of testimony revolves around feudal norms and values of jurisprudence. Briefly, the truth-value of the pre-modern eyewitness's testimony is based upon their status within an ethical community, its members serving as witnesses to his or her moral integrity, lending support (or not) to their standing as a credible person, which mattered more than ascertaining the accuracy of specific testimonial claims. In counterpoising ethical eyewitnessing with the epistemic eyewitnessing slowly gaining stature in the law courts during the fourteenth and fifteenth centuries, Frisch identifies a shift partly attributable to the impetus provided by writing in juridical procedures. 'When a physically absent witness addresses an anonymous audience, pre-modern ethical modes of testimony reach the limits of their efficacy, and the model of the witness as a second person is fundamentally transformed', she writes; 'No longer a matter of "being here" to bear ethical witness among familiars, witnessing becomes associated with the notion of "being there," alone, to have an epistemic experience of something alien or unprecedented' (2004: 17). It is precisely this tension between the conditions of oral exchange and those of written communication, she argues, that eventually gives rise to the preference for first-person singular in eyewitness histories.

While at first glance the pertinence of sixteenth-century French eyewitness travel accounts of the New World scrutinised by Frisch to illustrate her thesis may seem far removed from our purposes here, I would hope this discussion begins to show how efforts to compare and contrast varied conceptions of witnessing in early genres of writing may prove rewarding, with insights relevant to today's priorities. Histories of eyewitnessing in journalism will benefit from explorations into possible connections with these genres, I would suggest, not least in light of their respective investment in sustaining a claim to facticity inscribed in the perceived authenticity of first-hand experience. In addition to facilitating fresh thinking about how discursive conventions consolidate over time, this line of enquiry also encourages us to consider how current protocols of witnessing continue to evolve in relation to a myriad of factors.

To clarify, the journalistic presupposition that an individual becomes a witness the moment she or he acquires knowledge of an occurrence (visually or otherwise) through first-hand experience providing quasi-objective information – what Frisch, once again, calls modern or epistemic witnessing – is frequently asserted without due attention given to its varied inflections in different reportorial contexts. To what extent, we may ask, are customary conceptions of the witness open to reconsideration, not least as new technologies create spaces for re-imagining its imperatives in ways that render problematic more traditional epistemic definitions of testimony? One need not subscribe to a conception of testimony mired in postmodern relativism – effectively detached from a meaningful engagement with the materiality of the social world – to appreciate that the figure of the witness is being sharply redrawn by digital media and the capacities for social networking their uses engender.

'Seeing is believing'

Media-centred approaches invite further questions about modes of witnessing and their persistence in journalism, particularly where discourses of impartiality claim their purchase. In his book *Seeing things: Television in the age of uncertainty*, John Ellis (2000) places the concept of witnessing under sustained, thoughtful scrutiny in a manner that similarly chimes with our purposes here. 'The twentieth century has been the century of witness', he suggests, a claim informed by what he regards to be a profound shift in the way that we perceive the world existing beyond our immediate experience (2000: 9). As he explains:

> During this century, industrial society has embarked upon a course that provides us as its citizens with more and more information about events that have no direct bearing upon our own lives, yet have an emotional effect upon us simply by the fact of their representation and our consequent witness of them. The fact that the representation, on the news, is necessarily skimpy and inadequate, snatched from the living event, makes our role as witnesses all the more difficult. The events cannot be poignant because they are radically incomplete: they exist in almost the same moment as we do when we see them. They demand explanation, they incite curiosity, revulsion and the usually frustrated or passing desire for action. We need, in other words, to work them through. (2000: 80)

This Freudian inflection of 'working through' is important to Ellis because it helps to highlight how the media process forms of visual evidence – effectively worrying them over until they are exhausted – when striving to explain the witnessable world in all of its complexity. Television, in particular, 'works over new material for its audiences as a necessary consequence of its position of witness', he writes. It 'attempts definitions, tries out explanations, creates narratives, talks over, makes intelligible, tries to marginalize, harnesses speculation, tries to make fit, and, very occasionally, anathemizes' (2000: 79). For Ellis, then, it is the ensuing 'sensation of witness' that is a crucial, yet largely unexplored dimension of this process of mediation, only part of which is expressed in the familiar phrase 'seeing is believing' so often used to characterise this dynamic of perception.

Media imagery, it follows, draws us into the position of being witnesses, where what is rendered visible in front of the camera becomes undeniable. 'We live in an era of information', Ellis maintains, 'and photography, film and television have brought us visual evidence. Their quasi-physical documentation of specific moments in specific places has brought us face-to-face with the great events, the banal happenings, the horrors and the incidental cruelties of our times', which makes it impossible for us to claim ignorance as a defence (2000: 9–10). By this logic, we are necessarily implicated as 'accomplices' in the events in question, namely because we have seen what happened when they transpired (or, more typically, their distressing aftermath) in the media reportage. Our 'complicity' is engendered by this relationship to what is seen, Ellis argues, because knowledge of an event implies a degree of consent to it. Even though we may be witnesses in another time or a different space, the event depicted makes a silent appeal to our conscience: 'You cannot say you did not know.' Still, he cautions, this is not to suggest that to witness an event 'in all of its audio-visual fullness' is the equivalent of being present at the scene in question; 'There is too much missing, both in sensory evidence (no smell, no tactile sense) and, more importantly, in social involvement' (2000: 11). At stake, Ellis contends, is the way in which the audio-visual, as a form of witness, offers what he terms 'a distinct, and new, modality of experience'. This feeling of witness may be one of separation and powerlessness (events unfold, regardless) or, alternatively, the opposite: 'It enables the viewer to overlook events, to see them from more points of view than are possible for someone physically present: to see from more angles, closer and further away, in slow and fast motion, repeated and refined' (2000: 11). Television news, to the degree it affords the viewer a sense of co-presence with the event it seeks to document, turns the act of witness into an everyday, intimate act in the private home.

In the years since the publication of *Seeing things*, a number of theorists have sought to elaborate further similar lines of enquiry. John Durham Peters (2001), taking his cue from Ellis, proposes that witnessing 'is an intricately tangled practice', one that 'raises questions of truth and experience, presence and absence, death and pain, seeing and saying, and the trustworthiness of perception – in short, fundamental questions of communication' (2001: 707). Whilst concurring with Ellis in the main, Peters places greater emphasis on the positive aspects of this 'common but rarely examined term' of 'witnessing', briefly highlighting how three different domains – law ('the procedures of the courtroom'), theology ('the pain of the martyr') and atrocity ('the cry of the survivor') – have endowed it with 'extraordinary moral and cultural force'. In seeking to clarify matters, he points out that, in journalism, 'a witness is an observer or source possessing privileged (raw, authentic) proximity to facts', a commitment it shares with law, as well as literature and history. 'A witness', he writes, 'can be an actor (one who bears witness), an act (the making of a special sort of statement), the semiotic residue of that act (the statement as text) or the inward experience that authorises the statement (the witnessing of an event)' (2001: 709). As a verb, he adds, 'to witness' signals a double quality: it can be a sensory experience, involving one's own eyes and ears in the witnessing of an event, as well as a discursive act, where one's experience is stated for the benefit of an audience elsewhere. 'Witnesses', in this latter regard, 'serve as the surrogate sense-organs of the absent' (2001: 709). Nevertheless, he readily concedes, this proclaimed 'presence-at-a-distance' is fraught with difficulties, which warrant much greater attention than they have typically received. 'In media events', he writes, 'the borrowed eyes and ears of the media become, however tentatively or dangerously, one's own. Death, distance and distrust are all suspended, for good and evil' (2001: 717).

A continuum of sorts is thus apparent between Ellis, with his emphasis on the ordinary, even mundane everydayness of witnessing via television, on the one end, and Peters, who underlines its extraordinariness, involving 'mortal bodies in time' quite likely to be in 'peril and risk', on the other. Tamar Ashuri and Amit Pinchevski (2009), while aligning themselves with the general position adopted by Peters, attend to alternative emphases. Different events, they suggest, 'give rise to different modalities of witnessing', because 'the ontology of witnessing is dependent on its context' (2009: 133). Being a witness, it follows, 'is subject to constant struggle, not privilege; it is something to be accomplished, not simply given' (2009: 136). In theorising witnessing as a practice 'entangled with conflict and power', they succeed in accentuating the importance of attending to the 'contested ground of experience' in a manner that complicates rationalist, reason-based models in advantageous ways. Carrie Rentschler (2004, 2009) similarly stresses the need to think through questions of experience, maintaining that to witness 'means far more than to just "watch" or "see"; it is also a form of bodily and political participation in what people see and document that is often masked by their perceived distance from events' (2004: 298). In proposing that witnessing be regarded as a form of participation necessarily implicated in the pain or suffering of others, then, she draws out of the concept of mediation certain tensions associated with complicity highlighted by Ellis (2000) above. 'Witnessing needs to become part of a larger political and ethical mobilisation towards the eradication of violence', she argues, which will demand a 'different kind of media documentation, one that can help teach people how to act as responsible citizens, with a commitment to social justice, through acts of witness' (2004: 302; see also Ellis, 2012).

Spectacles of suffering

Few would dispute the globalization of media is crucial in this regard, even if attendant public spheres, as John Keane (2003) argues in *Global civil society?*, 'are still rather issue-driven and more effective at presenting effects than probing the intentions of actors and the structural causes of events' (2003: 169; see also Papacharissi, 2010). Anticipating Rentschler's point above about the teaching of citizenship, he suggests that global audiences are frequently being taught lessons in 'flexible citizenship', where boundaries between 'native' and 'foreigner' blur, just as a sense of ethical responsibility converges with a cosmopolitan affectivity (2003: 170). In his words:

> by witnessing others' terrible suffering, at a distance, millions are sometimes shaken and disturbed, sometimes to the point where they are prepared to speak to others, to donate money or time, or to support the general principle that the right of humanitarian intervention – the obligation to assist someone in danger, as contemporary French law puts it – can and should override the old crocodilian formula that might equals right. (2003: 171)

Related issues associated with 'distant suffering', a recurrent theme in pertinent scholarship, assume an added complexity when considered in relation to how journalistic mediations of witnessing encourage (as well as dampen, or dissuade) a shared sense of pathos – the 'politics of pity', as Hannah Arendt (1990) described it, or news 'saturated with tears and trauma' as Carolyn Kitch (2009) contends – amongst those looking on from afar.

'The spectacle of the unfortunate being conveyed to the witness, the action taken by the witness must in turn be conveyed to the unfortunate', Luc Boltanski (1999) observes; 'But the instruments which can convey a representation and those which can convey an action are not the same' (1999: 17). Public opinion is at stake where effecting change is concerned, which brings the role of the news media to light, namely their position in a chain of intermediaries offering the spectator a 'proposal of commitment' to negotiate (important to the spectator for a number of reasons, but particularly when he or she is unable to grasp adequately, let alone interrogate, the intentions of those presenting the unfortunate's suffering). 'The spectator can accept the proposal made to him [or her], be indignant at the sight of children in tears being herded by armed soldiers; be moved by the efforts of this nurse whose hands are held out to someone who is starving; or feel the black beauty of despair at the execution of the absolute rebel proudly draped in his crime', he writes; 'He [or she] can also reject the proposal or return it' (1999: 149). Of critical significance, it follows, are conditions of trust, which render abstract notions of mediation concrete in highly affective terms (see also Couldry, 2012; Tester, 2001).

'Trust', as Roger Silverstone (2006) reminded us, 'is a slippery thing; it is always conditional, requiring continuous maintenance and evidence of fulfilment' (2006: 124). To the extent the world has taken a 'pictorial turn' (Mitchell, 2011), television news elevates the paradigm of the witness as trustworthy arbiter of visual evidence in a way that recurrently valorises immediacy as preeminent news value (see also Huxford, 2004; Pantti and Bakker, 2009). Eric Taubert (2012) contends:

> Modern audiences have come too far – they can't turn back now. They want more than talking heads juxtaposed against lackluster images of smoky ashes. They want the flames. They want the fire. They want to understand what the people who witnessed the unfolding news event experienced. They want to see what breaking news looks like through the eyes of those who saw it. They want to live vicariously through pixels. They expect a 360 degree view of the story. (Taubert, 2012)

And 'we' want it *now*, it seems. 'Live footage is the genre of the witness, par excellence', Lilie Chouliaraki (2006) points out. The near-instantaneous presence of the camera at the scene, instrumental to live news's claim to factuality, she argues, claims to 'bring back home' an event in all of its raw contingency. 'This "mechanical witness," however, needs to be combined with verbal narratives that harness the rawness of the event and domesticate its "otherness"', thereby offering an explanation of what is happening while, at the same time, protecting viewers from the risks of trauma associated with the act of witnessing (2006: 159). In rendering suffering both 'cognitively intelligible' and 'emotionally manageable', live footage transforms a tragic scene into a television spectacle. Here Chouliaraki (2010a) suggests witnessing works as an economy of regulation in this regard – that is, to the extent it manages the boundaries of taste, decency and display in ways that invest imagery with a 'force of authentic testimony', it leaves little space for the 'truth' of the reported event to be questioned. Witnessing, without being explicitly political, she writes, 'produces forms of pity that primarily rely on the beautification or sublimation of suffering, thereby strategically participating in the political project of imagining community' (2010a: 522). This invocation of community may well create a sense of shared solidarity between viewers, but in so doing there lurks the danger that suffering will be represented in a manner that construes it as beyond, or simply irrelevant to, direct action as a response.

Chouliaraki's emphasis on witnessing as an economy of regulation privileging certain modes of seeing suffering as authentic (or not, as the case may be) usefully underscores the tensions in the duality of journalistic reporting, namely its requirement to both record (eyewitnessing) and to evaluate reality (bearing witness) in productive ways (2010a: 528, 529). She quotes a statement from the BBC College of Journalism – 'Good journalism in the field is about bearing witness to events that others may wish to hide or ignore; or which are simply too far out of sight for most people to care about' – which neatly illustrates the assumed subjunctive connection between reporting on events and engaging viewers' capacity to care (cited in Chouliaraki, 2010b: 305). Precisely what this entails in news media terms, however, is only now gradually becoming clear. She points out that the BBC has appropriated citizen journalism in its own 'cosmopolitan vision', thereby encouraging more collaborative conceptions of news increasingly open to 'ordinary' voices (see also Silverstone, 2006). The nature of journalistic witnessing is being transformed as a result, she maintains, with the term 'ordinary' signifying 'precisely this break with the monopoly of professional witnessing in favour of a valorisation of the "person on the street" as the most appropriate voice to tell the story of suffering' (2010b: 308). More than widening narrative parameters to be more inclusive, as important as such a strategy often proves to be, this valorisation makes possible an alternative epistemology of authenticity. Specifically, it works to 'relativise the empiricism of facts in television news, by placing it side by side with the empiricism of emotion' (2010b: 308). Hierarchical boundaries between professional and citizen notions of fact become blurred, she argues, so that the immediacy of experience redefines what counts as news – and in so doing, endows it with a new moralising force (see also Bell, 1997; Mirzoeff, 2005).

In contrast with the pessimism that tends to underlie critiques of journalism's potential to forge points of solidarity amongst distant peoples around the world, let alone help to fashion global public spheres of dialogue and debate, this more optimistic appraisal discerns cracks in the façade of corporate media hegemony. Still, Chouliaraki cautions, much work remains to be done to investigate how the act of witnessing itself is evolving.

Blurring distinctions

Reflecting on the challenges he has faced in the field, Jon Snow (2005) of Britain's *Channel 4 News* emphasises the value of subverting professional labels. He observes how in desperate circumstances, in this case when reporting on the aftermath of Hurricane Katrina in the US, the journalist as witness can be transformed into 'reporter as rescuer'. He writes:

> such is the chaos of federal failure that once on the water, we are alone on 39th Street, beseeched by an African-American man wading up to his chest to save his grandfather and his own children. The old man is 84, incontinent in a filthy bed in a saturated downstairs living room. We heave him, leaking, into the boat in his bed sheet. He's conscious but barely speaks. I think he is probably dying. There is congealed blood on his large stomach. The children are tiny and frightened as I lift them into the boat. The reporter as rescuer. Surely this breaks the rules. But this is flood, this is humans, this is contact with the epicentre of levy failure, Bush failure, America failure. (Snow, 2005)

Breaking the rules, as Snow aptly characterises it, refers to a violation of the unspoken codes of impartiality, which dictate the journalist as storyteller does not become the story. Even more telling in this particular example is the correlation he draws between the plight of those struggling to survive with the perceived failure of the Bush administration to muster an adequate response. When impartial reporting is restricted to the 'who?', 'what?', 'where?', 'when?' and 'how?' of events, efforts to answer 'why?' will likely prove contentious, transgressing as they do the boundary invoked between objective fact and subjective interpretation.

In the aftermath of the earthquake that devastated Haiti in January 2010, several news organisations were praised by some – and condemned by others – for decisions made by their journalists to cross the line from dispassionate witness to impassioned participant. 'In a disaster this huge, television reporters are the heralds of the fund-raising effort', Alessandra Stanley (2010) pointed out in the *New York Times*. News organisations interwove into their coverage updates on how and where to donate money for the relief effort, enabling them to remind 'viewers – and earthquake victims – that journalists serve as a pillar of the rescue mission, on the scene to do more than just gather information'. CNN, in particular, found itself under scrutiny for its blurring of these positions otherwise counterpoised. The network's Chief Medical Correspondent Sanjay Gupta appeared onscreen attending to victims as patients over several days, even performing surgery under the glare of television lights (although it was 'The Gupta Effect' that attracted headlines, ABC, CBS and NBC also deployed journalists qualified as doctors who offered medical assistance on camera, including splinting broken bones, assisting with an amputation, delivering babies, and so forth). Having followed the sound of gunshots to a shop being looted, CNN correspondent Anderson Cooper observed a small boy injured by a piece of concrete thrown into the crowd. Swiftly gathering him in his arms, he hurried down the street to safety. 'I could feel his warm blood on my arms. I stood him up, but he was clearly unable to walk. He wiped his bloody face, and I tried to reassure him', Cooper (2010) wrote on his blog afterwards; 'He had no idea where he was, and he clearly couldn't walk, so I picked him up again and handed him over to someone behind that makeshift barricade.'

Whether these types of actions were to be lauded for exhibit-

ing compassion above and beyond the call of journalism, or condemned for self-congratulatory, overly emotional and therefore
manipulative reportage, which happened to make for visually
arresting television, divided commentators (some critics believing the repetitive broadcast of this type of footage to be a cynical
effort to enhance corporate news reputations and boost ratings).
A key point of contention proved to be the proper status of the
journalist as witness under such tragic circumstances. It is hard
to criticise a reporter who 'puts being a decent, caring, empa-
thetic human being ahead of practicing some unattainable goal
of "objective" journalism', Jamie McIntyre (2010), formerly of
CNN, commented; 'And Haiti is a story that pulls unceasingly at
one's heartstrings. I'm not there, but I can just imagine the emotions that any decent person would feel bearing witness to all that
suffering' (see also Balaji, 2011).

Considering the issues at stake from the professional journalist's perspective, a recent study by Simon Cottle (2013) of
the practices adopted by Western journalists bearing witness
to disasters proves valuable. Drawing on several interviews, he
notes how those engaged in this type of reporting will frequently
acknowledge that certain calculations are inevitably entered into
when decisions need to be made about the relative saliences –
and silences – of news coverage. News organisations exhibit an
institutionalised, seemingly naturalised, 'calculus of death', he
argues, which is ethnocentric and politicised – being shaped by
geo-political interests, cultural outlooks, competitive pressures,
technological resources, narrative formats and the like – in the
course of routine, pragmatic judgements about newsworthiness
and audience appeal. 'The calculus of death operative inside the
world of journalist practices today produces a peculiarly myopic
and amoral – if not immoral – "witnessing" of disasters, death and
dying', he writes. This is 'a witnessing that falls short of "bearing
witness" in the morally infused sense', but may 'yet serve to under-
pin a cosmopolitan outlook and sense of responsibility for others'
(2013; see also Hanusch, 2010; Richards, 2010).

Discernible here is a different professional disposition at work,
Cottle contends, one which gives expression to journalists' personal

commitments, even when held in tension with the institutionally expedient calculus of death. For those journalists striving to ensure that their audiences engage, care about what is being presented to them, the experiential ontology of witnessing (underwriting the claim to be the 'eyes and the ears' of disaster) blurs into the epistemology of witnessing (active narratives of news storytelling) to engender a sense of shared humanity with those caught up in catastrophic events. Cottle describes this confluence of witnessing as journalism's emergent 'injunction to care', which, contrary to the conventions of dispassionate, detached reporting, recognises the bonds of moral responsibility. Such sentiments chime with a more 'cosmopolitan outlook', he writes, being 'professionally enacted through journalism's acceptance of the primary ontology of witnessing as seeing and "being there", experienced through bodily immersion and beneficent embedding in the disaster zone'. They are enacted in epistemological terms, in turn, 'through crafted narratives designed to humanize, *"sense-ize"* and "bring home" the plight of distant others – strangers still – but people not so unlike ourselves and deserving of our recognition and care' (2013: 13). It is in attending to the complexities in negotiating the competing tensions between the calculus of death and the injunction of care, it follows, that journalists will be better placed to facilitate new forms of connectivity.

This question of connectivity necessarily highlights the contributions made by ordinary individuals who find themselves – quite unexpectedly, more often than not – spontaneously giving expression to a civic compulsion to intervene. In this performative sense, it is often possible to discern in citizen witnessing an elaboration of this injunction to care in the motivation people demonstrate to share their experiences under trying, even dangerous circumstances. The reasons why individuals prove willing to put themselves in harm's way, where the risk of physical violence may be less emotionally traumatic than the sheer frustration of being unable to help those in desperate difficulty, will almost always be left unspoken. Efforts to identify a single, rational explanation overlook the intimate imbrication of subjectivities likely to be conveyed by anyone asked to explain themselves with the benefit of hindsight. Intermingled within such accounts, however, may well be personal commitments to the ideals of citizenship, if not to those of citizen journalism in formal terms.

In the next section of this chapter's discussion, we turn to consider in close detail a further example of crisis reporting with a view to discerning additional contours of what I am describing here as citizen witnessing. The year 2008 had seen a number of initiatives emerge which, to varying degrees, were interpreted as signifying the consolidation of citizen journalism as a movement making its presence felt across the mainstream newscape. In May of that year, YouTube's channel Citizen News was launched, joining CNN's 'i-Report', the BBC's 'Your News', the 'You Witness News' venture jointly launched by Yahoo and Reuters, and MSNBC's Newsvine, amongst others in signalling further collaboration – or appropriation, in the eyes of some – blurring the professional/amateur divide. Interestingly, Twitter's potential as a real-time news tool was also being increasingly recognised by journalists and their editors at this time. Crisis incidents in which Twitter proved an invaluable resource for breaking news coverage included natural disasters in Myanmar and China in May (Black, 2008, Nip, 2009), as well as an earthquake in Southern California in July (Guynn, 2008), but it was the violent siege in Mumbai, India, in November that brought the site to the fore of news media attention – and with it, micro-blogging's potential for citizen witnessing.

Tweeting terror

Widely dubbed as 'India's 9/11', the attacks – evidently perpetrated by ten members of a Pakistan-based militant organisation – began to unfold in Mumbai on the evening of 26 November 2008. Several different sites were targeted, including the city's main train station, Chhatrapati Shivaji Terminus (CRT), where commuters were shot indiscriminately; Nariman House, associated with the Jewish Chabad Luvavich movement, where 13 hostages were taken (5 of whom were murdered); the Trident-Oberoi Hotel, where 30 people were killed; and the Taj Mahal Palace Hotel, where most of the casualties took place as the assailants moved from floor to floor in a killing spree. In total, at least 172 people died, and over 300 others were injured, during a sixty-hour siege that transfixed news audiences around the globe.

During the crisis, the highly sensationalised forms of news coverage provided by the Indian news media – what critics called the 'TV terror' of the 24-hour news channels – were widely condemned for reporting 'exclusives' which more often than not proved to be wildly inaccurate rumours (Pepper, 2008; Sonwalkar, 2009; Thussu, 2009). Attracting much more positive attention, however, was the surprising role played by ordinary citizens in gathering information, with the micro-blogging service Twitter regularly singled out for praise as a vital source for real-time citizen news (see also Bahador and Tng, 2010; Matheson and Allan, 2010). 'At the peak of the violence', a *New York Times* report observed, 'more than one message per second with the word "Mumbai" in it was being posted onto Twitter, a short-message service that has evolved from an oddity to a full-fledged news platform in just two years' (Stelter and Cohen, 2008). Twitter, the report added, represented the latest example of how technology was 'transforming people into potential reporters' (see Bahador and Tng, 2010; Ibrahim, 2010; Mortensen, 2012; Reading, 2009; Tait, 2011).

Vinukumar Ranganathan's first thought was to grab his digital camera when he heard the explosions outside his home in Mumbai's Colaba district, he explained afterward. 'When I heard two loud reverberating [noises] in the night around 10:45pm, I picked up my camera bag and headed out', he told Wired.com; 'As I was stepping out my sis said there are reports of firing at CST (train station) – but I suspected it was [a] bomb as it was pretty loud. Turns out they were grenades' (cited in Stirland, 2008). Ranganathan, a 27-year-old business development manager, soon determined that the 'grenades were thrown by the terrorist from the terrace of the building on to the adjacent gas station. And they have taken some families hostage . . . the situation is still not in control. I have heard 5 gun shots in the last hour (12 hrs after start of the incident!)', he added. Amongst the 112 images he uploaded to the photo-sharing site Flickr – 'a chilling slideshow', in the words of an Australian news site (Moses 2008) – an hour and a half later were several documenting the destruction left in the wake of the attacks. London's *Daily Telegraph* credited him with providing 'perhaps the most amazing and harrowing first-hand account of the Mumbai attacks', in a report praising his 'series of photos showing mangled cars, bloodstained roads and fleeing crowds' (Beaumont 2008). Andy Heath (2008), in a post on the Demotix: News by You site, noted how Ranganathan's 'atmospheric and moving images emerged before professional photographers could move into action, and received thousands of views as the crisis unfolded'. Further images were posted over the next three days as he continued to walk the streets. 'The pictures are blurry and raw, but, taken together, provide a compelling portrait of this week's chaos and carnage', Sam Dolnick (2008) of the Associated Press commented. Regarding his motivation to be involved, Ranganathan explained in an interview: 'I just felt that there were lots of people I was communicating with who were also my friends, so it was about the personal connection' (cited in Dolnick, 2008).

Arun Shanbhag, visiting Mumbai from his home in Boston, where he teaches at Harvard Medical School, similarly felt obliged to contribute as he watched one of the fires at the Taj Mahal Palace Hotel burn, as well as ambulances departing from the Nariman House, from the vantage point of a nearby terrace. In order to relay what he saw and heard, he turned to Twitter to describe the 'thud, thud, thud' of gunfire, and to his personal blog and Flickr to upload photographs. An image of the Taj ablaze against the night-time sky was captioned:

Dome of the Taj is nearly all burn't out! Only the central post remains; the base of the dome is still burning! TV Cameras are located on diagonally opposite side of Taj and cannot see the dome; TV coverage only shows glow from burning dome! TV is now saying that shots are heard inside the Taj and all the terrorists are NOT YET cleared! (Shanbhag, 2008)

The next image, a close-up of the fire, was captioned:

> OMG! One of the domes of the Taj is on fire; It is burning like a bonfire! I can actually see the structs/frameworks under the tiles in full blaze. OMG! NO! This can't be happening!
> ~ Hand held; rested my elbow on the sill!; Sorry for blurry images from ~ 10:45 pm. (Shanbhag, 2008)

Evidently unaware of the term 'citizen journalism' at the time, he later told the *New York Times* that it aptly characterised the reportorial role he was performing. 'I felt I had a responsibility to share my view with the outside world', Shanbhag explained (cited in Stelter and Cohen, 2008). The *Times* was not the only news organisation to acknowledge the value of this material from well-placed individuals. Agence France-Press (2008), for example, credited him with providing 'a gripping and emotional eye-witness view of the events around the Taj Mahal Hotel', while Canada's *CTV News*, in a news report remarking on the 'small army of citizen journalists' involved, stated 'first-hand reports from people like Shanbhag gave global audiences a unique, local perspective – something which traditional media reports can never hope to duplicate' (Stuffco, 2008).

Major news organisations in India and around the globe struggled to cope with the amount of 'raw data' relayed via Twitter feeds, desperately trying to separate fact from conjecture for their live reports in what was fast becoming a curatorial role being defined under intense pressure. Further examples of 'tweets' (posts being limited to 140 characters) included the following:

> Mumbai terrorists are asking Hotel Reception for room #s of American citizens and holding them hostage on one floor (@dupree_)

> One terrorist has jumped from Nariman house building to Chabad house – group of police commandos have arrived on scene (anonymous, #mumbai channel)

> Special anti-hijacking group called Rangers entering Nariman House, at least 80 commandos (scorpfromhell)

Hospital update. Shots still being fired. Also Metro cinema next door (mumbaiattack)

Blood needed at JJ hospital (aeropolowoman)

Fascinating. CNN is filling airtime; #mumbai channel is full of tidbits posted by witnesses (yelvington)

At least 80 dead, 250 injured. American and British targeted (ArtVega)

Tagging posts with the hashtag #mumbai made them easily searchable for other users to find. Saad Khan (2008), at the Green & White blog, described a 'Tweets frenzy' when 'minute-by-minute updates about the location of the blasts/skirmishes, positions of the security forces, location of the journalists and safe passages for stranded commuters', amongst other topics, were shared. While agreed details were in short supply, there was little doubt that users gained a keen sense that news was breaking in 'real time' in an extraordinarily dynamic, interactive environment.

'The witnesses are taking over the news'

Belying the steady stream of messages was the fact that very few of the individuals behind them were actually bearing witness to what was transpiring at the scene. Some bloggers, angered by the 'ripple effect' of inaccurate, unfounded – or simply outdated – claims being 're-tweeted' (re-distributed), challenged the notion that Twitter deserved recognition as a news source. Posting in the early hours of the events was Tom on TomsTechBlog.com, for example, who wrote:

> The facts ARE THE NEWS. Nothing else is relevant. In fact, the noise that twitter generates in situations like these is downright cruel and dangerous.
> Let me give you the perfect example of what I mean.
> If you watch Twitter you'll see people reporting an attack at the Marriot Hotel in Mumbai. The problem is there was NO ATTACK

on the Marriot. The Ramada hotel next door was attacked by several gun men but nothing's happened at the Marriot.

Now imagine, if you're someone who has family or friends at the Marriot right now. You'd be scared out of your mind over information that's completely false.

I'm sorry but it really makes me angry. What you have here are people who simply don't care if they get the news right. They're turning the most dire of situations into entertainment by using Twitter to 'be involved in the story.' They throw their little tweets out not caring who they scare half to death and then brag about how great Twitter is for 'beating the mainstream media at reporting the news. (TomsTechBlog.com, 26 November 2008)

Blogger Tim Malbon of 'Made by Many' described how his positive impression of the coverage on Twitter soon gave way to alarm:

I was awestruck by the live feeds provided at #Mumbai and others (such as Twitter Grid). Having looked around elsewhere, my initial reaction was that the main old-school news agencies like Reuters, CNN and the BBC just weren't providing the coverage, in contrast to the truly MASSIVE volume of tweeting going on. But as the evening continued my feelings changed about this, and I started to see [an] ugly side to Twitter, far from being a crowd-sourced version of the news it was actually an incoherent, rumour-fueled mob operating in a mad echo chamber of tweets, re-tweets and re-re-tweets. During the hour or so I followed on Twitter there were wildly differing estimates of the numbers killed and injured – ranging up to 1,000. (Made by Many, 27 November 2008)

In the hours following the early reports, the majority of tweets were either relaying secondary observations taken from mainstream news reports, correcting previous messages or offering links to online sources for fresh perspectives. Examples of the latter were links to sites such as Google map, which documented the location of the attacks, as well as Wikipedia and Mahalo which constantly updated known details. Videos in the dozens were being uploaded to YouTube, while Flickr displayed users' photographs ('Vinu' posting particularly grisly images). Sites such as Metblogs Mumbai, GroundReport, Global Voices, NowPublic,

Poynter.org and iReport.com, amongst countless others, were busy aggregating citizen reports. Meanwhile major news organisations were moving swiftly to gather insights. In addition to using tweets as source statements, several news organisations endeavoured to interview users for exclusive insights. Reuters drew upon blogging posts, such as one from Dina Mehta's blog ('I've been tweeting almost all night, too, from Mumbai. Upset and angry and bereft'), to supplement its coverage (cited in Lee 2008). The *New York Times*, via its blog 'The Lede', asked its readers in the city to email photographs or to insert a written description of events in the 'comment field' on its webpage.

In the case of BBC News Online, the site's running account supplemented information provided by the Corporation's correspondents with details from news agencies, Indian media reports, official statements, blog posts, emails and Twitter messages – 'taking care to source each of these things', as Steve Herrmann (2008), editor of BBC News Interactive, explained. In his words:

> As for the Twitter messages we were monitoring, most did not add a great amount of detail to what we knew of events, but among other things they did give a strong sense of what people connected in some way with the story were thinking and seeing. 'Appalled at the foolish ness of the curious onlookers who are disrupting the NSG operations', wrote one. 'Our soldiers are brave but I feel we could have done better', said another. There was assessment, reaction and comment there and in blogs. One blogger's stream of photos on photosharing site Flickr was widely linked to, including by us. All this helped to build up a rapidly evolving picture of a confusing situation. (Herrmann 2008)

Despite these advantages, however, Herrmann and others were aware of the risks associated with using material when its veracity could not be independently verified. One instance of false reporting, repeatedly circulated on Twitter, claimed that the Indian government was alarmed by what was happening on the social network. Fearful that the information being shared from eyewitnesses on the scene was proving to be useful to the attackers, government officials – it was alleged – were urging Twitter users to cease their efforts, while also looking to block Twitter's access to the country itself. On the BBC's Mumbai live event page, it was reported: '*1108 Indian government asks for live Twitter updates from Mumbai to cease immediately. "ALL LIVE UPDATES – PLEASE STOP TWEETING about #Mumbai police and military operations," a tweet says.*' The BBC was criticised by some commentators for reporting a claim which was later revealed to be untrue. Speaking with the benefit of hindsight, Herrmann responded to questions regarding the decision to post it:

> Should we have checked this before reporting it? Made it clearer that we hadn't? We certainly would have done if we'd wanted to include it in our news stories (we didn't) or to carry it without attribution. In one sense, the very fact that this report was circulating online was one small detail of the story that day. But should we have tried to check it and then reported back later, if only to say that we hadn't found any confirmation? I think in this case we should have, and we've learned a lesson. The truth is, we're still finding out how best to process and relay such information in a fast-moving account like this. (Herrmann, 2008)

Bearing these constraints in mind, he believed it was justifiable for the BBC to be sharing what it knew as quickly as possible, even before facts had been fully checked, as a general principle. In this way, users gain an insight into how a major story is being put together, even when it entails having to accept some responsibility for assessing the quality – and reliability – of the information being processed.

In assessing the implications of what had happened for online journalism, several commentators – despite misgivings about the quality or reliability of much of the information being conveyed – recognised that some sort of transitional moment, if not a major tipping point, had occurred. 'Mumbai is likely to be viewed in hindsight as the first instance of the paradigmatic shift in crisis coverage', Alexander Wolfe (2008) of *Information Week* declared; 'namely, journalists will henceforth no longer be the first to bring us information. Rather, they will be a conduit for the stream of images and video shot by a mix of amateurs and professionals on scene.' Jeff Jarvis (2008), in his assessment of the news coverage of the crisis, concurred. 'The witnesses are taking over the news', he argued. Reports from witnesses relayed via Twitter, blogs, Flickr, Wikipedia and the like – as well as citizen-powered sites such as GroundReport, Global Voices and NowPublic – proved vital. People's 'urgent need to share what they knew' compelled them to get involved, adopting 'journalistic functions – reporting, gathering, organising, verifying – that anyone can now take on'.

Twitter, time and again, won plaudits for capturing the rawness of the tragedy in reportorial terms. 'Last night', Claudine Beaumont of the *Daily Telegraph* pointed out, 'the social web came of age' (*Daily Telegraph*, 27 November 2008). Stephanie Busari (2008) of CNN agreed: 'It was the day social media appeared to come of age and signaled itself as a news-gathering force to be reckoned with.' This was not to deny its limitations as a trustworthy news source, but rather to acknowledge the potential of social networking for first-hand crisis news, and thereby as an important dimension to digital war reporting (see also Matheson and Allan 2009). 'It was Twitter's moment', wrote Brian Caulfield and Naazneen Karmali (2008) in Forbes.com, the service having been transformed from one specialising in 'distributing short, personal updates to tight networks of friends and acquaintances into a way for people around the world to tune into personal, real-time accounts of the attacks'. The challenges in making the most of this resource were formidable, they pointed out, not least with the blurring of professional and amateur roles. 'In other words, we're all journalists now', they added; 'Let's just hope none of us wind up being combat reporters, as so many in Mumbai did this week.'

The compulsion to narrate

In seeking to elaborate the concept of what I am calling 'citizen witnessing', it has proven necessary to disrupt the conceptual purchase of the familiar binarisms associated with the professional versus amateur debate. The emphasis placed on discerning the subtle dynamics of journalistic and citizen witnessing has been shown to be advantageous, in my view, not least because it encourages us to attend to issues otherwise at risk of being glossed over in ongoing disputes over who is entitled to lay claim to the authority of 'journalism' as privileged testimony. The ensuing discussion of witnessing during the Mumbai attacks, in particular, has highlighted the varying degrees of investment individual citizens were prepared to make in defining their contributions in reportorial terms. Equally noteworthy has been the extent to which the desire to bear witness, to document and evaluate what it meant to 'be there' on the scene, informed their commitment to share what they experienced first-hand with distant others.

To the extent the act of witnessing is a conscious choice – and the decision to bear witness (or not) most certainly is a self-reflexive commitment – it may well resonate with a feeling of social obligation, if not a more formal sense of citizenship or public service. It is important not to overstate relations of intentionality in the nature of this act, though, for in contrast with the self-declared citizen journalist deliberately pursuing newsmaking with particular aims or objectives in mind, the citizen witness temporarily grasps this protean subject positionality in order to cope with exigent circumstances. It is likely to be in the process of narrating what is or has been seen, heard or felt (the precise point where observation begins to inform testimony) that the imperative of witnessing will claim its sense of performativity. The distinction between truth and truth-claim is a vital one in this regard, given that witnessing appeals to the former while revolving around the latter. Testimony is no guarantor of truth, but rather a personal attestation to perceived facticity; in other words, to be truthful does not imply possession of Truth. The citizen as witness seizes the opportunity to affirm their truth-claims for reasons that may or may not be made evident there and then, either to themselves or to others. While likely to be self-critiqued on the basis of honesty or sincerity – in contrast with journalistic criteria of accuracy, credibility or corroboration – these motivations cannot be simply read off the compulsion to narrate or its discursive outcomes.

Confronted with crisis situations, major news organisations tend to mobilise certain preferred, ritualised strategies and procedures to process truth-claims that necessarily implicate them in a discursive politics of mediation. This chapter has sought to identify a number of the ways in which citizen witnessing is helping to reconfigure this geometry of informational power, namely through the evolving capacity of individuals to reclaim the discursive terrain of 'the field of media witnessing', as Ashuri and Pinchevski (2009) designate it. Professional decision-making concerning the priorities of witnessing – routinely enabled and constrained by appeals to impartiality – proves open to contestation when the normative criteria giving shape to tacit rules of inclusion and exclusion are recast by citizen-centred perspectives rendered by mobile digital technologies harnessing the power of social networks. Bearing witness consistently encounters formidable difficulties, however, not least because incidents deemed 'witnessable' will always prove unruly, disruptive and frustratingly elusive. 'Witnessing traffics in pieces, parts, and circumstantial details', Peters (2009) points out, 'not in stories with beginnings, middles, and ends (which are the province of active witnessing, of saying rather than seeing)' (2009: 45). And yet, paradoxically, it is the invocation of storyness – news storyness – that underwrites the journalist's imperative to narrativise the fleeting realities of potentially traumatic events. The challenge for online journalism, it follows, is to create spaces for citizen witnessing with the capacity to foster points of human connection, and in so doing affirm principles of trust, responsibility and emphatic engagement to counter the forms of social exclusion endemic to the 'us' and 'them' dichotomies otherwise permeating so much news reporting of other people's misery.

5

News, Civic Protest and Social Networking

With what would later be described as 'the slap heard around the world', Mohamed Bouazizi, a 26-year-old fruit vendor in the provincial town of Sidi Bouzid, Tunisia, was sharply rebuked by a female police officer confiscating his unlicensed wooden cart and its contents on the morning of 17 December 2010. Publicly humiliated by the loss of his livelihood, and with his subsequent effort to complain to local municipal officials frustrated, Bouazizi poured fuel over himself and ignited it in a suicidal protest that would further galvanise a fledgeling popular uprising. Longstanding antagonisms over poverty, injustice and corruption were already converging in articulations of open defiance and dissent in the streets, but few would have predicted that the dictatorial regime of President Zine al-Abidine Ben Ali, who had ruled the country for twenty-three years, would soon topple and collapse. News of Bouazizi's act of self-immolation had spread across the region, primarily due to ordinary citizens – many of them students – posting videos and updates of the ensuing unrest on Facebook. From there they were picked up by an Al Jazeera journalist who, alert to the wider implications, promptly reported what was happening as news of social unrest rapidly intensifying (Fahim, 2011). Taking inspiration from the Tunisian revolt, further upheavals began to spread over the days and weeks ahead, first in Egypt and then Yemen, followed by Bahrain, Libya and Syria. 'The Sidi Bouzid picture spread like wildfire on the internet', Omar Amar of the Libyan Youth Movement later recalled; 'Everyone could see what happened and then they organised the protests via social media. Everyone was informed – straightaway it was right there on your homepage.'[1]

There is little doubt that the significance of events at the heart of what is currently being described as the Arab Spring will be defined by outcomes we can only begin to anticipate today. In following journalistic accounts of what is transpiring, it is intriguing to note the extent to which young people's use of internet and social media – such as Facebook, Flickr, Twitter, YouTube and the like – have proven to be newsworthy topics in their own right within the coverage. In a news article headlined 'A Tunisian–Egyptian link that shook Arab history', David D. Kirkpatrick and David E. Sanger (2011) of the *New York Times* underscore this point:

> As protesters in Tahrir Square faced off against pro-government forces, they drew a lesson from their counterparts in Tunisia: 'Advice to the youth of Egypt: Put vinegar or onion under your scarf for tear gas.'
>
> The exchange on Facebook was part of a remarkable two-year collaboration that has given birth to a new force in the Arab world – a pan-Arab youth movement dedicated to spreading democracy in a region without it. Young Egyptian and Tunisian activists brainstormed on the use of technology to evade surveillance, commiserated about torture and traded practical tips on how to stand up to rubber bullets and organize barricades. (Kirkpatrick and Sanger, 2011)

The article proceeds to explain that the young protestors have been 'breaking free from older veterans of the Arab political opposition' over recent years so as to form an Egyptian youth movement intent on challenging state corruption and abuse. Informal online networks, using a Facebook group as their nexus, have succeeded in setting in motion a range of tactics to articulate resistance.[2] While their relative success is impossible to determine at this point in time, one may be forgiven a certain cautious optimism that virtual civic spheres enlivened by public participation, deliberation and engagement are currently emerging with the potential to empower ordinary people to renew their efforts to extend democratic change and human rights.

In assessing the specific features of the uprisings unfolding across the Middle East, it is important not to overlook the fact that these forms of citizen protest have been years in the making. Bold, even at times triumphalist, claims about digital technologies have featured prominently in impassioned discussion across the media-scape. Cyber-enthusiasts have heralded them as tools of liberation responsible for ushering in near-instant revolutionary change. Contrary views have tended to be sharply dismissive, insisting that conventional types of political mobilisation and protest are being overlooked in the hype. A more measured appraisal, situated between these two polarities, would necessarily recognise the structural imperatives underpinning these ostensibly spontaneous eruptions of dissent. Important here, I would suggest, is the need to look beyond otherwise starkly rendered assertions in order to investigate the lived, complex – and frequently contradictory – forces giving shape to collective re-imaginings of civic cultures. This is particularly the case where young people's identity politics are concerned. Social networks facilitated by digital technologies help to engender the conditions whereby they learn to become citizens willing and able to engage in the world around them.

This chapter's elaboration of citizen witnessing takes as its focus young people's active negotiation of emergent forms of digital citizenship, devoting particular attention to the articulation of protest and dissent. Taking Manuel Castells's (2007, 2011) notion of 'mass self-communication' within the 'network society' as its conceptual point of departure, it will be shown that young people – many of them having little experience with civic issues beyond student politics – are actively recrafting social media as resources in the service of elaborating interactive, peer-sustained forms of personal engagement in public life. Time and again, diverse strategies of citizen witnessing give voice to the voiceless in a dialogic politics of alternative newsmaking.

Communicating in the network society

The concept of Web 2.0 has become a buzzword of sorts, with its varied inflections typically highlighting the fluidly dynamic ways in which the web is evolving to facilitate participatory cultures of interactivity, sharing and collaboration consistent with the aims and interests of diverse virtual communities. For Manuel Castells, this rise of 'mass self-communication' has profound ramifications for the communicative construction of reality. 'The diffusion of Internet, mobile communication, digital media, and a variety of tools of social software', he writes, 'have prompted the development of horizontal networks of interactive communication that connect local and global in chosen time' (2007: 246). The familiar dynamics of top-down, one-way message distribution associated with the mass media are being effectively, albeit unevenly, pluralised. Ordinary citizens are appropriating new technological means (such as digital wifi and wmax) and forms (SMS, email, IPTV, video streaming, blogs, vlogs, podcasts, wikis and so forth) in order to build their own networked communities, he argues, and in so doing are mounting an acute challenge to institutionalised power relations across the breadth of the 'network society' (Castells, 2000, 2009; see also Allan, 2007; Allan and Matheson, 2004).[3]

The term 'mass self-communication' is employed by Castells to highlight the ways in which these horizontal networks are rapidly converging with the mass media. In his words:

> It is mass communication because it reaches potentially a global audience through the p2p networks and Internet connection. It is multimodal, as the digitization of content and advanced social software, often based on open source that can be downloaded free, allows the reformatting of almost any content in almost any form, increasingly distributed via wireless networks. *And it is self-generated in content, self-directed in emission, and self-selected in reception by many that communicate with many.* We are indeed in a new communication realm, and ultimately in a new medium, whose backbone is made of computer networks, whose language is digital, and whose senders are globally distributed and globally interactive. (Castells, 2007: 248; emphasis in original)

Although one may question the use of 'mass' in this context – Raymond Williams's (1963: 289) observation that: 'There are in fact no masses; there are only ways of seeing people as masses' being called to mind – Castells is usefully elucidating the countervailing ethos helping to shape the contours of this communicative terrain. Similarly, despite the emphasis placed on the technological imperatives driving convergence, he takes care to acknowledge that a given medium does not determine message content, let alone its impact, in linear zero-sum terms. Rather, he draws attention to the ways in which communication flows 'construct, and reconstruct every second the global and local production of meaning in the public mind' in diverse, intensely contested social realms. Thus 'the emerging public space, rooted in communication, is not predetermined in its form by any kind of historical fate or technological necessity', he contends; 'It will be the result of the new stage of the oldest struggle in humankind: the struggle to free our minds' (2007: 259).

Castells's approach has proven to be suggestive of fresh ways to investigate the geometry of power unfolding around us. The phrase 'the network society' serves as a form of analytical shorthand to characterise the global forces transforming collective action and institutions from one national context to the next. Regarded as the social structure of the Information Age, it is being organised around relationships of production/consumption, power and experience. Its prevailing logic, while constantly challenged by conflicts, nevertheless gives shape to the pervasive infrastructure of cultural life in most societies – albeit with unpredictable outcomes. From this perspective, the familiar notion of an 'information society' can be safely discarded. In its place, Castells seeks to elaborate a grounded theory of information technology-powered networks. The distinguishing feature of the network society, he believes, is its dialectical interaction between modes of production (goods and services are created in specific social relationships) and those of development (especially technological innovation). This interaction is neither linear nor mechanical in the manner in which it operates. Nor, crucially, is it contained within the authority of the nation-state. Rather, the network society is indicative of a new power system, whereby the once sovereign nation-state's very legitimacy is tested by factors largely beyond its control.

In documenting the contours of the network society, this approach underscores the ways in which information has become the 'privileged political weapon' in the age of the internet. The displacement of human values by commercial ones is rendered especially sharp where the uneven structures of the digital divide are concerned. As Castells points out, being 'disconnected, or superficially connected, to the Internet is tantamount to marginalization in the global, networked system' (2001: 269). Precisely how the dynamics of differential access unfold in different social contexts is largely a matter of possessing the capacity – or not – to adapt to the speed and uncertainty of change. 'The differentiation between Internet-haves and have-nots', he observes, 'adds a fundamental cleavage to existing sources of inequality and social exclusion in a complex interaction that appears to increase the gap between the promise of the Information Age and its bleak reality for many people around the world' (2001: 247). These and related issues highlight several of the reasons why Castells's conceptual formulations continue to figure so prominently in academic research, but also with respect to strategic thinking in relation to real-world interventions to effect social change.

Beginning in the next section, we turn to consider how these issues resonate in young people's efforts to secure their own forms of media-making. More specifically, we consider the ways in which the digital tools of do-it-yourself composition and critique provide them with the means to render visible social injustices. It will be shown that attendant protocols of citizen witnessing are inescapably political, particularly discernible where the materiality of testimony calls into question hierarchical relations of discursive power. Politics, in this sense, is more likely to be shaped by a communal awareness of shared experience of a crisis, however, than by politics in a more partisan or activist sense, although the latter can be crucial in certain situations, as will be shown in this chapter. The citizen witness aligned with a group or movement making its claim to affirm a collective presence on contested space will likely strategise about how best to re-inflect their conditions of visibility to advantage. This shift in positioning may well entail a corresponding decision to embrace a more self-consciously journalistic role as an extension of an activist commitment, however fleetingly, as events unfold before them. In so doing, a proclaimed status as a witness will be recast; that is, it will be almost certainly presumed to be guided by an interested perspective, and thus to be selective in its purview, as opposed to the ostensibly 'neutral' observation of the disinterested bystander suddenly caught up in the heat of the moment. These subtle gradations matter, particularly for journalists moving swiftly to mediate between and across competing forms of testimony (eyewitness accounts, visual imagery, tweets and the like) in a manner consistent with their interpretive authority.

Making meaning

While young people's interest in media-making is hardly a new development, it is often framed in related academic discussions as a matter of 'media literacy', whereby instruction in the critique of mainstream media forms and practices serves as a worthy end in its own right. Interesting to observe in this regard is the extent to which early considerations of how 'old media' ideas about literacy have been recast by the interactive, network technologies highlighted above.

Douglas Kellner (2002) argued over a decade ago that we need to develop 'multiple literacies' so as to respond better to the globalizing demands for a more informed, participatory and active citizenry in political, economic and cultural terms. Literacy, in this conception, 'comprises gaining competencies in effectively using socially constructed forms of communication and representation' (2002: 92). More specifically, media literacy 'helps people to use media intelligently, to discriminate and evaluate media content, to dissect media forms critically, and to investigate media effects and uses' (2002: 93). In the new multimedia environment, Kellner maintained, this type of literacy had never been more important, especially with regard to the development of skills to create 'good citizens' motivated to play an active role in social life. He pointed out that the same technologies of communication capable of turning 'spectators into cultural zombies' may, at the same time, be used to invigorate democratic debate and participation. The problem, then as now, was how to bring about the latter on the terrain of the former. That is, how to take seriously the texts of popular culture enjoyed by young people, recognising and respecting their ideas, values and competencies, without 'romanticizing' views that 'may be superficial, mistaken, uninformed and full of various problematical biases' (2002: 94). One way forward, Kellner suggested, is to adapt new computer technologies to education so as to facilitate the development of new literacies.

In seeking to expand upon familiar conceptions of literacy, Kellner drew attention to emergent forms of what he terms 'computer literacy'. Important here, he argued, is the need to push this concept beyond its usual meaning, namely as the technical ability to use computer programs and hardware. A broader definition, it followed, would attend to information and multimedia literacy as well. That is to say, Kellner's extended conception of computer literacy would include learning how to use computers, locate information via search engines, operate email and list servers, and construct websites. Computer and information literacies, he wrote, involve 'learning where information is found, how to access it, and how to organize, interpret and evaluate it' (2002: 95). At the same time, they also entail 'learning how to read hypertexts, to traverse the ever-changing fields of cyberculture, and to participate in a digital and interactive multimedia culture that encompasses work, education, politics, culture and everyday life' (2002: 95; see also Allan, 2002; Hassan, 1999; Lievrouw and Livingstone 2002; Sefton-Green 1998; Warnick 2002). Clearly at stake here, then, is the teaching of more than just technical forms of knowledge and skills. By stretching the notion of literacy to include new strategies of reading, writing and researching and communicating abilities appropriate to a larger 'computer culture', Kellner was helping to discern the conceptual space necessary to engage with an array of different, yet interrelated, types of information processing that possessed the potential to open up opportunities for alternative types of media practice to emerge.

Reading this and related research with the benefit of hindsight, one recognises the extent to which early discourses of 'computer literacy' inform certain formulations of media literacy today, namely those striving to interweave relevant aspects of 'news literacy', 'information literacy', 'visual literacy' and 'digital literacy' to advantage. The scholarship devoted to these and related conceptions of literacy is voluminous, and need not be rehearsed here. Rather, it is sufficient to note for our purposes the growing awareness amongst researchers and practitioners of the reasons why 'literacy' must necessarily stretch to encompass creative forms of making, sharing and collaborating in a manner alert to a community's – lived or virtual – collective priorities. 'When people have digital and media literacy competencies, they recognize personal, corporate and political agendas', Renee Hobbs (2010) observes, 'and are empowered to speak out on behalf of the missing voices and omitted perspectives in our communities.' Moreover, she adds, by 'identifying and attempting to solve problems, people use their powerful voices and their rights under the law to improve the world around them' (2010: 17). While as a broad assertion this risks sounding a little idealistic, Hobbs is usefully underscoring – at least in my reading – the importance of discerning how and why such competencies become socially relevant, and thereby politicised in normative terms (see also Mihailidis, 2012).

In danger of being overlooked in discussions of young people's skills in negotiating the affordances and constraints of digital technologies, I would suggest, is the extent to which a politics of citizenship informs their participatory cultures. Such a view, I readily acknowledge, problematises the oft-rendered assertion that young people are apathetic, even cynical, about the prospect of active involvement in their communities. What may appear to be passive disengagement, however, is most certainly political nonetheless (indeed, all the more so because it is seldom recognised as such). Where 'politics' is allowed to be defined narrowly within a discourse of partisanship, it is safely contained within the domain of voting and political parties – this when young people's everyday negotiations of social hierarchies, divisions and exclusions will be much more likely to be considered by them to be relevant to their lives. It follows that sweeping claims regarding their apparent disaffection are open to challenge on these grounds, yet it is telling how often their use of digital media – especially where social networking is concerned – is singled out for attention, if not moral censure.

Amy Mitchell's (2010) research contends, for example, that 'Social media tools and mobile connectivity provide citizens with a deeper and more direct relationship with the news', one which suggests that 'news grazers' are anything but 'aimless wanderers'. Mobile devices not only bring new information sources into the mix, she maintains, they dramatically alter what happens to news reports after they appear. Young people, in particular, will be inclined to search, filter, react to and share with one another news they consider interesting, often relying on social networking to serve as a 'personal editor' of sorts helping to 'determine their front page information' (2010: 27; see also Pew, 2011). Mizuko Ito (2010), in describing the apparent 'generational gap' in how people of different ages regard social media, points out that disagreements over 'what participation in public life means' are often at issue. 'Whether it is teachers trying to manage texting in the classroom, parents attempting to set limits on screen time, or journalists painting pictures of a generation of networked kids who lack any attention span', she writes, 'adults seem to want to hold on to their negative views of teens' engagement with social media' (2010: 18). Given that young people deliberately sidestep 'institutional gatekeepers' wherever possible, she adds, literacy becomes a 'byproduct' of social engagement. Larry Rosen (2010) reaffirms this observation, maintaining that, as 'the pace of technological change accelerates, mini-generations are defined by their distinctive patterns of media use, levels of multitasking, and preferred methods of communication' (2010: 25). Efforts to identify the 'distinctive digital habits of mini-generations', it follows, need to be aware of differences 'in their values as well as levels of social and political activism' (2010: 25–6). Precisely what counts as political activism varies considerably across these mini-generations, of course, but several researchers have sought to highlight the ways in which social networking is recasting familiar assumptions about civic participation.

One of the first instances when the political implications of these emergent forms of connectivity attracted media attention in their own right occurred in Greece in December 2008. Indeed, the *Guardian*'s Paul Mason (2012), in his book *Why it's kicking off everywhere: The new global revolutions*, maintains that this uprising in Athens was 'the clearest precursor event for the new unrest', the disturbances creating a template of 'social explosion' – that is, 'an uncontrolled and randomly provoked reaction to economic crisis, in which students and uneducated urban youth come together to make mayhem' (2012: 32; see also Cottle and Lester, 2011). In the next section, our attention turns to consider the ways in which these protestors called upon social media to shape the articulation – and co-ordination – of their dissent. Moreover, it will be shown that equally important were their contributions of citizen witnessing to real-time reportage of violence on the streets, not least in recasting the priorities of mainstream, corporate journalism.

The politics of protest

'Rebellion is deeply embedded in the Greek psyche. The students and school children who are now laying siege to police stations and trying to bring down the government are undergoing a rite of passage', the BBC's Malcolm Brabant reported. 'They may be the iPod generation, but they are the inheritors of a tradition that goes back centuries', he added, before turning to describe the 'current wave of violence' testing the limits of social stability. Brabant, like other journalists on the scene, was struggling to make sense of events that defied easy explanation. Most news accounts agreed that the spark that ignited the student protest was the shooting of a 15-year-old student, Alexandros Grigoropoulos, by a police officer – for no apparent reason – on the evening of 6 December 2008 in the centre of Athens. The incident received extensive coverage, and 'near-universal condemnation' (Gemenis, 2008), in the Greek media. Where accounts differed was at the level of context – that is, when presenting the details necessary to enable distant audiences to understand the nature of the ensuing crisis, as well as its larger significance. Brabant's references to the 'Greek psyche' as having a predisposition to rebellion were one way to explain the forces involved; another was to frame events historically, where previous examples of police brutality were held to be suggestive of a larger pattern over recent decades. Still another strategy, however, revolved around the gathering of insights being generated via social networks amongst the protestors themselves.

Pavlos Tsimas (2008), a commentator with Mega TV in Athens, described his sense of how events were unfolding in a speech to the Global Forum for Media Development shortly thereafter:

> [At] 9:00 in the evening of Saturday a boy was shot dead. For no reason. In cold blood.
>
> I learned about the fact 80 mintues [*sic*] later by email. Turned on the TV set and there was nothing on. Just commercials and nice shows. I turned to the Internet and there in some blogs extensive coverage of the event. I kept receiving messages. The clock struck midnight. People took to street to protest the murder. Victim's name nobody knew.
>
> Even radio stations were late to get the news.
>
> Thousands of people in the street protesting murder of a boy whose name they didn't know. Established media have not yet reported the event. TV stations came in a little late. The next day the newspapers did not carry words of the event with the exception some sport papers that carried the story due to late night printing (due to reporting of a football match).
>
> Greece plunged into the deepest crisis in recent memories – people watched fire burning in neighborhoods and saw smashed windows. Radio and TV stations, most of them choose to open the airwaves non stop with call-in shows where listeners expressed themselves and newspapers tried to find out what else to do. (Tsimas, 2008)

Internet and social networking sites, the latter including Facebook, MySpace and Twitter, proved to be playing a pivotal role in mobilising protestor collaboration in real-time. Bloggers posting accounts of what had happened – together with links to a YouTube video which appeared to contradict police claims – led the way. Photos uploaded to Flickr, via mobile telephones and laptop computers, recorded the violent turmoil. Twitter – via tags such as #griots – relayed reports of what was happening on the streets, as well as information for protestors to help co-ordinate their efforts – that is, to relay details about where to meet, what to do, and how best to protect themselves. 'Several Greek Web sites offered protesters real-time information on clash sites, where demonstrations were heading and how riot police were deployed around the city', Paul Haven (2008) reported for AP; 'Protest marches were arranged and announced on the sites and via text message on cell phones.' Here it quickly became apparent not only that the shooting needed to be situated in relation to protracted civil unrest in Greek public life, but that the protestors themselves did not form a single, monolithic group. The majority of those involved were students, primarily from secondary schools, engaged (peacefully, in the main) in marches and rallies. A second, smaller element, was composed of groups of 'anarchists' (or 'koukouloforoi' – 'the hooded ones') intent on seizing the moment to articulate dissent in any way possible – which included torching cars and smashing shop windows. Not surprisingly, the actions of the latter figured prominently in news reports. 'Without a doubt', Alexis S (2008), a 'peaceful protestor from Thessaloniki' observed, 'such coverage focused on the most sensational, frightening, collective and dramatic cases of the countless incidents that took place in Greece's major cities since Saturday night'.

For journalists looking beyond sweeping claims about 'the iPod generation' – or the '€700 generation' (a phrase used by some to describe the modest monthly wage they hope to earn after university, if they gain employment) – it was important to connect with young people to understand better what they were feeling, and why. Traditional news media, Andrew Lam (2008) noted, 'were trying to play catch up in a world full of Twitterers and bloggers', a challenge made worse by the need to 'filter real news from pseudo news' under intense time pressure. Social network sites proved to be especially valuable resources in this regard, rapidly extending alternative forms of connectivity initially set in motion via an IndyMedia bulletin board. In addition to providing live reports, personal accounts, photos and videos (most in English, if not in Greek), they afforded journalists with a different level of connection. *The Economist* described this level as being indicative of a 'new era of networked protest':

> A tribute to the slain teenager – a clip of photos with music from a popular rock band – appeared on YouTube, the video-sharing site, shortly after his death; more than 160,000 people have seen it. A similar tribute group on Facebook has attracted more than 130,000 members, generating thousands of messages and offering links to more than 1,900 related items: images of the protests, cartoons and leaflets.
> A memorial was erected in Second Life, a popular virtual environment, giving its users a glimpse of real-life material from the riots. Many other online techniques – such as maps detailing police deployments and routes of the demonstrations – came of age in Athens. And as thousands of photos and videos hit non-Greek blogs and forums, small protests were triggered in many European cities, including Istanbul [and] Madrid. Some 32 people were arrested in Copenhagen. (*The Economist*, 18 December 2008)

For Evgeny Morozov (2008), the networked protest in Greece provided a 'glimpse of what the transnational networked public sphere might look like', and as such signalled the rise of a new global phenomenon. Readily acknowledging that the internet has helped to make protest actions more effective in the past, he nonetheless believed that what happened in this case was 'probably the first time that an issue of mostly local importance has triggered solidarity protests across the whole continent, some of them led by the Greek diaspora, but many of them led by disaffected youth who were sympathetic of the movement's causes'.

While their actions were widely condemned by the authorities, the success of their intervention – its ethos spelled out in banners such as 'Stop watching, get out into the streets' – was such that then Conservative Prime Minister Costas Karamanlis conceded in a speech to parliamentary colleagues: 'Long-unresolved problems, such as the lack of meritocracy, corruption in everyday life and a sense of social injustice disappoint young people' (cited in BBC News Online, 17 December 2008). Few had anticipated the scope and intensity of the student outrage, nor their fluency in new forms of digital communication. Journalists were as surprised as anyone else, a point underlined in a headline from the Reuters (2008) news agency: 'Protestors rule the web in internet backwater Greece.' More to the point, the crisis provided evidence that every citizen could be a front-line correspondent, a prospect which called into question the viability of the mainstream news media – not least their capacity to set the news agenda (see also Matheson and Allan, 2010). New media – ranging from established blogs and forums to 'radicalised' Facebook pages – 'directed the flow of information' in the larger 'struggle for interpretation', Maria Komninos and Vassilis Vamvakas (2011) argued, leaving mainstream media, especially commercial TV, 'reduced to following and reporting, for the most part, information originating via the Internet' (2011: 160).

'Twitter revolutions'

Further instances of young people's use of social media for organisational and news-making purposes – sometimes dubbed a 'Facebook protest' or 'Twitter revolution' – attracted periodic attention in the mainstream media over the following months. In Moldova in April 2009, for example, young protestors took to the streets to condemn what they regarded as election fraud involving members of the Communist Party. 'We decided to organise a flash mob for the same day using Twitter, as well as networking sites and SMS', explained one of the organisers; 'we expected at the most a couple of hundred friends, friends of friends, and colleagues', she added. 'When we went to the square, there were 20,000 people waiting there. It was unbelievable' (cited in Stack, 2009). Violent clashes ensued, with tweets relaying images and video clips of confrontations with police, as well as the destruction of windows and furniture in the Parliament building. Shortly thereafter, then-President Vladimir Voronin relented, agreeing to a recount of the votes.

Social networking strategies proved similarly indispensable during the G20 summit in London the same month. Amongst the estimated 35,000 people demonstrating peacefully were a small number of protestors, some involved with anarchist groups, intent on violent confrontations with the police. Citizen-rendered still and video imagery, much of it shot using mobile telephones, recorded several clashes in shocking detail. One incident, in particular, ignited a major controversy – namely, the actions of a police officer knocking passer-by Ian Tomlinson to the ground. Tomlinson, a newspaper seller, collapsed and died after being hit by a baton (see Greer and McLaughlin, 2010, 2011). The Metropolitan Police's initial denial that an officer had been involved was flatly contradicted by evidence revealed by the *Guardian* six days later, namely a video clip documenting the assault, handed over to it by an American visitor to the city. For journalist Nik Gowing (2009), the citizen bystander who 'happened to bear witness electronically' represented a telling example of how non-professional 'information doers' were 'driving a wave of democratisation and accountability' redefining the nature of power. 'The new ubiquitous transparency they create', he observed, 'sheds light where it is often assumed officially there will be darkness.'

June of that year saw major public demonstrations in the aftermath of Iran's disputed presidential election, with many young Iranians performing roles akin to citizen journalists in order to document what was happening (Western journalists having been barred from reporting the protests). 'Social media's power to present unmediated reality has never been better demonstrated', journalist Paul Mason (2012) argued, with citizen imagery circulating via Twitter, Facebook and SMS affording 'micro-detail of social responses to unrest' that proved invaluable to mainstream media. 'The moment of the protests', he observed, 'fed off this cycle of guerrilla newsgathering, media amplification, censorship and renewed protest' (2012: 35). Amongst the images assuming an almost iconic status were those taken from grisly mobile-telephone footage of 27-year-old Neda Agha-Soltan bleeding to death on the street (she had been shot in the chest, reportedly by a Basij paramilitary). Relayed to the world's news media, this 'amateur footage' captured by a bystander and uploaded to YouTube on 20 June 2009 transformed Neda into a symbol of the opposition, galvanising support in Iranian diasporas as well as focusing international attention (see also Anderson, 2012; Ghanavizi, 2011; Hänska-Ahy and Shapour, 2012; Mortensen, 2011: see also Khiabany and Sreberny, 2009). 'The killing of Neda Agha-Soltan, the grisly images of blood spreading across her face, have become perhaps the defining sequence in the 10-day uprising against the regime in Tehran', Robert Tait and Matthew Weaver (2009) of the *Guardian* observed at the time. 'Like much of the footage that has emerged from Tehran in recent days, the authenticity and circumstances behind the video could not be verified', they added. 'But Agha-Soltan was quickly lionised by an engaged online community inside and outside Iran', effectively 'mythologised as a martyr to the opposition's cause, a rallying call for a protest movement in need of a hero'. Roger Cohen (2009b) in the *New York Times* went even further: 'Never again will [the Ahmadinejad regime] speak of justice without being undone by the Neda Effect – the image of eyes blanking, life abating and blood blotching across the face of Neda Agha-Soltan.'

In July, demonstrations by Uighur protestors (a Turkic-speaking Muslim group) in the western region of Xinjiang, China, were met by police officers wielding fire hoses and batons, sparking 'ethnic riots' that reportedly left 156 people dead and more than 800 injured. The central government, in the words of a *New York Times* reporter, took 'the usual steps to enshrine its version of events as received wisdom: it crippled Internet service, blocked Twitter's micro-blogs, purged search engines of unapproved references to the violence, saturated the Chinese media with the state-sanctioned story' (Wines, 2009). Nevertheless, once again young people's use of social media succeeded in offering real-time personal updates, even though official censors were moving swiftly to respond. 'When we heard that something had happened in Xinjiang, we all went online to try to find some information', one Beijing-based writer, Woeser, stated. 'There were some people posting their own personal accounts of what was happening on [social media sites, such as Youku and Fanfou, as well as Facebook, Twitter, YouTube and MSN messenger: see RSF, 2009]. But these were often removed very soon after posting. I'm talking about a matter of minutes', she said (cited in RFA, 2009). Within hours of the protests getting underway, the flow of news and information had been reduced to a trickle by the authorities. 'It just goes to show that the government has a very advanced capability when it comes to controlling information online. They are very fast and efficient', Woeser added; '[After these accounts] were removed, the only voice that could still be heard was the official line' (see also HRW, 2009).

Inflected to advantage, network technologies engender improved, occasionally counter-intuitive, opportunities for political action, a point underscored by the examples considered above. 'Since state power and capital power is based on disconnecting people, workers, and citizens, so to make their common interests more opaque and their fighting chances less coordinated', Castells (2009) contends, 'anything that helps connection helps social change.' As these examples also indicate, however, when 'self-defined communities of resistance' become associated with violent confrontation, the institutionalised power of the state is almost certain to be invoked, and with considerable force.

London is burning

Time and again, news media framing of a crisis will privilege a decisive incident for purposes of narrativisation, one that can be identified as the unexpected spark that abruptly ignites simmering anger, grievances, suspicions or resentment into open defiance. Such was the case with the 'London Riots' of summer 2011. In the early evening of 4 August in Tottenham, North London, police officers pulled over a minicab carrying Mark Duggan, a 29-year-old black man, intent on arresting him on suspicion of involvement in a developing 'crime in action', to use police parlance. In the ensuing altercation, two shots were fired, one of which left Duggan fatally wounded in the chest; the other shot penetrated a radio worn by one of the officers. Typical of the initial news reports was the *Telegraph*'s account, headlined 'Man Killed in Shooting Incident Involving Police Officer', which began:

A policeman's life was saved by his radio last night after gunman Mark Duggan opened fire on him and the bullet hit the device.

Armed police immediately returned fire and Mark Duggan, 29, who was under surveillance, was shot dead in the street in north London. (*Telegraph*, 4 August 2011)

Evidence to support the contention that Duggan had shot first was attributed in the article to a spokesperson for the Independent Police Complaints Commission (IPCC), called in to investigate. It would later be revealed by a *Guardian* investigation, however, that ballistics tests indicated that the police had fired both shots, prompting the IPCC to issue an apology for accidently misinforming journalists.

In Tottenham at the time of the incident, many of those living in the local community considered it to be yet another tragic example of the police using excessive force when individuals from ethnic minority groups were concerned. Two days later, several of Duggan's relatives joined fellow residents in a peaceful protest to demand justice at Tottenham Police Station. Shortly thereafter the tenor amongst the crowd, now numbering about 300 people, began to change. Police on horseback, intent on dispersing the gathering, came under attack as objects, including rocks, bottles and fireworks, were thrown (youths from a nearby housing estate being blamed by some eyewitnesses). As tensions rose, two police cars were set alight, engendering a series of clashes with officers that would escalate into a fully fledged riot. Social networking sites exacerbated matters, some press accounts alleged, with 'trouble-makers on Twitter' relaying inflammatory claims and images certain to incite a 'frenzy' of violence (in the case of the latter, the *Daily Mail* reported: 'One picture of a police car on fire in the area was re-tweeted more than 100 times on the social networking site within an hour'; see Gallagher and Farrell, 2011). So-called 'copy cat riots', as they were promptly labelled in other reports, spread to further districts of London and, soon after, to other towns and cities across England, including Birmingham, Bristol, Manchester and Liverpool. Over the next four days, thousands of mainly young people were swept up in scenes of mayhem and public disorder, with rampant looting and arson leaving considerable destruction in their wake.

Militarist terms were frequently employed in the ensuing news coverage of towns and cities 'under siege', where certain neighbourhoods were described as 'battle zones' with protestors 'in control of the streets'. Several journalists themselves drew on this language, recounting violent skirmishes 'from the front lines', such was the risk to their personal safety at times. Efforts to broadcast live were frequently curtailed, with crews in satellite vans belonging to networks such as the BBC, ITN, Sky News and CNN forced to retreat. 'CNN reporter Dan Rivers, kitted out in a helmet and what looked like body armour under his jumper, and his cameraman were caught between rioters and a police line in Peckham', one reporter observed; 'They beat a hasty retreat as bottles and other missiles began to rain down' (Halliday, 2011b). Photojournalists were similarly concerned for their safety, their digital-SLR cameras making them all too conspicuous in the eyes of those alert to the risk of being identified in photographs made public (or secured by the police). The Press Association's Lewis Whyld, fearful of being singled out, watched in dismay as another photographer was targeted by an angry group. 'I put my bag on the ground and got my camera out, but as I did so the other photographer was grabbed by a mob of maybe ten or more men who immediately smashed his cameras and hit him to the ground', he later recalled; 'I quickly moved away into a crowd with them after me, feeling massively guilty about leaving the other photographer but knowing I had to leave immediately if I wanted any chance of keeping my cameras and not being beaten up' (cited in Hope, 2012). His professional equipment safely stowed in his car, he continued documenting the carnage around him using his Blackberry mobile phone, which also enabled him to relay the images to the newsroom without having to use his laptop. Several of them would duly appear in newspapers around the world.

Mindful of the need to blend into the crowd, photojournalists recognised that opting to use their telephones helped considerably, but still raised suspicions. Everyone taking pictures, it seemed, was being confronted by those anxious to determine whether or not they were 'Feds'. Photojournalist Fil Kaler left the protection of the police line in Brixton to enter a crowd outside an electronics store. 'Once I got in, I knew it didn't feel safe to film', he stated; 'I had my camera down by my side and took some shots on my phone and sent a few tweets and then out of nowhere I got punched in my face, my glasses were knocked off and my camera was nicked' (cited in L. O'Carroll, 2011). The *New York Times*'s London reporter Ravi Somaiya said in an interview that the 'rioters didn't like being photographed for obvious reasons, so I had to be subtle about the way I went about it'. The situation was too dangerous for broadcast media to cover the unfolding story, in his view, primarily due to the lack of an adequate police presence: 'In those circumstances – where there were no police to be seen – it wouldn't be possible for [a television crew] to be protected. It was difficult enough for me to sent Tweets and discreetly take photographs on my phone.' In many ways, he added, 'it was a story made for Twitter' (cited in Kemp and Turner, 2011).

Evidently Paul Lewis (2011) of the *Guardian* concurred, explaining that his efforts to document 'what felt like a country at war with itself' had been facilitated by social networking. 'The first portal for communicating what we saw was Twitter', he wrote; 'It enabled us to deliver real-time reports from the scene, but more importantly enabled other users of Twitter to provide constant feedback and directions to trouble spots.' Working alongside his film-maker colleague Mustafa Khalili, Lewis's five-day journey to cover the riots and disorder in different towns and cities was guided by his growing legion of Twitter followers: 'While journalists covering previous riots would chase ambulances to find the frontline, we followed what people on social media told us.' This collaborative relationship with citizens helped to refine the coverage, although did prove to be fraught at times, not least because of the constant danger that observations relayed via tweets would be taken out of context. Lewis realised precisely this problem had occurred when one of his reports about a 'minor skirmish', which had quickly turned viral, was being used by some to 'stoke fears of imminent racial conflict'. It was 'a sobering reminder of the power of social media', he maintained; 'The streets were in chaos, but so too was the internet, which was both the fastest source of reliable news and, unchecked, a means of spreading panic.'[4] Fears expressed about so-called 'Twitter mobs' and 'Facebook thugs' bordered on a moral panic discourse in some news reports, a number of which framed demands for greater CCTV surveillance as a necessary response to social networking spiralling out of control.

Separating facts from rumours

In addition to relaying online reports, residents taking to the streets to bear witness also captured still photographs and video footage of significant value to news organisations. An array of 'haunting images' chronicling the violence 'flooded the Internet over the past 24 hours', Lindsay Kalter (2011) of IJNet.com pointed out, with sites such as Flickr, Blottr, Instagram, Citizenside and The-Latest, amongst many others, offering particularly 'captivating images of the breaking story'. A relatively small portion of the imagery was shot by the participants themselves, including incriminating 'trophy' snapshots of one another standing in front of ransacked shops (Holehouse and Millward, 2011). News editors adopted a curatorial role, moving swiftly to repurpose diverse types of contributions from members of afflicted communities, many of them evidently intent on doing their part to extend the scope of mainstream coverage. Photographs were typically captioned with care, such as when the *Daily Mail* stated 'pictures on Twitter appeared to show the [Barclays Bank] building being looted', although the same news report declared that 'youths had stormed McDonald's and had started frying their own burgers and chips' based on an unsubstantiated tweet (Gallagher and Farrell, 2011). Videos on YouTube posted by eyewitnesses were valued for providing raw, frequently poignant, testimonies, although here too some proved seriously ill-informed upon closer inspection.

Similarly rich in prospective content were live-blogs hastily convened by ordinary citizens, several of which usefully supplemented those provided by news sites (the BBC, *Guardian*, Sky News, amongst others) striving to monitor breaking developments. Successful initiatives included journalism student Gaz Corfield and his ad hoc team of contributors, their hyperlocal site, the West Londoner, attracting some 1 million views in twenty-four hours. Describing the challenges they faced, Corfield stated:

> Our people on the ground have mainly been friends and volunteers who got in touch and offered their services. The vast majority of what we're doing is curating reports from Twitter [as well as Twitpic, Yfrog and Facebook] but having our own people on location has helped. One of our contributors, Sarah Henry, was in Hackney on Tuesday and was briefly caught up the violence there but got away unscathed – she tells me that the BBC reporter next to her was hit by a bottle.

In his view, their coverage stood out from other sites because of its resolute commitment to reporting factual, up-to-the-moment updates.

> Speed, accuracy and collation of information from the ground, sifting between rumours and facts. Debunking false rumours, where we felt confident enough to do so, also built up our readers' trust quickly. We weren't afraid to categorise our reports – if we had sketchy information about something, we'd tell our readers 'this report is unconfirmed' and work as quickly as we could to either confirm or deny it.
>
> We also made a conscious choice not to label the people we were reporting on, even though our sources mentioned vigilantes, ethnic groups and political groups. Given the already heightened situation I felt it would be irresponsible to put out sensitive information we couldn't directly check ourselves, so we stuck to just reporting movements of people. I think our readers appreciated that; our coverage was seen as being purely factual without any speculation, and therefore more valuable than other sources. I refused to report rumours about intended targets, which I think reassured a lot of people. (Corfield cited in McAthy, 2011)

Rather tellingly, fluidly dispatched, on-the-spot reportage mediated within the familiar strictures of impartial reporting was being prized over and above the forms of 'second-hand', near-instant 'armchair' analyses otherwise proliferating across the webscape. Erratic, unsubstantiated assertions, frequently given greater credence simply by sheer repetition (and thereby posing the risk of becoming self-fulfilling prophecies), disentangled when challenged by citizen witnessing conscientiously informed by personal knowledge and experience of local neighbourhoods.

'Tools of democracy'

As the violence waned, media commentaries recurrently highlighted differing perceptions of the reasons behind the civil unrest. 'While the television broadcast images of burned buildings and cars, Tottenham's new citizen journalists captured the full extent of the damage, reaching the corners that the press couldn't', one blogger, Reni Eddo-Lodge (2011), observed. Writing as someone who had grown up there, however, she expressed her sadness that it had taken a riot to highlight the complex problems blighting one of the most deprived areas in London.

The restoration of public order tended to be narrowly defined around social control measures, with Prime Minister David Cameron's declared 'fightback' strategy, permitting police to employ harsher tactics, being widely praised in news reports for finally quelling what was being called 'the biggest explosion of urban rebellion in a generation'. In the end, 5 deaths were attributed to the rioting, with at least 16 people left injured in its wake. Over 3,000 people were arrested, about one-third of whom were formally charged, with most offences concerning theft or property damage to vehicles, homes and shops (the Association of British Insurers estimating the cost to the insurance industry to be in excess of £200 million). It would take some time, though, before sensational headlines denouncing street gangs for perpetrating the riots were exposed as inaccurate. Too many press reports had elected to characterise the events as evidence of anarchy, or, in Cameron's words, 'mindless selfishness' motivated entirely by 'criminality pure and simple' to wreak havoc. 'Images of burning buildings, cars aflame and stripped-out shops may provide spectacular fodder for a restless media, ever hungry for new stories and fresh groups to demonise', Nina Power (2011) observed at the time, 'but we will understand nothing of these events if we ignore the history and the context in which they occur.'

Gradually, more informed reporting began to emerge, with in-depth examinations of the underlying structural divisions and hierarchies prevailing in young people's lives receiving some, albeit limited, treatment. Criticisms of the coverage were sharply polarised, typically corresponding to divergent views over whether the rioting was to be condemned outright, or to be regarded as understandable, even justifiable, given wider social factors. Few could dispute, however, that official assertions about the necessity of 'fiscal austerity measures', 'budgetary efficiencies', 'belt-tightening' and the like were rarely aligned with the deprivation of those confronted with the harsh realities of economic hardship, unemployment and impoverishment of life-chances on the streets of inner-city communities. For many of those denigrated for belonging to what then Justice Secretary Ken Clarke (2011) described as a 'feral underclass', the riots were acutely political in their articulation of deeply entrenched civil dissent. News media indifference to their plight compounded the problem.

Poverty, together with related forms of structural inequality, is seldom regarded as sufficiently newsworthy to warrant sustained attention. During the riots and their immediate aftermath, this remained the case for most news organisations, evidently reluctant to delve into the politics of social exclusion as a hard news story. That said, however, discourses of 'moral decay', 'social disintegration' and the like featured in press commentaries, at times stretching to include the powerful, who occasionally found themselves openly chastised for preserving class privilege in ways detrimental to the interests of the wider democratic society. 'The culture of greed and impunity we are witnessing on our TV screens stretches right up into corporate boardrooms and the Cabinet', the *Telegraph*'s chief political commentator, Peter Oborne (2011), remarked; 'It embraces the police and large parts of our media. It is not just its damaged youth, but Britain itself that needs a moral reformation.'

Rather than engaging with such issues in depth, however, news reports in the main were much more inclined to focus elsewhere. All too predictably, fierce criticisms surfaced blaming social networking sites (particularly Twitter and Facebook), as well as mobile telephone makers, for 'orchestrating criminality' and 'spreading contagion' that led to scenes of destruction. 'Everyone watching these horrific actions will be struck by how they were organized via social media', Prime Minister Cameron stated; 'And when people are using social media for violence we need to stop them' (cited in Pfanner, 2011). BlackBerry promised to co-operate with the police as evidence emerged that its encrypted messenger service had proven to be widely used by those implicated in co-ordinating gatherings and encouraging vandalism and looting. While some commentators wondered aloud about how best to curtail future disturbances through the imposition of severe censorship over digital media, others saw in the very popularity of such devices evidence of young people's 'alienation', stemming from their 'moral detachment' from wider social norms, values and beliefs.

More thoughtful assessments highlighted the apparent double-standard between the use of social networking – often likened to 'tools of democracy' – by those organising to overthrow corrupt regimes in the Arab world, on the one hand, and British citizens employing similar strategies to articulate their embittered frustration with the inequalities endemic to their society, on the other. Meanwhile, as the debate raged on, social networks were being pressed into service to help to mobilise public responses, with #riotcleanup and #riotwombles on Twitter and Facebook's 'Post riot clean-up' pages proving useful to assemble volunteers to begin the slow work of rebuilding devastated communities.

New York is occupied

Public criticisms of the deepening income gap between a privileged elite and the vast majority of citizens have continued to intensify as the global economic crisis grinds on, with state austerity measures producing severe hardship for many of society's most vulnerable citizens. Social antagonisms, typically receiving scant media attention as issues in their own right, have largely remained hidden in plain sight.

In the month following the London riots, a fledgeling protest movement on the other side of the Atlantic was beginning to garner news coverage by bringing to bear an unusual set of strategies and tactics. An initiative of the Canadian activist group AdBusters, Occupy Wall Street launched its intervention – symbolised in its rallying cry 'We are the 99%' – in Zuccotti Park, in New York's Wall Street financial district on 17 September 2011. As a gathering estimated to number about 1,000 people gradually coalesced into a loosely organised demonstration, the New York Police Department (NYPD) endeavoured to stop them from erecting tents in the park, soon after re-named Liberty Square. News organisations, initially slow to report on the protest (demonstrations being a routine feature of the city's life), had begun to monitor developments more closely by the end of the first week.[5] Coverage sharply intensified on the eighth day, when protestors marched uptown.

The NYPD moved in to arrest over eighty individuals, primarily for obstructing traffic, with a smaller number of disorderly conduct charges. Some participants shouted 'cameras, cameras', while others sang in unison 'The whole world is watching! The whole world is watching!' in the heat of what was transforming into a media spectacle of open dissent. Many of the protestors were image-savvy, carrying cameras and mobile phones, even in some cases audio equipment, laptops and webcams in order to upload and relay live footage. Self-consciously alert to the importance of fashioning their 'grassroots media' to articulate a visual politic consistent with the aim of legitimising their cause, they soon found what they regarded as their democratic right to bear witness to police activity was challenged. Several incidents flared up that day, but one senior officer's use of pepper spray against a 'kettle netted' (surrounded and detained) group of young female marchers proved particularly controversial. Citizen-shot video footage of the unprovoked attack, which left two of the four women screaming in pain, provided – in the words of Clyde Haberman (2011) of the *New York Times* – 'a vital shot in the arm for the nascent anti-Wall Street movement', the officer's 'improvidence' being a 'game changer'.

Distinctions between journalists with press credentials and their citizen counterparts tended to be ignored by police officers in the immediate aftermath of the incident. One professional reporter shocked to find himself in handcuffs was MetroFocus web editor John Farley (2011), who had attempted to interview the women in question. Some thirty-five men were held in custody with him, most of whom were protestors but a small number were passers-by arrested for 'snapping souvenir photos'. One such individual, Sam Queary, who had been working at a café near Union Square that day, was described by Farley as an 'inadvertent, spontaneous citizen journalist'. Queary told him: 'I heard a commotion and went outside to find cops macing women and arresting people and hitting people with nightsticks, so I started taking pictures.' Soon after, he said, 'I followed a young, black male as he was being accosted by five cops. As I tried to take a picture I was pushed away. I asked why I was pushed away and then the next thing you know I was being judo flipped' (cited in Farley, 2011). The NYPD later denied that it had been deliberately targeting people with cameras, but many of those on the ground engaged in citizen witnessing felt strongly that their civil rights had been violated by officers employing excessive force.[6]

Tanya O'Carroll (2011), a member of 'Occupy Media' at the time, recalled her experience as an activist reporter that day:

> I saw them [the NYPD] take down one of the live stream guys and smash his computer. I jumped in under one of the police officers' legs to get the shot of it because they were literally pushing his head, the camera and the computer into the ground. And then a moment later I see several white shirts charging him and I step in front thinking they will stop the charge and they knock me to the ground too. Up until that moment I had been treated as a journalist because I was shoot-ing with a camera and shoulder rig. At that moment I realized I had stepped on to the frontlines. There were no lines between citizens and the media. (T. O'Carroll, 2011)

In the days to follow, additional material gathered and posted online by 'the army of citizen documenters', to borrow O'Carroll's phrase, further galvanised the rapidly growing Occupy movement, leading *The Economist* (2011) to observe: 'what's going on in America right now may be the world's first genuine social-media uprising'. By the end of its first month, protest marches and rallies were being organised in other parts of the US, with others following soon after elsewhere in the world in solidarity with the struggle to demand action to curb the undue influence of corporations on government, and to redress social and economic inequalities. 'If it were not for Facebook, Twitter, YouTube, email, this would have been squashed on Wall Street', Eugene 'Roy' Sherrill of Occupy San José told the *Mercury News*; 'Without the open public media, this movement wouldn't have gone national and global. It can't be slowed by big corporate media' (cited in Boudreau, 2011).

Civic cultures

Writing with the benefit of hindsight, it is readily apparent that 'big corporate media' have proven a more formidable adversary than some of the movement's activists may have anticipated. In seeking to explore the implications for citizen witnessing, however, there can be little doubt that familiar assumptions regarding citizenship require examination afresh.

Peter Dahlgren's (2009) reformulation of 'civic cultures' is helpful in this regard, I would suggest, because of the way it attends to the conditions giving shape to civic agency as a dynamic process of identity formation amongst young people. 'Civic cultures', he writes, 'refer to cultural patterns in which identities of citizenship, and the foundations for civic agency, are embedded' (2009: 103). To the extent they generate a compelling sense of 'we-ness', it follows, they 'operate at the level of citizens' taken-for-granted horizons in everyday reality', which necessarily entails examining 'those features of the socio-cultural world that serve as preconditions for people's actual participation in the public sphere and political society' (2009: 104–5). While an array of factors impacts upon civic cultures, Dahlgren suggests that 'family and schools lay a sort of foundation', before pointing to the influence of 'group settings, social relations of power, economics, the legal system, and organizational possibilities', amongst others.

Singled out for attention in this regard is the 'ever-evolving media matrix', which makes possible new kinds of civic practices while, at the same time, demanding new skills for citizenship. Interactive media, in particular, offer significant resources for civic identities, especially at the level of lived experience where the 'dialectical interplay of possibilities and their actualizations' construct new contexts of use. 'The ease of interacting, reformatting, remixing, adding on to existing texts, and so forth', Dahlgren contends, 'promotes the participatory uses of these technologies – and alters forever the traditional premises whereby mass audiences receive ostensibly authoritative, centralized information in a one-way manner' (2009: 154). Nevertheless, he cautions, it is simply too early to say how the social transformations underway will be incorporated into civic cultures. In calling for a 'realistic grasp' of the complexities involved, he acknowledges that there is little prospect that digital technologies will deliver a 'quick fix' or 'shortcut to democracy' anytime soon.

Just as the availability of news and information does not in itself ensure an informed citizenry, it is similarly apparent that no corresponding relationship can be presumed to exist between young people's involvement in social networking and their aptitude for civic participation. One in no way prefigures the other, but this is not to deny that individuals conversant in the uses of technologies widely associated with 'Web 2.0' will be well placed to advance personalised, affective forms of engagement with issues they consider relevant to their concerns (see also Allan and Thorsen, 2009; Atton, 2010; Moeller, 2009b). Taken together, the types of political intervention highlighted over the course of this chapter may be read as broadly indicative of an emergent, uneven and frequently contested ethos of digital citizenship. A word of caution, however: this is not to suggest that those involved self-identify with specific roles, duties or obligations consistent with traditional (that is, prescriptive) ideals of democratic responsibility. Discourses of citizenship may or may not resonate with young people's performative identities, let alone their sense of belonging within a shared community. Instead, their actions are more likely to be defined in these terms by commentators anxious to reaffirm 'real' tenets of political mobilisation and protest in the face of 'virtual' alternatives. Consequently, I would argue that citizenship must be rethought in a manner alert to its multiple, socially contingent re-inflections within a new media ecology where such dichotomies have long ceased to claim a conceptual purchase.

Current discussions about how to address the changing imperatives of citizen witnessing within the network society, to use Castells's evocative phrase, have much to gain from revisiting earlier instances of rapid technological change being criticised for ushering in undesirable forms of media content. Echoes of Walter Lippmann's warning about relying on 'untrained accidental witnesses' – lest democracy descend into mob rule – can be heard to reverberate in reservations expressed about young people's media activities, even where care is taken to avoid overtly elitist claims about harmful influences. The disdain frequently expressed in news reports about their use of Twitter or Facebook, for example, can take the form of a 'cyber-scepticism' that chastises them for being isolated from reality – in effect, a generation of 'slacktivists' too lazy to engage in face-to-face communication, let alone inform themselves about political issues with a view to getting involved (see also Gerodimos and Ward, 2007; Morozov, 2011; Turkle, 2011). Related criticisms about emotional dislocation, detachment, inauthenticity – and thereby 'weak ties' to the community – would not sound out of place in John Dewey's (1927) *The public and its problems*, published all those years ago (for whom 'instability, disintegration and restlessness' characterised 'the present epoch'). At risk of being overlooked is the extent to which social networking is intimately interwoven into the fabric of young people's everyday lives, as well as the reasons why connectivity is so deeply valued. Dahlgren's (2009) conception of 'civic cultures' reminds us that there are many ways of being a citizen, of 'doing democracy' – civic identities, in his words, 'are not static, but protean and multivalent' (2009: 119). Examinations of citizen witnessing, it seems to me, ignore these lived contingencies at their peril.

In the course of its exploration, this chapter has examined a number of examples drawn from a myriad of alternatives. Much of the news coverage of these protests has highlighted how young people have learned to exploit the capacity of social networking tools to advance their causes, often under extraordinarily difficult circumstances, in the name of social justice. Still, pressing questions remain about the nature of civic agency being engendered. Efforts to rethink its provenance, I would argue, need to understand better how personal experience gives shape to the ways young people relate to their communities beyond 'citizenship' narrowly defined. It is in the gaps, silences and fissures of more traditional definitions that the basis emerges for envisaging alternative networks of civic participation firmly situated in the politics of the everyday. Important here, in my view, is the need to discern how young people may be encouraged to embrace their civic selves, that is, to recognise themselves as prospective participants contributing to democratic cultures in self-reflexively meaningful, purposeful ways. In opening up a wider debate concerning how best to improve the quality of citizen witnessing in this regard, it follows, every effort must be made to ensure young people's views, experiences and perspectives inform the ensuing dialogue about what it means to be a citizen in a digital age.

6

WikiLeaks: Citizen as Journalist,
Journalist as Citizen

'Everytime we witness an act that we feel to be unjust and do not act we become a party to injustice', Julian Assange (2006), founder of WikiLeaks, wrote in a treatise describing the website's ethos. He continued:

> Those who are repeatedly passive in the face of injustice soon find their character corroded into servility. Most witnessed acts of injustice are associated with bad governance, since when governance is good, unanswered injustice is rare. By the progressive diminution of a people's character, the impact of reported, but unanswered injustice is far greater than it may initially seem. Modern communications states through their scale, homogeneity and excesses provide their populace with an unprecedented deluge of witnessed, but seemingly unanswerable injustices. (Assange, 2006)

This conception of witnessing brings to light a further dimension of citizen witnessing, namely by recognising the role of the whistle-blower as a progressive form of civic engagement. WikiLeaks, a website dedicated to bringing 'important news and information to the public' so that readers 'can see evidence of the truth', relies on ordinary citizens to forward to it source materials in their possession which they believe belong in the public domain. Personal accounts, descriptions or opinions are insufficient; witnessing, in this context, signifies the reading, assembling and sharing of private, possibly classified items (documents, still images, video footage and the like) in order to further the public interest.

Histories of journalism alert to questions of freedom of expression and the rights of the press help to illuminate contrasting definitions of the public interest, particularly where an ordinary individual has taken it upon themselves to pass along information to a journalist with the aim of exposing corruption, maleficence or injustice. The list of celebrated cases is likely to be a lengthy one in any modern democracy, where invariably the individual involved has witnessed something alarming by virtue of their privileged access within an organisation. Hollywood films have contributed to a certain mythology surrounding whistleblowing, *All the President's Men*'s (1976) depiction of the covert informant 'Deep Throat' in the Watergate scandal being an especially well-known example, with others including *The China Syndrome* (1979), *Norma Rae* (1979), *Silkwood* (1983), *The Insider* (1999), *The Constant Gardener* (2005), *The Informant* (2009) and *The Whistleblower* (2010), amongst others. In real life, whistleblowers almost always strive to remain anonymous, not least for reasons of their personal safety, thereby relying on the journalist to uphold the principle of 'protecting their source' to safeguard them from reprisals. If journalist–source dynamics can be challenging to negotiate at the best of times, however, negotiations with whistleblowers can be especially fraught.

Prior to the emergence of citizen journalism on the web, the status of the citizen witness engaged in whistleblowing could be counterpoised against that of the journalist in relatively straightforward terms. The relationship was symbiotic, with both parties benefiting from the other's involvement, as well as hierarchical in that the decision of whether or not to proceed rested with the journalist's news organisation (with the benefit of legal advice). In other words, the whistleblower was reliant upon the journalist to translate what they had witnessed – typically evidenced in a document of some description – into a news story of interest to the public, justification for this resting squarely on the grounds of its fulfilment of a public interest test. In a digital age, however, the normative rules of this reciprocity have been recast, with the whistleblower increasingly able to bypass the journalist altogether.

New forms of whistleblowing are flourishing across diverse platforms, inviting a host of questions about this dimension of citizen witnessing and its implications for both citizenship and journalism. This chapter, as its title suggests, seeks to hold these two categories in conceptual tension. Beginning in the next section, we turn to examine WikiLeaks, the 'world's most dangerous website' as one of its former members called it (Domscheit-Berg, 2011), and the controversy it sparked over the citizen's right to bear witness as a journalist in the digital age. In the course of examining several of its reportorial interventions, with particular attention given to the Afghanistan war logs posted in 2010, differing views about its perceived potential to reinvent journalism in the public interest will be assessed. WikiLeaks's alternative conception of 'scientific' journalism – whereby readers are afforded access to a whistleblower's witnessing of original source material so as to determine for themselves its relative significance – is shown to challenge the prescribed ideals of professionalism, revealing them to be riven with ideological fissures and contingencies that severely curtail the impartial journalist's capacity to speak truth to power.

Re-writing rules

WikiLeaks eludes straightforward definition. While commentators are inclined to characterise it as a singular institution, closer scrutiny shows that the website's provision is underpinned by a multiplicity of convergent networks reliant on dozens of servers dispersed around the globe. Since its launch in December 2006 by The Sunshine Press (WikiLeaks.org having been registered two months earlier), the site has undergone a series of changes in its strategic rationale and objectives. A careful reading of its 'About' or FAQ pages appearing over the years helps to document this gradual evolution, frequently revealing subtle re-inflections of self-definition in light of changing circumstances. One recurrent point is the acknowledgment that the 'wiki' in its name was introduced due to the initial intention to adopt an operational model similar to that of Wikipedia, the free-content online encyclopaedia created in 2001. This model – envisaged as enabling the website's users to edit or comment on the posted data – was quickly abandoned by Wikileak's organisers, however, in favour of a safer, more restrictive approach reliant upon volunteers to select and research submissions.

'A Wiki for Whistle-Blowers' was the title of a January 2007 *Time* magazine article by Tracy Samantha Schmidt (2007) about the fledgeling website, one of the very first blips on the mainstream media's radar. Described as a 'bold new collective experiment in whistle-blowing', WikiLeaks's organisers ('Chinese dissidents, mathematicians and start-up company technologists, from the US, Taiwan, Europe, Australia and South Africa') were credited with putting into motion – 'in theory' at least – a system that would 'protect leakers' identities while exposing government and corporate corruption worldwide'. With the prospect of more than 1 million leaked documents being posted online by March, when it was anticipated the website would go live, *Time* enthused about its potential as a global forum for examining otherwise confidential materials, despite the 'suspicion building around it' (namely 'conspiracy theories' that it was a 'front for the CIA or some other intelligence agency'). While conceding that it is not possible to determine 'what shadowy organization is behind WikiLeaks', Schmidt's assessment of the site's relative merits led her to maintain:

> Savvy web users, of course, know that public wikis are never trusted for their authenticity for the simple reason that anyone can post or edit them. Instead they're viewed as a first step in the research process. And if WikiLeaks is used with a healthy dose of skepticism, it could become as important a journalistic tool as the Freedom of Information Act. (Schmidt, 2007)

Little would she know that this qualified suggestion that WikiLeaks 'could become as important a journalistic tool as the Freedom of Information Act' would be promptly placed on the site's home-page for publicity purposes, where it has remained ever since. In addition to ostensibly affording it a major news organisation's endorsement, however, WikiLeaks's decision to use the quotation was arguably indicative of a desire to cast its remit in journalistic terms from the outset.

Tensions regarding the precise nature of the journalistic underpinnings of WikiLeaks's operational rationale continued to mount throughout 2007. For most news organisations it was less a question of how best to describe the website's role in providing access to sensitive information than an issue of whether to acknowledge it at all.[1] Journalistic attention would seldom be directed at WikiLeaks in the months ahead, even though the number of news stories based on documents it put into public circulation steadily enhanced its reputation for whistleblowing amongst hackers, activists, campaigners – and investigative reporters. Documents the site released helped to generate and sustain a number of news reports, including stories focusing on the treatment of prisoners at the detention centre in Guantánamo Bay, Cuba; allegations of corruption in a Swiss-based bank; secret information about the internal organisation of the Church of Scientology; Republican Vice Presidential candidate Sarah Palin's use of private email to sidestep public record laws; and details about the far-Right British National Party (BNP) membership.

If largely ignored by the mainstream media, however, WikiLeaks's growing reputation within internet circles was increasingly subject to polarised debate in the blogosphere. Advocates enthused about its 'fourth estate' role as a vital 'check against tyranny' in the fight for a 'more open and transparent society'. Detractors, in sharp contrast, pounced on what they perceived to be the site's reckless violation of secrecy for its own sake, issuing grave warnings about detrimental implications for national security. Meanwhile several news outlets, somewhat begrudgingly, began to acknowledge the site as a 'journalistic tool' (*Time*'s initial definition) to pry loose stories otherwise being concealed. This status was reinforced, in turn, by related forms of public recognition for the site's activities, such as *The Economist*'s 2008 New Media Award as well as credit from the *Index on Censorship* for being 'an invaluable resource for anonymous whistleblowers and investigative journalists'. In June of 2009, WikiLeaks earned a second new media award, this time from Amnesty International for exposing 'extra-judicial killings and disappearances' in Kenya. 'The material was important', the site's co-founder Julian Assange told Journalism.co.uk in an interview at the time; 'It was difficult to get Western press attention to it. We ran it on our front page for a week. Most journalists didn't care about it. Even regular [WikiLeaks] readers didn't care about it' (cited in Townend, 2009).

Further examples of 'censorship attacks', to use Wikileaks's turn of phrase, continued to surface throughout 2009. Scandals included a multinational oil trading company's efforts to impose a gagging order on news organisations – not least the *Guardian* – striving to report on a health crisis associated with toxic waste dumped in Côte d'Ivoire, Africa; 'Climategate', when more than 1,000 emails and 2,000 documents from the University of East Anglia's Climate Research Unit were posted online by WikiLeaks, some of which appeared to suggest that statistical information inconsistent with scientific assumptions about climate change was being suppressed; and the posting of more than 500,000 pager messages sent in the immediate aftermath of the September 11, 2001 attacks. In light of these and related initiatives, by early 2010 it was fast becoming apparent that WikiLeaks warranted regular monitoring by journalists anxious to scoop rivals with breaking news of leaked disclosures.

This threshold was finally crossed when WikiLeaks became front-page news in its own right in early April 2010, following its posting of a video documenting US military action in Iraq. Shot in black-and-white from an Apache helicopter gunship hovering over a Baghdad neighbourhood on 12 July 2007, the thirty-nine minutes of classified footage shows a group of men, including two employees of Reuters, being slaughtered – and in a manner that seemed to many of those watching as jocular as it was arbitrary. Minutes later, a second airstrike is shown, this time targeting a van arriving on the scene, with the effect of killing the civilian driver and wounding his two children passengers. 'Collateral Murder', as the video was titled, garnered media attention around the globe (the seventeen-minute version having gone viral via YouTube), igniting a bitterly acrimonious debate – not least in the blogosphere – about the ethics of WikiLeaks's decision to release it on its website. Voices weighed into the controversy from across the political spectrum. Some expressed their outrage at what they perceived to be a war crime, contending that Geneva Conventions for the humanitarian treatment of casualties had been violated. Others debated the nature of 'murder' in WikiLeaks's choice of title, calling into question the legal complexities associated with the US military's 'rules of engagement'. Still others blamed the 'fog of war', insisting that the incident was little more than a regrettable example of what can happen in the heat of battle.

As the controversy unfolded, WikiLeaks became the subject of intense media interest for the first time. In observing how the video had garnered attention for a 'once-fringe Web site', the *New York Times* suggested that this 'clearinghouse for sensitive documents' was 'edging closer toward a form of investigative journalism and to advocacy' in a manner certain to be a thorn in the side of authorities. 'That's arguably what spy agencies do – high-tech investigative journalism', Assange is quoted as stating in an interview with the paper. 'It's time that the media upgraded its capabilities along those lines' (cited in Cohen and Stelter, 2010). WikiLeaks itself appeared to have adopted enhanced capabilities furthering its claim to be evolving beyond source status to embrace a journalistic role, most notably with regard to the steps taken first to decrypt and then to verify the authenticity of the Apache video footage. The latter entailed Icelandic journalist Kristinn Hrafnsson and cameraperson Ingi Ragnar Ingason travelling to Baghdad to find the two children injured in the attack (the interview was later broadcast on Icelandic television), while Assange himself, working out of a 'bunker' in Iceland, endeavoured to help to supply context and analysis. 'This week marked the international coming-out party for a new media organization that could upend the sacred cows of traditional journalism', Jonathan Stray (2010) of *Foreign Policy* observed. In describing WikiLeaks as 'an Internet-savvy investigative journalism outfit', he suggested it represented the type of 'accountability journalism' made famous by Carl Bernstein and Bob Woodward of Watergate fame. If praise for the website was rare, in public at least, due to its controversial tactics, Stray commented that 'no journalist I've spoken to will speak ill of

WikiLeaks in private: Every reporter understands that WikiLeaks is the thin end of the wedge. If they can't run a dangerous story, no one can.'

Revealing human consequences

This commitment, typically expressed as a 'publish and be damned' declaration in journalistic folklore, was tested almost to breaking point when WikiLeaks released over 91,000 pages of US military documents in July 2010. The compendium, promptly labelled 'the Afghanistan war logs' by the press, consisted primarily of classified memos and reports written by soldiers and intelligence officers, typically describing lethal military actions, over the period between January 2004 and December 2009. Some 15,000 items were held back from the archive for further review, the site explained, 'as part of a harm minimization process demanded by our source'.

In a significant departure from previous form, the co-operation of major news organisations – namely, the *Guardian*, the *New York Times* and *Der Spiegel* (in its German and English on-line editions) – had been negotiated beforehand. Each was given the opportunity to examine the items several weeks in advance, subject to agreeing to withhold publication of their news reports until 25 July. The public interest in the material was so significant, the three ascertained, that the agreed embargo was a price worth paying.[2] The *Guardian* characterised the 'huge cache of secret US military files' as offering a 'devastating portrait of the failing war in Afghanistan, revealing how coalition forces have killed hundreds of civilians in unreported incidents, Taliban attacks have soared and NATO commanders fear neighbouring Pakistan and Iran are fuelling the insurgency' (Davies and Leigh, 2010). The *New York Times* concurred that the documents presented 'an unvarnished, ground-level picture of the war in Afghanistan that is in many respects more grim than the official portrayal' (Chivers et al., 2010). *Der Spiegel* maintained: 'Never before has it been possible to compare the reality on the battlefield in such a detailed manner with what the US Army propaganda machinery is propagating' (Gebauer et al., 2010).

This capacity to afford documentation of the lived experiences of soldiers reporting from the field in a warzone was the most significant feature of the logs. The members of the 'strong journalistic team', to use Assange's phrase, each prioritised different aspects of the material in relation to their respective judgements about relative news value. Whether or not WikiLeaks itself was part of the team, or simply the purveyor of material for others to process, proved a contentious point. *Guardian* journalist Nick Davies (2010), in a personal account headlined 'Story Behind Biggest Leak in Intelligence History', revealed several details regarding how the 'huge trove of data' amounting to a 'secret record of the world's most powerful nation at war' came to light via WikiLeaks and a 'unique collaboration' between the three news outlets. The original source of the material – a citizen witness – is identified as 'Bradass87', who initiated a series of instant messages with Californian computer hacker Adrian Lamo, including one which asked: 'hi ... how are you?... im an army intelligence analyst, deployed to eastern bagdad ... if you had unprecedented access to classified networks, 14 hours a day, 7 days a week for 8+ months, what would you do?' In the days that followed, 'Bradass87' explained that someone he knew (presumably 'Bradass87' himself, later alleged to be a 22-year-old intelligence analyst named Bradley Manning) had been downloading, compressing and encrypting the data on to blank CDs, labelled as Lady Gaga's music, before uploading it to Assange of WikiLeaks. 'i want people to see the truth', he is quoted as stating; 'its open diplomacy ... its Climategate with a global scope and breathtaking depth ... its beautiful and horrifying ... It's public data, it belongs in the public domain.' Evidently Lamo, two days into their exchange of messages, had contacted the US military, who sent officers from its criminal investigations department to meet him at a Starbucks. Lamo provided them with a printout of Bradass87's online chat, Davies maintains, which led to Manning's arrest the next day at the operating base where he was stationed, 25 miles outside of Baghdad. 'I wouldn't have done this if lives weren't in danger', Lamo told Wired.com following Manning's arrest; 'He was in a war zone and basically trying to vacuum up as much classified information as he could, and just throwing it up into the air' (cited in Poulsen and Zetter, 2010).

Assange, fearful of his own arrest, went to ground. The *Guardian*, drawing on a series of intermediaries, made contact with him in a Brussels café. There a plan began to form whereby a small team of its specialist reporters would sift through and decode the logs with a view to publishing key insights. The decision to share the database with the *New York Times* and *Der Spiegel* was taken as a strategy intended to reduce the risk of the authorities imposing a gagging order, not least because it ensured publication would occur in three different jurisdictions. 'Under the arrangement', Davies (2010) noted, 'Assange would have no influence on the stories we wrote, but would have a voice in the timing of publication.' WikiLeaks meanwhile prepared to publish simultaneously much of the raw data itself (some material having been withheld to protect human sources), thereby facilitating efforts to compare and contrast the actual logs with claims made about them in the ensuing news reports. This strategy was a useful check on newspapers' selection and interpretation, and as such indicative of tensions in the relationship. These tensions, not surprisingly, broke out into the open soon after.

'What this war looks like and feels like to the soldiers'

Bill Keller, Executive Editor at the *New York Times*, explained to readers in a 'Talk to the Newsroom' Q and A forum that the paper 'has no control over WikiLeaks – where it gets its material, what it releases and in what form. To say that it is an independent organization is a monumental understatement.' He proceeded to point out that the decision to post the military archive on the web was taken by WikiLeaks, and was going to happen regardless of whether or not the *Times* elected to be involved. Recognising that the fact that the site had obtained secret material in the first place was 'newsworthy in itself', Keller's (2010) comments positioned the site strictly as a source, with the paper performing the journalistic work of studying the material, assessing its value and credibility, weighing it against *Times*' reporters experience of the war, and determining its larger significance. 'In doing so', he added, 'we took great care both to put the information in context and to excise anything that would put lives at risk or jeopardize ongoing military missions.' While carefully vetting the material for disclosures, patterns and, of course, scoops was of primary importance, it was the effort made to process raw details into more personal narratives that enabled the paper, in his view, to 'give readers an intimate sense of what this war looks like and feels like to the soldiers in the field'.

The response from the Obama administration was swift. National Security Advisor General James Jones (2010) condemned the leak as 'irresponsible', issuing a statement the same day declaring: 'The United States strongly condemns the disclosure of classified information by individuals and organizations which could put the lives of Americans and our partners at risk, and threaten our national security.' White House frustration over the leak, not surprisingly, meant the motives of the leaker were called in question, with Jones contending: 'WikiLeaks made no effort to contact us about these documents – the United States government learned from news organizations that these documents would be posted.' An administration official, this time in an email to journalists (subject line: 'Thoughts on WikiLeaks'), underscored the point in sharper language: 'As you report on this issue, it's worth noting that wikileaks is not an objective news outlet but rather an organization that opposes US policy in Afghanistan.' The unnamed official also used the opportunity to outline a defensive posture, stressing that the events occurred before the President had announced his new strategy, and that the information revealed was of little significance in any case.

Herein lay the definitional problem for the government, evidently determined to characterise WikiLeaks's actions as a harmful threat ('a breach of federal law') while, at the same time, insisting the leaked material was of little value (documents consisting of 'unvarnished, unvetted, uncorroborated reporting' from people in the region who may have 'agendas'). Meanwhile those weighing into the growing controversy included Senator Joe Lieberman (2010), who echoed the White House line by stating that 'WikiLeaks is not an objective news organization' before going even further, arguing that it was 'an organization with an ideological agenda that is implacably hostile to our military and the most basic requirements of our national security'. It was important, he warned, to be 'wary of drawing conclusions based on materials selectively leaked by WikiLeaks, as it seeks to sap support for the Afghan war among the American people and our European allies'. Time and again, critics levelled the charge that WikiLeaks had put the lives of US soldiers at serious risk. 'Somebody ought to be wearing an orange jumpsuit', Missouri Senator Kit Bond, ranking Republican on the Senate Intelligence Committee, told Fox News (2010).

Several commentators assumed a decidedly more upbeat stance, however, perceiving in WikiLeaks's actions grounds for cautious optimism. '[T]he truth is that we don't really know what WikiLeaks *is*, or what the organization's ethics are, or why they've become such a stunningly good conduit of classified information', Alexis Madrigal (2010) of the *Atlantic* observed. 'In the new asymmetrical journalism, it's not clear who is on what side or what the rules of engagement actually are', he added; 'But the reason WikiLeaks may have just changed the media is that we found out that it doesn't really matter. Their data is good, and that's what counts.' This conception of a 'new asymmetrical journalism' resonated with several other assessments on offer. Roy Greenslade (2010), in his *Guardian* blog, suggested that the WikiLeaks revelations were rightly hailed as a triumph of 'data journalism', and as such the site deserved credit – along with the news organisations involved – for performing a public service. 'We journalists should be delighted because our central task has always been one of disclosure, of revealing public interest material that others believe wish to be kept secret', he wrote; 'The emerging form of disclosure through the internet, pioneered so successfully in the past couple of years by WikiLeaks, deserves our praise and needs to be defended against the reactionary forces that seek to avoid exposure.'

It was this strategy to elude control from any government or legal system that academic Jay Rosen (2010), in his blog Pressthink, sought to highlight by proposing that WikiLeaks be regarded as 'the world's first stateless news organization'. In his words:

> Appealing to national traditions of fair play in the conduct of news reporting misunderstands what WikiLeaks is about: the release of information without regard for national interest. In media history up to now, the press is free to report on what the powerful wish to keep secret because the laws of a given nation protect it. But WikiLeaks is able to report on what the powerful wish to keep secret because the logic of the Internet permits it. This is new. Just as the Internet has no terrestrial address or central office, neither does WikiLeaks. (Rosen, 2010)

For Rosen, government confusion over how to engage with WikiLeaks ('we're gonna hunt you down/hey, you didn't contact us!') is symptomatic of the 'new balance of power' being established. 'In the revised picture', he wrote, 'we find the state, which holds the secrets but is powerless to prevent their release; the stateless news organization, deciding how to release them; and the national newspaper in the middle, negotiating the terms of legitimacy between these two actors.' For the prospective whistle-blower with explosive documents, he continued, WikiLeaks is a much more attractive proposition (it 'has no address, answers no subpoenas and promises to run the full cache if they can be verified as real') than a newspaper subject to the laws of a nation, which may or may not restrict its capacity to protect sources.

Pasts justifying futures

A recurrent feature of the more positive appraisals of WikiLeaks appearing at this time was the effort made to situate it within a broader journalistic tradition of investigative reporting. Much was made of perceived connections with the *Washington Post*'s reliance on a secret informant to break open the Watergate scandal

that toppled the Nixon administration. Even stronger parallels were drawn with the 'Pentagon Papers' case in 1971, when
Daniel Ellsberg, an analyst at the RAND Corporation, handed
over to Neil Sheehan, a *New York Times* correspondent, several
sets of photocopies he had painstakingly prepared of classified
documents pertaining to a top-secret Pentagon study of official
decision-making concerning the lead-up to the Vietnam War and
its conduct.

The scale of deception revealed in the US government's secret
escalation of the conflict while making public assurances to the
contrary was astonishing, with the Johnson administration, in
particular, shown to have systematically lied to Congress. Shortly
after the *Times* had taken the brave decision to publish excerpts of
the 7,000-page document on 13 June (outside legal counsel having
advised against publication), the Nixon administration succeeded
in obtaining a federal court injunction prohibiting the newspaper from publishing further articles. While the *Times* appealed
against the temporary injunction – only three days of instalments
having being published at that point – other newspapers began
publishing their own reports, before they too were restrained. On
30 June, the Supreme Court ruled in a 6–3 decision against the
government's case for censorship based on prior restraint. 'Only
a free and unrestrained press can effectively expose deception in
government', Justice Hugo Black stated; 'And paramount among
the responsibilities of a free press is the duty to prevent any part of
the government from deceiving the people and sending them off to
distant lands to die of foreign fevers and foreign shot and shell.'[3]

Differing opinions regarding whether or not WikiLeaks's disclosure of the Afghan war logs amounted to a landmark case for press
freedom akin to the Pentagon Papers frequently revolved around
diverging assessments of its journalistic importance. Ellsberg
(2011) himself remarked: 'The WikiLeaks' unauthorised disclosures of the last year are the first in 40 years to approach the scale
of the Pentagon Papers (and even surpass them in quantity and
timeliness).' His one regret was that 'the courageous source of
these secret, field-level reports . . . did not have access to top secret,
high-level recommendations, estimates and decisions'. Further

points of connection were identified by Michael Wolff (2010), who observed that 'One of the burdens and wonders of the Pentagon Papers leak was the sheer logistics of copying, storing, and delivering all that material. The WikiLeak makes leaking – leaking on a historical level – just a digital transfer.' In light of this development, Wolff maintains that a new model is emerging, one which holds the promise of effectively 'saving' journalism. 'As Daniel Ellsberg, and then Woodward and Bernstein, remade journalism into a transaction of reporters and sources', he contended, 'now it will be a hackers function.'

Telling in this regard, at least in my reading, is the decision taken by Assange, dubbed 'the Robin Hood of hacking' in some reports, to describe himself as 'a journalist and publisher and inventor' in an interview published at the time. 'There is a bit of a desire to romanticize what I do', he told *Time* magazine; 'But like war correspondents who go to various countries, I do the same thing. I travel to different countries where we have supports and where I need to follow stories.' Evidently, most of his attention is focused on 'logistics', drawing on a longstanding interest in cryptography and steadfast commitment to free speech. This 'combination of skills has proved coincidentally extremely effective in what WikiLeaks does in terms of protecting people', he added, 'using encryption technology and being engaged in political and policy debate and producing information that will push reforms' (Assange, 2010a). Possible reasons for Assange's inclination to assume the mantle of either 'journalist' or 'publisher' invited scrutiny from commentators, especially in light of his remarks during an interview with *Der Spiegel* when asked about his personal motivations. 'I enjoy creating systems on a grand scale, and I enjoy helping people who are vulnerable', he commented; 'And I enjoy crushing bastards. So it is enjoyable work' (Assange, 2010b).[4]

Several critics incensed by this stance – the phrase 'crushing bastards' proving remarkably tweet-worthy – sought to transform Assange into a figure of hate. Others condemned him for disguising malicious intent in the language of 'whistleblowing'. Jamie McIntyre (2010), a former Pentagon correspondent for CNN, expressed his deep misgivings on this point:

As a professional journalist I have been on the receiving end of hundreds of leaks, and they have been invaluable in helping me sort out unvarnished fact from official fiction, which after all is at the core of my job. . . . I bristled a bit Sunday night when the story first broke and I heard several news organizations shorthand WikiLeaks as a 'whistleblower' group. A whistleblower is someone who exposes wrongdoing. To apply the label to WikiLeaks is not only imprecise but unfair, in that it creates a preconceived perception that the released material 'blows the whistle' on illicit activity.

McIntyre continued, stating:

Let's be clear: WikiLeaks is an anti-privacy, anti-secrecy group, whose primary tenet is that nothing should be kept from the world, not military secrets, not sources or methods of intelligence gathering, not even the secret rituals of fraternities and sororities. Governments, Corporations, Private citizens all have some right, even responsibility to keep some secrets. WikiLeaks' only allegiance seems to be to the source of its leaks. By remaining agnostic on the consequences of its actions, WikiLeaks seems to me to be functioning less in the tradition of good old-fashioned muckrakers, and more like anti-privacy terrorists. If I were the *New York Times*, I would not be happy about being described as one of WikiLeaks' 'media partners' on the organization's website. (McIntyre, 2010)

Meanwhile others celebrated the boldness of Assange's personal audacity, employing terms such as 'maverick', 'crusader' or 'info-hacker' to suggest that WikiLeaks's efforts should be recognised as a modern-day continuation of a long, proud tradition of journalistic muckraking. Several accounts called forth details of achievements secured by reform-dedicated reporters in early twentieth-century US history, perceiving in the website's mission a welcome return to 'digging dirt' at a time when investigative journalism is all too often reduced to celebrity tittle-tattle. 'WikiLeaks founder Julian Assange has publicly eschewed the role of impartial journalist, embracing instead the role of a muckraker – using modern technology to do what he says the mainstream media are not doing enough of', Noam N. Levey and Jennifer Martinez (2010) suggested in the *Pittsburgh Post-Gazette*. Their observation echoed a number of similar accounts already circulating in the months leading up to the Afghanistan war logs story, including a *New York Times* article headlined 'Pentagon Sees a Threat From Online Muckrakers' (see Strom, 2010).

Differing views over whether WikiLeaks was aptly regarded as a 'whistleblower' or 'muckraker' website frequently hinged on presumptions made about where it belonged on the journalist–source continuum. Steve Myers (2010), managing editor of Poynter.org, offered an alternative view however, contending that WikiLeaks had effectively situated itself between source and publisher. The site, he argued, 'has shifted power away from the monoliths that once determined what is news and toward the people who, before the Web, would have been stopped in the newspaper lobby before they could see a reporter'. The three news organisations, in agreeing to WikiLeaks's terms in 'striking a bargain' to gain access to the logs, 'found themselves not as gatekeepers of information, but as guests with VIP access'. At the same time, however, 'WikiLeaks needed these titans of old media. It needed their reporting, their reach, their distribution networks, their reputation.' WikiLeaks's determination to 'play both sides' suggests to Myers an emergent advocacy role intended to influence traditional media, but not replace them. 'The power of self-publication isn't quite enough', he argued; 'To achieve the most impact, to get people to pay attention to this story, WikiLeaks needed to broker a deal with traditional media.' In striving to enhance its credibility via its relationships with major news outlets, WikiLeaks took a significant step toward garnering public trust for its actions. Far from being a neutral player, its priorities were readily apparent.

'Deep Throat had an agenda. Ellsberg had an agenda', Keller of the *New York Times* told Myers (2010) in an email. 'That doesn't invalidate the information they provide us. If we refused to work with sources whose motivations we didn't share, a lot of important stories would go untold.' For Keller, the 'critical thing is what we do with the material – check its authenticity, draw our own conclusions from it, put it in context, and lay it all out for readers on our terms, not the source's terms'.

Shifting the burden of verification

This insistence that WikiLeaks was a source, and not a 'media partner' as the site itself claimed, was reinforced by Keller's colleague at the *Times*, reporter Eric Schmitt, when recalling his experiences in 'the bunker' preparing the materials for publication. 'I've seen Julian Assange in the last couple of days kind of flouncing around talking about this collaboration like the four of us were working all this together', he maintained. 'But we were not in any kind of partnership or collaboration with him. This was a source relationship. He's making it sound like this was some sort of journalistic enterprise between WikiLeaks, *The New York Times*, *The Guardian*, and *Der Spiegel*, and that's not what it was' (cited in Hendler, 2010). Davies of the *Guardian* concurred that Assange's involvement was limited to that of a source, stressing that collaboration was limited to the three news organisations involved.[5] Assange himself countered this position, however, stating in a London press conference that WikiLeaks decided to work with the three publications because they 'were the best newspapers in the world for investigative research', and because each was willing to co-operate with the website in its media strategy intended to achieve the maximum impact for the benefit of its secret source. 'We can't have a journalistic coalition which is too large . . . for logistical reasons. With three or four we could get into a room and agree on all the conditions', he stated; 'The task of good journalism is to turn this material; who, when, where, how, how many, into something which emotionally engages people' (cited in McAthy and Gunter, 2010).

In a follow-up interview with Amy Goodman on her *Democracy Now* programme, Assange (2010c) described what he termed the 'journalistic coalition' WikiLeaks mobilised to process the material, highlighting the role of the site's own 'journalistic teams' in extracting the data, before noting, in turn, how this 'unusual collaboration' revolved around a sense of partnership. This was not to deny, however, that certain tensions existed. He conceded that WikiLeaks was not 'totally happy' about the way the *New York Times* had characterised its relationship with the website in

'defensive' terms, suggesting it seemed 'a little bit unprofessional'.
He added:

> So, as an example, the *New York Times* stated that it chose not to
> link to our website. I mean, it is just ridiculous. The public can see
> that and Google it, if they want. If the *New York Times*, for whatever
> reason, wants to not link to WikiLeaks for its own defensive politics,
> then it can do that, and it's perfectly entitled to. But to deliberately say
> that that is being avoided smacks of unprofessional conduct, to me.
> Now, that doesn't mean it's been approved by the editor to do that,
> but it does seem to be quite pusillanimous to be engaging in that kind
> of defensive conduct, instead of pursuing the real meat of the story.
> (Assange, 2010c)

Assange was similarly concerned about the coalition's decision,
evidently at the insistence of the *Times*, to show the White House
the documents prior to publication in order to help redact sensitive
information of possible harm to people on the ground. '[T]here is
a bit of a difference between . . . how the American press tends to
deal with government agencies prior to publication and the standards that we have and the standards the European press has', he
stated:

> We don't see that . . . in the case of a story where an organization
> has engaged in some kind of abusive conduct and that story is being
> revealed, that it has a right to know the story before the public, a right
> to know the story before the victims, because we know that what
> happens in practice is that that is just extra lead time to spin the story.

Independent, 'scientific' journalism, he suggested, demanded
something different: 'It seems to us that a journalist's relationship
should be with the public, on the one hand, and with their sources,
on the other hand, who are providing them with information to
give to the public' (Assange, 2010c). 'Scientific journalism', it
follows, aspires to a higher standard, effectively enabling members
of the public to corroborate for themselves what they are being
told.

Alerted to Assange's criticisms, Keller responded in an email to
The Daily Beast website. 'Obviously our decision not to link to the

WikiLeaks archive would not deter anyone who wanted to find it', he acknowledged; 'All we could do was make this gesture to show we were not endorsing or encouraging the release of information that could cause harm.' In his view, the public interest was served by work of the three news organisations to 'mine the data for news and analysis' for a 'large audience that would take this seriously'. That said, he promptly levelled criticism of his own against Assange: 'His decision to release the data to everyone, however, had potential consequences that I think anyone, regardless of how he [or she] views the war, would find regrettable' (cited in Jacobs, 2010). No explanation was forthcoming concerning the reason why he considered the public release of the data 'regrettable', particularly when the site had gone to such lengths to involve its 'media partners' to help ensure the documents were carefully scrutinised (and withheld those deemed to be too risky) before releasing them in the name of openness and transparency.

In any case, some commentators wondered aloud whether a more important point wasn't being missed. Assange should 'bite his tongue', was the view of Craig Silverman (2010) commenting for the *Columbia Journalism Review*. 'The *Times*'s decision to check with the White House was of great service to WikiLeaks, because it was one of several processes that served to remove any doubts about the authenticity of the Afghanistan documents', he argued. In this way, he reasoned, the ensuing controversy focused on matters other than the origin of the documents themselves. Assange was to be credited, he believed, for having 'expertly removed accuracy and verification from the conversation by placing the burden for these elements on the shoulders of *The New York Times*, *The Guardian* and *Der Spiegel*.' The *Times*, he added, placed some of that burden on the White House, as did the other two news organisations, albeit to a lesser extent.[6] The end result of this 'unprecedented verification challenge' was a 'big win' for WikiLeaks, Silverman concluded, recognising 'a certain brilliance in the way Assange shifted the burden of verification and analysis away from WikiLeaks, while at the same time ensuring he was able to call out mistakes made by the very news organizations that supplied the all-important credibility to his data'.

Improvising journalism

In rounding out this chapter's discussion, we return once again to the tensions between journalism and citizenship, tensions which WikiLeaks reformulates to advantage in striving to create alternative spaces for the citizen witness as whistleblower. Such an aim, I have endeavoured to show, strikes something of a discordant note with customary projections of journalists' collective identity, particularly where they prove unduly mechanistic in their rendering of certain mythologised images of journalists' affinity. While I hesitate to suggest that it is possible to discern a general set of principles from WikiLeaks's creative use of 'internet technologies in new ways to report the truth' (Assange, 2010d), it seems to me that there is little doubt that the website's insistent transgression of journalistic boundaries puts paid to conventional assumptions about how power is – and should be – distributed within new media ecosystems where witnessing is concerned.

In daring to occupy ground claimed by mainstream, corporate news organisations, WikiLeaks calls into question their discursive authority, helping to render transparent their vested interests in preserving the status quo. To pause and consider Assange as an improvising journalist of sorts, deliberately eschewing 'objective' reporting in order to expose social injustice through tactics lawful and otherwise, is to recognise the precarious nature of this authority ('To be completely impartial is to be an idiot', he told one interviewer: see Khatchadourian, 2010). Perceived threats to its legitimacy become all the more acute when set in the context of the wider crisis confronting these organisations as they struggle to re-negotiate the terms of their relationship with distrustful audiences, many of whom are increasingly inclined to regard them as compromised or, even worse, irrelevant. To the extent it is appropriate to characterise journalism as an interpretive performance, it follows, it is necessary to attend to the ways in which certain values associated with professionalism risk reinforcing a normative order that excludes those committed to journalism as a public service.

In seeking to lay claim to a citizen witness-centred conception of journalism, WikiLeaks has thrown into sharp relief the ways in which this normative order is maintained, repaired and, when necessary, policed. 'WikiLeaks is not a news organization, it is a cell of activists that is releasing information designed to embarrass people in power', George Packer of the *New Yorker* insisted; 'They simply believe that the State Department is an illegitimate organization that needs to be exposed, which is not really journalism' (cited in Carr, 2010). Marc Thiessen (2010) went further in a *Washington Post* op-ed column, castigating the website for being a 'criminal enterprise'. One may presume that his call for the site to be shut down, 'and its leadership brought to justice', met with the approval of those accustomed to believing that journalism's formulation of the public interest should correspond with corporate priorities. WikiLeaks, in its ad hoc fashioning of an alternative news culture, threatens to unravel this relationship of equivalence, not least by providing the opportunity for citizens to actively re-write the rules of membership for journalism as an imagined, interpretive community.[7]

Reforming journalism that taps into the passion, innovation and expertise of ordinary people prepared to blow the whistle over what they witness is certain to disrupt traditional hierarchies of power and privilege in its advocacy of reporting aligned with the public right to know. No one should be under any illusion about the formidable nature of this challenge, however, or the reluctance of news organisations to confront it. 'One day, the WikiLeaks uproar was sparking a once-in-a-generation debate about the disclosure of classified information, the audacious role of a stateless organization beyond the reach of sovereign nations, and the old media's complicity in packaging the 91,000 pages of Afghanistan war documents', observed press commentator Howard Kurtz (2010). 'The next day, the media establishment seemed to yawn: Old news. Recycled stuff. Kinda knew that. See ya. Hey, is Lindsay Lohan still in jail?'

7

'The Global Village of Images'

The figure of the citizen witness, whilst of formative influence in giving shape to our conceptions of citizen journalism (and thereby citizenship and journalism more generally), has proven a rather elusive quarry throughout this book's discussion. This is as it should be, of course. Discourses of witnessing, as we have seen, recurrently stretch to encompass multiple modalities.

At first glance, these modalities may appear to be crisply differentiated from one another as separate positions along an imagined continuum. At one end is the otherwise indifferent viewer, listener or reader. Confronted with breaking news reporting of distant suffering, she or he may enact a sense of civic commitment by being moved to care, possibly even to respond to the plight represented before them. At the opposite end of this continuum is another individual, similarly engaged in everyday activities, who suddenly finds themselves caught up in unexpected, quite possibly dangerous events. Much to their own surprise perhaps, she or he may feel compelled to document some fleeting aspect of what's unfolding around them, perhaps in order to share their perspective with others, or maybe to help render it affectively meaningful. To the extent either person self-identifies as a citizen witness, or some variation thereof highlighting their capacity to bear witness (either vicariously from afar or at first-hand on the scene), the occupied role is likely to be understood to be as human(e)ly subjective as it is ephemeral. Complicating matters still further is a third subject position, situated in a shifting, even contested (at times) relationship to the other two, namely the citizen self-reflexively engaged in purposeful witnessing – such as the activist determined to challenge injustice, the NGO worker revealing a humanitarian crisis, the combatant recording the grisly realities of conflict, or the whistleblower exposing corruption.

Multiple modalities of citizen witnessing invite, in turn, varied responses from the journalist, formally charged with the obligation to perform witnessing on behalf of their publics (with all of the tensions this entails). Firmly intent on wielding the cultural authority of expertise necessary to adjudicate truth-claims – both their own and, crucially, those of others – the journalist strives to sustain what can be a fraught process of mediation, and endeavours to do so in a manner at once impartial, dispassionate and responsible. There can be little doubt his or her claim to professional witnessing effectively rests on managing, if not containing, the discursive threat to this authority posed by the amateur, citizen witness. Hence one of the reasons journalistic scepticism, if not outright hostility – usually tinged with defensiveness – comes to the fore when the value of citizens' contributions to newsmaking is heralded as evidence of a broader democratisation of news reporting.

In the course of our enquiry, efforts to discern these alterable, evolving modalities have served to enrich, deepen and occasionally upset familiar assumptions about witnessing, not least by showing how these diverse positionalities mutually implicate one another in complex, frequently contradictory ways. Indeed, even to speak of them as separate points of identification along our imagined continuum would quickly prove problematic were it understood too literally. Closer inspection will qualify otherwise bold assertions about witnessing invoked for the sake of theoretical convenience. At issue, I have argued, is the risk of reifying into place analytical categories that gloss over the very social contingencies that need to be brought to light to further our investigations. Varied discourses of witnessing belie inchoate ideological commitments, each one of which can be shown to register its respective investment in sustaining a preferred definition of what it means to lay claim to apprehending the real in a language of truthful testimony. In other words, modalities marked for purposes of analytical clarity must not be conflated with actual empirical, lived positions in any mechanistic sense. Too often we may be tempted to smooth over inconsistencies in the search for stable categories, rather than encouraging deliberative space for the recognition of subtle nuances of inflection, however troublesome they may seem for the task at hand.

Time and again, however, it has been shown that the capacity to generate first-person epistemic knowledge is contained within a narrower set of questions focusing on the social dynamics of technology. The journalist's competence as a professional witness is routinely judged on the basis of their relative skill in handling the multifarious contingencies of technical demands, especially where improvisation under pressure makes good an opportunity otherwise denied those less proficient. Histories of war reporting, in particular, recurrently bring to light the technological impera-tives underwriting journalistic witnessing, ranging from the advent of the telegraph and still camera in covering the US Civil War, the motion-picture camera making possible World War I's silent newsreels, the immediacy of minute-by-minute live radio reports in World War II, the role of television news in relaying the battlefields of Vietnam into 'the living room war', 24-hour satellite news of the Persian Gulf War, the 'first internet war' in Kosovo, and so forth (see Matheson and Allan, 2009; Neuman, 1996; Perlmutter, 1999). References to aspects of what we are describing as citizen witnessing occasionally feature across the array of such instances, to varying degrees, though seldom drawn out for scrutiny in their own right given the emphasis placed on pinpointing advances ushered in via significant technological breakthroughs.

In examining this emergent ecology of citizen witnessing, we have sought to open up for analysis and critique the ways in which myriad modes of reportorial form, practice and epistemology – all too often obscured by apparent 'revolutions' in technology – have been crafted through the exigencies of crisis reporting. This chapter, in bringing together the book's themes, proceeds to push beyond technology-centred conceptions of witnessing so as to elucidate wider ethical implications for revisioning citizen newsmaking.

Technologies of witnessing

Journalists themselves have been at the fore in thinking through these issues. British broadcaster Jon Snow (2005), for example, has offered several pertinent observations in the course of describing what he calls the 'human connection' at the heart of good reporting:

> Technology has given us the wonder of instant, the knowledge of the suffering now, but not what it means human to human. Technology has given us the global village of images ready to weave into as comprehensive an account as mankind has ever known. We have invested in technology. But we have neglected the human. We have danced to the music of endless pictorial options. We have dispatched willing writers to editing devices to wax poetic about scenes they have often seen but rarely, if ever, witnessed. (Snow, 2005)

Images, however compelling, are of secondary importance to witnessing – 'one pair of eyes, one camera' – which he regards as primary. 'The core is the human', he writes, 'the reporter as witness. And despite the brilliance and comprehensiveness of the global village, nothing has replaced her or him.' To the extent the technological is prioritised over and above the human, the quality of the ensuing reporting is compromised. '[W]e are still wowed by the instantaneous whiz-bang of it all', Snow (2011) argues in a later essay. 'For the reporter the sheer business of "going live" so preoccupies and undermines the journalistic endeavour, there is little time left to retrieve the unique content his or her pair of eyes should be giving us.' Where personal observation is concerned, the traditional commitment of 'one pair of eyes witnessing a story' is increasingly being replaced by a new emphasis on what he calls 'sausage machine telly' where 'the work of many pairs of eyes' is put together into a single 'package' of an event. Too often the end result, he contends, is a news report appropriate to a 'competitive multiplatform age', yet neither sufficiently distinctive nor interesting enough to engage the concern of the viewer about the human suffering they are being shown.[1]

There would appear to be a growing chorus of journalists expressing their misgivings that first-person witnessing is in a marked state of decline because of this incessant drive to exploit the speed and access afforded by new digital technologies. Some focus on the economic restructuration besetting the news industry, contending that an emergent geo-politics of news and information threatens to prove detrimental to the range and quality of foreign news provision. Diminished resources compound longstanding logistical difficulties, translating into ever-stretching commitments to cover the world's trouble-spots – leaving some crises under-reported, while others are ignored altogether. Others point to the growing casualisation of news-gathering teams, that is, the transference of responsibility from professional news correspondents to local citizens pressed into journalistic service. This re-writing of obligations is rarely acknowledged as the outcome of budgetary decisions, however – news organisations being more inclined to justify their changing priorities on the basis of perceived risks to the safety of their employees in the field.

Regrettably, this frequently proves to be all too pressing a concern. The number of journalists killed when reporting from conflict and crisis zones in recent years suggests military authorities do not always endorse the validity of their role as dispassionate observers. Evidence continues to mount that an increasing number of journalists are being deliberately targeted by soldiers determined to stop them from bearing witness, either there and then on the ground, or later when making formal testimony before commissions and courts (Allan and Zelizer, 2004; Cottle, 2009; Hoskins and O'Loughlin, 2010; Seib, 2010; Tumber, 2010). Confronted with this bind, journalists can opt to make themselves suitably conspicuous as members of the press or, alternatively, strive to blend into crowds of bystanders. In the case of the latter, the mobility of portable newsgathering technology (iPhones, handy-cams, flip-cameras, BGAN satellite terminals and the like) becomes a more practicable consideration than standard-sized equipment.

When reporting from the Middle East, simply avoiding having equipment confiscated at security checkpoints is an achievement, but the real challenges emerge when trying to keep one step ahead of the efforts of authorities determined to curtail independent reportage. Roger Cohen (2009a,b) of the *New York Times* describes how his departure from covering ordinary people amassing in Tehran to protest the violation of their country's Constitution left him feeling bereft. One of the last Western journalists to leave the city in June 2009, he had ignored the revocation of his press pass in order to continue documenting as long as possible a story he knew demanded his presence to witness, despite both the risks and the costs.

> To bear witness means being there – and that's not free. No search engine gives you the smell of a crime, the tremor in the air, the eyes that smolder, or the cadence of a scream.
>
> No news aggregator tells of the ravaged city exhaling in the dusk, nor summons the defiant cries that rise into the night. No miracle of technology renders the lip-drying taste of fear. No algorithm captures the hush of dignity, nor evokes the adrenalin rush of courage coalescing, nor traces the fresh raw line of a welt. (Cohen, 2009a)

Readily acknowledging that Iranians themselves had borne witness 'with cellphone video images, with photographs, through Twitter and other forms of social networking', he nonetheless found it almost unbearable to leave. At stake, in his view, was a professional responsibility to tell the story: 'Images multiply across the Web but the mainstream media, disciplined to distill, is missed.' It is the capacity of journalists ('expelled, imprisoned, vilified') working for news organisations to perform this role of distillation where otherwise 'raw material' is concerned that is of paramount significance. Assessing the news coverage since he left, he reaffirmed his conviction that it is in the making of choices – 'whether in words or image, made in pursuit of presenting the truest and fairest, most vivid and complete representation of a situation' – that presence on the ground is required (Cohen, 2009b). 'Because part of the choice lies in something ineffable – the air you breathe, the sounds you hear, the shadow light as a bird's wing that falls across fearful eyes – something that cannot be seized or rendered at a distance.'

The problem of distance, namely the necessity of being there to bear witness, risks being overstated in the eyes of some. Cohen's belief in 'truth as seen and distilled from the ground' was hotly rebuked by Arianna Huffington (2009) of the Huffington Post. She chastised him for his 'bizarre' attempt 'to attack the tools of new-media-fueled reporting by citing the very event that highlights the power of those tools'. It was these tools – she cites 'search engines, news aggregation, live-blogging, and "miracles of technology" such as Twitter, Facebook, and real-time video delivered via camera phones' – that succeeded in playing 'an indispensable part in allowing millions of people around the world to "bear witness" to what was happening in Iran'. In admonishing Cohen for failing to learn the lessons of what took place there, she nonetheless conceded the 'tremendous value' in being an eyewitness. Still, she insisted, the 'truth is, you don't have to "be there" to bear witness. And you can be there and fail to bear witness.' The limitations of 'Cohen's credo', in her view, revolve around the 'the eyewitness fallacy' (a phrase she attributes to Malcolm Muggeridge), namely 'the tendency of people to see, in eyewitness accounts, what they want to see'. She proceeds to list several examples where well-known professional journalists, claiming to bear witness, failed to capture the essence of an important news story. Hope for improvement, she believed, rested with ordinary people engaged in news reporting. 'New media is not replacing the need to "bear witness," it is spreading it beyond the elite few', she writes, 'and therefore making it harder for those elite few to get it as wrong as they've gotten it again and again – from Stalin's Russia to Bush's Iraq.' Cohen (2009b), writing in response, argued her criticisms were wide of the mark. 'You can't bear witness from afar any more than you make an omelet without cracking eggs', he countered; 'Seeing is different and has a price, sometimes even the ultimate price.'

This disagreement matters, not least because it helps to

illuminate precisely the tensions otherwise obscured in discussions of news reporting that reduce its diversity of forms, practices and epistemologies to underlying technological imperatives. One need not revisit earlier critiques of the excesses of technological determinism to recognise this tendency in certain celebratory journalistic accounts. All too often, questions of human agency are answered on the basis of social media devices and platforms, such as when – under the rippling banner of a 'Facebook Revolution' or a 'Twitter Uprising' – it seemed the smartphones were doing the talking while Facebook plotted the strategy, Twitter organised the demonstration, Flickr captured images and YouTube relayed video footage to the outside world. Digital technology may be credited with facilitating relationships across incipient communities of practice, but it remains important to bear in mind these ad hoc relationships are under fluid negotiation between people rather than inanimate actors in a networked system removed from specific contexts. Where human beings making choices or decisions blur into faceless 'nodes' personifying inexorable technological drivers, the ensuing analysis will be impoverished, particularly where the analysis of the social contingencies of witnessing are concerned.[2]

To think through these contingencies, the lived materiality of technological proficiencies, affordances and constraints becomes a starting point for enquiry rather than a presumed explanation in its own right. Time and again, the examples discussed on this book's pages have pinpointed how they shape the embodiment of citizen witnessing in times of crisis, when the harsh, even violent dictates of circumstance necessitate a discursive shift from impassive looking to affective communication. Bearing witness entails much more than digitally recording for purposes of informational relay; rather, it is to acknowledge self-reflexively a responsibility to proclaim one's presence through testimony, to engage in personal documentation for the benefit of others. Still, we may ask, wherein lie the normative limits of witnessing? That is, how to discern the ethical boundaries giving shape to its epistemic truthclaims, once digital technology ceases to be upheld as panacea or disparaged as scapegoat?

Hyper-realities

If it is difficult to identify the factors that make certain photographs recognisably newsworthy over and above alternative ones, it is even more challenging to explain why a mere fraction of them will acquire 'iconic' status (see Hariman and Lucaites, 2007; D. Mitchell, 2011). Much debate has ensued over the defining image of the Arab Spring uprisings, but it seems fair to say – looking across the mediascape over recent months – that it may well be a young man or woman holding their mobile telephone at arm's length in a tumultuous scene. As *Guardian* correspondent Peter Beaumont (2011a) writes:

> She's in the Medina in Tunis with a BlackBerry held aloft, taking a picture of a demonstration outside the prime minister's house. He is an angry Egyptian doctor in an aid station stooping to capture the image of a man with a head injury from missiles thrown by Mubarak's supporters. Or it is a Libyan in Benghazi running with his phone switched to a jerky video mode, surprised when the youth in front of him is shot through the head.
>
> All of them are images that have found their way on to the internet through social media sites. And it's not just images. In Tahrir Square I sat one morning next to a 60-year-old surgeon cheerfully tweeting his involvement in the protest. The barricades today do not bristle with bayonets and rifles, but with phones. (Beaumont, 2011a)

Aware of how certain commentators have characterised the effectivity of social media in the 'Twitter revolutions', Beaumont's personal experience – 'what I witnessed on the ground in Tunisia and Egypt' – leads him to argue that historic crises are shaped by the means of personal expression. 'The instantaneous nature of how social media communicate self-broadcast ideas, unlimited by publication deadlines and broadcast news slots, explains in part the speed at which these revolutions have unravelled, their almost viral spread across a region', he contends; 'It explains, too, the often loose and non-hierarchical organisation of the protest movements unconsciously modelled on the networks of the web.' Twitter and WikiLeaks were important, but young people's use of

Facebook proved crucial in these two countries, in part because of the ease with which imagery could circulate in defiance of state censorship. Having asked a group of young Tunisians what they were photographing with their telephones, he was told: 'Ourselves. Our revolution. We put it on Facebook ... It's how we tell the world what's happening.' Another explained, 'I put up amateur video on Facebook. For instance, a friend got some footage of a sniper on Avenue de Carthage', before adding: 'It's what I've been doing, even during the crisis. You share video and pictures. It was if you wrote something – or made it yourself – that there was a real problem' (cited in Beaumont, 2011a).

This performative engagement with imagery, which I am inclined to suggest is indicative of what Edward Said (1977) described as the challenge of reclaiming self-presentation, complicates stereotypical conceptions of 'the protestor' in the Arab world. Such stereotypes, as the *Guardian*'s Paul Mason (2012) contends, help to explain why so few Western commentators recognised the early signs of what would become the Arab Spring. 'Nobody had seen this coming. Nobody with any influence, anyway', he writes; 'The stock image of Arabs in the Western media was of a passive but violent race, often filed under the categories of "terrorism" and "insoluble problems"' (2012: 25). Here Mason echoes a related point Said (1990) made years earlier, when discussing the representation of Islam in news reporting. 'Very little of the detail, the human density, the passion of Arab-Moslem life has entered the awareness of even those people whose profession it is to report the Arab world', Said wrote. Instead, news reports portray 'a series of crude, essentialized caricatures of the Islamic world presented in such a way as to make that world vulnerable to military aggression'. Media 'obsession' with Islam as a threat, he argued, almost always rendered complexity into 'flatness, ignorance and stereotypes' of almost 'blinding uniformity' (see also Barkho, 2010; Karim, 2011; Mellor, 2011; Said, 1997). Mason's assessment helps to reveal the extent to which such precepts permeated the early reporting of the uprisings as they swept from one country to the next in the region.

The journalistic impulse to narrativise the ambiguities of

uncertainty into newsworthy events is a precarious achievement, one which in this case saw certain conceptions of the uprisings recurrently framed in a manner broadly consistent with Western values, beliefs and perspectives. Kevin Marsh (2011), Director of OffspinMedia, contends that an overarching 'super narrative' set down the terms of the 'hyper reality' of specific incidents, driving what news organisations looked to cover and, equally importantly, what they elected to ignore. Once it was decided that 'The Arab Spring' was a 'domino' story, it became apparent how it would be told as a news story. The guiding presupposition, Marsh suggests, held that: 'One Arabic despotism after another would fall to Western ideas of liberal democracy' (2011: 114). He adds:

> And before long, we journalists became familiar with the modalities. There would be a 'Day of Rage', linked often to Friday prayers – so we made sure the cameras were there. Articulate young men and women would find the TV cameras, or the cameras would find them, and they would speak in polished Harvard English about freedom and democracy and law and the burning desire for justice. And we would show how Facebook and Twitter and SMS were their communication tools of choice.
>
> And because we knew these were Muslims we looked for the hidden hand of the Muslim Brotherhood in Egypt and the machinations of Islamic fundamentalism elsewhere. We speculated on whether 'The Arab Spring' would weaken or strengthen al Qaeda . . .
>
> [The] pictures and themes and interviews we selected were all images of the hyper reality we called 'The Arab Spring.' We collected and shared them as if to confirm that what *must* be taking place really was taking place. (Marsh, 2011: 114–15)

Topics, themes or even questions that seemed inconsistent with this narrative, which could not be made to conform to its truth-telling, tended to be passed over as a result. Largely overlooked, Marsh argues, have been 'the millions in every country who did not become involved in the popular uprisings, either out of fear, lack of interest, distance or because they sustained in themselves a weary cynicism that nothing was changing, nothing would change' (2011: 115).

Further, Marsh points to how the mundane issues of everyday life were usually disregarded, as well as more pressing ones concerning the absence of Arab nationalism, the involvement of non-Arab actors in certain situations, as well as 'the role of tribalism, personal fear, vengeance, familial loathing' and so forth. 'The Arab Spring' defined as a political movement made it that much more difficult for journalists to attend to the complexities of ostensibly non-political dynamics, as well as the distinctive ways they shaped the unique characteristics of each uprising in turn. The 'narrative certainties' of 'The Arab Spring' created by journalists, he maintains, 'were built on ideas which, to those who do not share the Western view of mankind's inevitable "progress", look like, feel like and are intellectual imperialism' (2011: 119; see also Cottle, 2011; Smith and McConville, 2011).[3]

'Blurring what it means to be a journalist'

In the case of Libya, over the months leading up to the start of the multi-state coalition's military intervention (initially led by Britain, France and the United States before NATO assumed control of the air campaign targeting pro-government ground forces), problems of misperception were compounded by the near-absence of Western journalists on the ground to cover the initial signs of popular dissent emerging on the streets of places such as Benghazi, Bayda and Zintan. Muammar Gaddafi's regime had imposed strict control over the circulation of news and information within the country's borders, severely limiting freedom of speech to ensure conformity with official doctrine (the national broadcaster, like the majority of newspapers and the one internet service provider available, being state-owned and effectively policed).

Fear of reprisals, including arrest and imprisonment, meant Libyan journalists felt pressured to exercise self-censorship to protect themselves and their sources. Few foreign journalists were allowed into the country; for those able to negotiate access, official minders monitored them closely, wary of any sign of investigative initiative. 'The "trick" in Tripoli (when covering events as a "guest" of the Gaddafi government)', the BBC's Wyre Davies (2011) recalled, 'was to give your minders the slip and try to report from a capital under siege where many people were clearly too afraid to protest' (2011: 52). Restrictions were sharply entrenched still further on 24 January 2011, when government authorities blocked several foreign-based portals, including Libya Al Youm, Al Manara, Jeel Libya, Akhbar Libya, and Libya Al Mostakbal. YouTube was similarly censored, the site having featured videos of demonstrations thought to have angered officials. 'These web sites were the one recent sign of tangible progress in freedom of expression in Libya', Sarah Leah Whitson, Middle East Director at Human Rights Watch pointed out at the time; 'The government is returning to the dark days of total media control' (HRW, 2010).

Restrictions steadily worsened as uprisings took shape first in Tunisia and then Egypt, so that by the time Libyan citizens launched a Day of Rage on 17 February 2011 to demand basic freedoms and human rights, independent news reporting from within the country had been almost entirely curtailed. 'The Libyan authorities have been imposing a media blackout on the actual developments in the country', the BBC's Muhammad Shukri (2011) reported; 'TV, which initially ignored the protests, has been trying to depict the demonstrators as saboteurs and foreign agents. Most airtime has either been dedicated to showing recorded images of pro-Qadhafi rallies or patriotic songs and music.' Foreign journalists eluding official sanction were labelled 'outlaws' by frustrated officials vehement in their criticisms of Western 'interference' and 'disruptions'.

The regime's struggle to effect control over the web, intended to prohibit the posting of anti-Gaddafi material while also restricting protestors from organising their efforts online, was only partially successful – the Twitter hashtag #Feb17 helping to shape a collective identity for numerous web-savvy rebels. At the same time, distant members of the Libyan diaspora also endeavoured to actively relay information – occasionally intermingled with political strategy – via email, texts, blogs and other social media. Many were acutely aware of the relatively small share of the population with access to the internet in comparison with other countries in the region, but persevered nonetheless. 'I can call Benghazi or Tripoli and obtain accurate information from people on the ground and then report it straight on Twitter to thousands of people', Omar Amer, the Manchester-based head of the Libyan Youth Movement told Channel 4 News (2011a). 'There are no more "Chinese whispers" – accurate information is spreading real-time.' International news sites, especially Al Jazeera's and Al Arabia's respective provisions, also proved to be vital resources in this regard, affording a continuous stream of updates for Libyans desperate to know what was happening within their own country (Topol, 2011).

In the days that followed, as it became apparent the country was teetering on the brink of civil war, Western news media moved swiftly to respond. The eastern border proved the easiest way in, with checkpoint officials greeting journalists with requests such as 'Tell the world of our revolution' (Poole, 2011: 20). The BBC's Jon Leyne (2011) was well aware that journalists were 'witnessing history' in the making, but added 'like it or not, wc journalists are more than just witnesses, we are playing our part'. That is, in his view, if 'no journalists had made it into eastern Libya, then surely the pressure would never have built up for a no-fly zone and the subsequent NATO-lcd military intervention' (2011: 42). This convergence of journalistic and military interests proved controversial in the eyes of critics challenging the legitimacy of the coalition's intervention, many of whom expressed their dissatisfaction with the quality of the ensuing coverage.

Here it is worth noting that a high proportion of the journalists and photographers able to enter the country were freelancers (or 'local hires', in journalese), a large share of whom were witnessing conflict for the first time in their lives. Hannah Storm of the International News Safety Institute remarked:

> You can understand why new journalists or journalists inexperienced in covering conflict were drawn to Libya. It was on the doorstep and there was a sense of being part of history. But it was so dangerous because it was not like a traditional war – it was fluid and unpredictable, with the anti-Gaddafi fighters often not very familiar with the weapons they were using. (Storm cited in Beaumont, 2011b)

In addition, she argued, a certain 'blurring of what it means to be a journalist', brought about by 'the rise of citizen journalism and journalist-activists', meant that the lure of this type of opportunity was difficult to resist, despite the dangers. Some of those involved struggled to cope without the benefit of training or adequate logistical support, often relying on 'fixers' to report what was happening, as individuals living in the area prepared to help were called. Suliman Ali Zway, otherwise employed as a construction worker, explained:

> I realised that without help the journalists weren't going to get the story out.
>
> It happened before in 2006. We had a revolution in Benghazi and it was controlled after 10 days because nobody could report it, nobody could get word out.
>
> I knew it would be important to help the journalists keep on top of things and to do everything it took to help them report the truth. . . .
>
> When you go to a frontline and its just an army of volunteers with AK-47s fighting against a regular army, it's dangerous. (Zway cited in Gunter, 2011)

Meanwhile some 130 foreign journalists in Tripoli were told by their official minders to remain in their hotel for their own safety when it was readily apparent the real reason was to stop them covering the demonstrations and the authorities' repressive responses to them. Shortly thereafter, according to one *New York Times* reporter, 'the government informed the journalists that it planned to fly them away from potential Friday protests to a Qaddafi stronghold in the south'. When the journalists objected, refusing to co-operate, 'the government temporarily locked them in their hotel, before arranging a bus trip to a central square that is a hub for pro-Qaddafi rallies' (Kirkpatrick, 2011; see also Coker and Dagher, 2011).[4]

'A snapshot of the chaos'

It was against this backdrop that the significance of reportorial contributions made by ordinary Libyans came to the fore. 'When protests first began in Libya', Al Jazeera (2011a) reported, 'the media presence there was scarce so the story filtered out via social media thanks to courageous citizen journalists.' Diverse forms of citizen reporting ('guerrilla journalism', as one professional called it) emerged via Twitter and Facebook, efforts to block them circumvented by using proxy servers, amongst other strategies. 'The citizen journalists provide an alternative to the official media in their portrayal of the protests and the turmoil across the country', BBC Monitoring (2011) observed. 'While state media showed only pro-Gaddafi protests, pictures and video from mobile phones told a different story.' Some individuals crossed neighbouring borders in order to upload eyewitness accounts and imagery to the web, despite guards at checkpoints reportedly confiscating cameras, memory sticks, hard drives and telephone SIM cards – virtually everything containing video footage or still photographs (see O'Neill, 2011).

Mohammed Nabbous set up an online television station, Libya Alhurra TV, in order to make available raw footage and commentary contributed by eyewitnesses sharing his commitment to citizen journalism. 'Long before international reporters made it to Libya, Alhurra TV was streaming footage online, allowing the world to see what was going on inside the country', the BBC's Jon Williams (2012) later recalled; 'The authorities tried to shut down the internet to silence the station but, thanks to the ingenuity of its founder Mo Nabbous and his colleagues, government blocks were bypassed and the webcast was able to continue.' Tragically, Nabbous was killed by government troops in the battle for Benghazi, details of which were announced by his wife Perdita on the site. 'Please keep the channel going, please post videos, and just move every authority you have to do something against this. There's still bombing, there's still shooting, and more people are going to die', she said in her short, tearful statement; 'Don't let what Mo started go for nothing, people. Make it worth it' (cited Washbrook, 2011).

Struggling to keep abreast of unfolding developments, news organisations found themselves relying on materials ostensibly shared by eyewitnesses, all too aware that independent verification was near-impossible at times. Noteworthy in this example from a blog on the *Los Angeles Times* site – 'LIBYA: Amateur video footage purportedly depicts battle scenes in Zawiyais' – is the qualified language employed to express this uncertainty. In describing three YouTube videos being shared, the post is careful to add further caveats, such as the 'fresh footage' is 'said to show the "bombing" of the city of Zawiya', while 'loud chants' are 'heard from what appears to be a nearby mosque'. In the case of the second of the three videos, the *Times*'s Alexandra Sandels (2011) writes:

> Below, another video posted on the Internet on Thursday purportedly depicts the situation in Zawiya. Crowds are seen roaming the streets chanting slogans honoring the fallen 'martyrs' as occasional shots rattle the air. At one point, the camera closes in on what could be a pool of blood in the street. As more gunfire is heard, the people in the crowd appear to turn increasingly defiant. Some of them climb up onto the hood of cars and start waving sticks and raise clenched fists into the air. (Sandels, 2011)

Tell-tale words such as 'purportedly', or phrases such as 'could be a pool of blood', signal this contingency, the unspoken acknowledgement that sometimes cameras – or, more to the point, the people holding them – do not always relay the truth. Sandel sets up the third video by stating: 'And here, crowds are gathered around what could be a body of a dead person shrouded in a white sheet. The video, also uploaded on Thursday, is said to show the "martyrs" of Zawiya.' Her byline indicates that she was in Beirut – where Western journalists were frequently based at the time – thereby implicitly underscoring the challenge for journalists endeavouring to cover a conflict they could not witness first-hand (senior Libyan officials having labelled correspondents 'al-Qaida collaborators' and, as such, 'terrorist sympathisers' who risked immediate arrest: see Halliday, 2011a).

It would seem fair to suggest that truth-claims hedged in such terms invited a nuanced relationship with readers, effectively crediting them with the interpretive skills necessary to differentiate subtle gradations in journalistic authority over contested evidence.

The sheer volume of such diverse forms of citizen imagery defied straightforward categorisation in any case. 'Without a doubt', journalist James Foley (2011) observed, 'home videos have played a huge role in the Libyan revolution', whether shot from 'clunky early '90s TV cameras' to newer handycams, or the ubiquitous cell or mobile telephones. Ranging 'from early videos of unarmed protestors being attacked in Benghazi, to shocking videos taken from captured Gaddafi troops filming their own atrocities', these images have 'sowed the righteous anger of thousands as they spread like wildfire on Facebook and YouTube'. So-called 'unauthorised media' compelled to bridge the gaps in Western news coverage included hacker groups, such as Anonymous, which played a key role in facilitating the creation of illegal parallel networks while also distributing imagery shot by eyewitnesses. 'We want to tell the world about the horror in Libya', one member explained to *Nouvel Observateur*, a French weekly; 'We're passing on pictures of burned and mutilated bodies. It's a bloodbath. Tripoli is a slaughterhouse' (cited in RWB, 2011).[5]

Much of this imagery was shot by rebel fighters engaged in active resistance, and promptly relayed outside the country by ad hoc networks of activists and protestors to distant journalists via Twitter. NPR's Andy Carvin, for example, curated a feed from Washington DC striving to offer up-to-the-minute news of what was happening on the ground. In his words:

I'm always looking for documentary evidence – photos and videos, as well as audio. Sometimes I don't know much context about a given media artifact, but I retweet it nonetheless and ask for help understanding it – figuring out the location, the time it took place, what's actually going on, etc. Lots of people also serve as translators for me. And I'm retweeting a lot of brutal stuff – horrible images depicting the results of violence because I want to give people a chance for themselves to understand what's going on. They don't have to open the link, of course, but if they feel the need to bear witness, they will. (Carvin, 2011)

This conception of bearing witness based upon accounts that 'give you a snapshot of the chaos' prefigures a certain scepticism on the part of readers, who must be prepared to recognise the uncertainties permeating Carvin's efforts to piece together reliable reportage. 'I try to have [followers] understand my Twitter feed is essentially an open, transparent news-gathering operation', he explains, 'not a stream of verified headlines'.[6]

Precisely what counted as credible, trustworthy information in a warzone was very much in the eye of the beholder, just as the status of 'journalist' seemed open to fluid re-negotiation across the citizen–professional continuum. Rana Jawad (2011a) had been 'off air' for six months from her BBC post reporting from Libya when she took a telephone call from the Corporation requesting that she commence filing updates on the uprisings. Her anxiety about arrest and subsequent 'disappearance' meant she would have to work undercover, so she informed the authorities that she was taking a career break for personal reasons. 'Life in hiding', she explained, 'is an uncomfortable term to use because I was not physically chased by anyone; just by the demons of paranoia at the simple knowledge of what might happen.' Learning to cope with the constant threat of discovery, she adopted a male persona under the by-line 'Tripoli Witness' for the BBC's online reportage, which afforded her sufficient anonymity to evade Gaddafi's secret police. The blog quickly proved to be a crucial resource, offering a series of first-hand accounts of events in the capital otherwise eluding BBC News efforts to cover them in adequate detail.

In the main, however, eyewitness reports from Libya were provided by citizen witnesses without the benefit of training, or the protection of anonymity in many cases. Amongst them were the rebels themselves, as noted above, capturing imagery of jubilant celebration, as well as combat destruction and the human misery left in its wake. Likened to 'battlefield tourists' by some, those risking their lives to overthrow the Gaddafi regime recognised the value of both cameras and Kalashnikovs in waging war, including in the battlefield over public opinion. For news organisations intent on processing this type of combatant imagery, however, thorny problems of mediation emerged, in terms of logistics as well as with respect to certain ethical implications. Differing views over what constituted appropriate, responsible and non-judgemental treatment, particularly where it risked being perceived as overly graphic or upsetting for distant audiences, simmered throughout the ensuing coverage.

'Sometimes truth is shocking'

These tensions boiled over when photographs and video clips of captured former leader Muammar Gaddafi, wearing heavily bloodstained clothing whilst surrounded by ecstatic rebel fighters near the town of Sirte, surfaced on 20 October 2011. Grainy, blurry images of what appeared to be his slumped body were soon followed by shaky, staccato flashes of mobile telephone footage of him being dragged down the street. A further clip showed him splayed on the bonnet of a pickup truck, much of his face covered in blood, violently jostled by jeering rebels (the sound of euphoric gunfire in the background), while another revealed him staggering to the ground where he was repeatedly kicked, evidently alive but clearly struggling to endure. Gaddafi's execution by his captors was not documented – or at least no imagery of it has appeared thus far – but photographs of his corpse, revealing a bullet hole in his left temple, were posted online soon after. Initial reports claiming that the former leader had been killed by crossfire when being transported to a hospital for treatment following his arrest were dispelled in no uncertain terms. Still, concerns about verification continued to linger, with some news organisations hesitating to declare the Libyan leader dead prior to official confirmation – CNN's qualified claim 'Video appears to show fmr. Libyan leader's body', was typical. Explanatory text from Al Jazeera and Agence France-Presse, the first relayers of mobile-phone imagery from the rebel fighters for many Western news organisations, frequently failed to accompany the clips as they were rapidly re-appropriated over and over again across the webscape.

Journalists and their editors around the world were scrambling to ascertain the authenticity of what they were seeing. Compounding difficulties with sourcing, the explicit nature of photographs and video footage – replete with close-ups of the bloodied, evidently lifeless body of the Libyan leader – posed awkward questions of ethical judgement where the risk of transgressing the normative limits of public sensitivities were concerned. Under intense time pressure, television and internet editors and producers typically opted 'to go graphic', journalist David Barron (2011) observed, which meant their audiences 'saw images that would have been unattainable before cellphone cameras and Internet sites and 24-second news cycles, and unimaginable before an era when news executives must make immediate, difficult choices in a competitive environment on which images are too gruesome to show'. Such decisions were seldom made on their own terms, not least when it was assumed that audience members would simply go online to find material otherwise left out of mainstream reporting (almost by way of mitigation, Barron cites an analyst's claim: 'We're spending a lot of money in Afghanistan, Libya and Iraq, and people want to see the snuff-out').

A news organisation electing to disregard this type of gruesome material risked appearing irrelevant, it followed, suggesting to several commentators that a tacit shift from 'Should we show this?' to 'How should we show this?' was becoming increasingly discernible. Verbal forewarnings to television viewers, like those cautioning internet users from clicking past certain checks (e.g., 'Warning: This gallery contains graphic images. Viewer discretion is advised'), revealed presumptions made about audience sensibilities. Judgements regarding what was reasonable (or at least palatable) were context-specific, corresponding to differing inflections of explicitness on the basis of what might be subsequently criticised for being exploitative, sensationalising, trivialising or simply 'bad taste'. Still, typically left unspoken was the further precept that presenting images of Gaddafi's battered corpse, or that of Osama bin Laden had they been made public, was deemed both morally and journalistically acceptable in a way that revealing images of the violated bodies of Westerners would not be.

Ethical quandaries demanded resolution in pragmatic terms where breaking news was concerned, with pressing decisions to be made about appropriate use – as opposed to sensational exploitation – of the imagery in the absence of agreed conventions. 'Did you need to see Gaddafi's corpse?' was the headline of a post by James Poniewozik of *Time* magazine, for example, who argued that because we live in the 'pix or it didn't happen' era, it was not surprising that 'the pix in and of themselves did not immediately prove that it happened' when first released. At the same time, disputes over the purpose such imagery served, he believed, missed a larger point.

> The job of journalism – at least of breaking-news reporting like this – is not to determine what people should and should not feel and then work backward to produce the images that will engineer the ideal emotional response in the name of right thinking. It's not to try to encourage the right public reaction or head off a dangerous one (whereas that might be the entirely appropriate worry of a government). It is to get at the truth of what actually happened in an event. (Poniewozik, 2011)

This refusal to privilege journalism's subjunctive claim on emotion, which some might typify as its moral duty to care (and to be seen to be caring), was recurrently reaffirmed on the basis of upholding a normative commitment to objectivity. The 'truth' of what had actually transpired took some time to establish, as noted above, which in Poniewozik's view was consistent with a 'conspiracy-minded age' of suspicion. 'What if someone dressed up a different corpse? What if the picture shows him wounded, not dead? What if it's Photoshopped? What if, what if?', he asked.

Even when veracity appeared to have been established, further questions remained regarding how best to display the imagery in a suitably responsible manner. Gaddafi's status as a dictator and war criminal meant he would not be accorded the respect that might be otherwise expected for a slain political leader. The extensive, repetitive play of video clips showing his evidently life-less body was justified as necessary, in part, in order to put paid to doubts that he was really dead (thereby providing a counterpoint of sorts to the controversy generated by the Obama administration's refusal to release the photographs of al Qaeda leader Osama bin Laden's body into the public domain). CNN's Laura Smith-Spark (2011) suggested that 'while the ethics of taking snapshots of dead dictators is still up for discussion, the ubiquity of cell phones equipped with cameras – and the way such images swiftly find their way to the waiting world – means such doubts are far less likely'. Steven Baxter (2011) of the *New Statesman* offered a blunter appraisal. Because 'we live in a "pics or it didn't happen" era', he argued, 'we don't trust the word of broadcasters and want to see for ourselves'. Hence one of the key reasons, he surmised, 'news outlets have been happy to splash the blood this time around', with 'the trophy-like nature of Gaddafi's corpse' proving a grisly spectacle.

As further digital photographs and video clips continued to emerge, the journalistic significance of this spectacle became increasingly problematic, not least with regard to the relative legitimacy of such graphic forms of citizen witnessing. A *Daily Mail* report by Damien Gayle describing one of the clips notes its attribution to 'Freedom Group TV' before explaining that according to the group's Facebook page, they were a 'group of citizen journalists [whose] mission is to let the world know what is happening in Libya' (cited in Gayle, 2011). BBC News's head of the multimedia newsroom, Mary Hockaday (2011), echoed this sense of documentary evidence, conceding in a blog post that while imagery of the Libyan leader in his dying moments was 'undoubtedly shocking and disturbing', it was editorially justified to quell 'the swirl of rumour'. Conveying the drama of unfolding events 'in the age of mobile phones', meant being clear with audiences what had been verified, and what had not been, where the origins of 'emerging photographic evidence' was concerned. 'We judged that it was right to use some footage and stills, with warnings about their nature', she insisted. As a news organisation, 'our role is to report what happened, and that can include shocking and disturbing things' (Hockaday, 2011; see also Halliday, 2011c).

Crossing ethical thresholds

Tacit rules of journalistic filtering become apparent when they are broken, one of the reasons why image-making in the hands of soldiers, activists and civilians can prove so unsettling, even emotionally traumatic. Michael Trice (2011), in noting the power of imagery from 'decidedly unprofessional venues', remarked that in his view the 'amateur nature and unrestrained viewpoints of such videos does not feel like journalism'. Still, he added, 'to dismiss raw history for no other reason than its naked display of the pain, chaos, and joy of war represents a terrible form of censorship', one that a society engaged in war could ill afford in its public discourse. For Susannah Breslin (2011) of Forbes, however, such imagery risked becoming the 'porn' of war. 'It's hard to look at the viral spread of Gaddafi's death images – being pulled through the street, slumped against someone's knee, covered in blood – and not think of pornography', she wrote. In contrast with news images created by photojournalists, those relayed by a mobile telephone by whoever happened to be nearby were likely to be taken up and used precisely because they aroused intense, emotional reactions. 'While journalists are supposed to maintain some kind of moral compass, random spectators are not', she argued; 'Therefore, with digital recorder running, there's no reason why you shouldn't record the fleeting moments of a self-proclaimed "King of Kings" being reduced to a corpse.' Recording such distressing eyewitness imagery is one matter, while preparing distant audiences for its affective impact is a different concern altogether.

While some heralded this latest instance of 'citizen journalism' as a potential 'game-changer' that 'raised the stakes' for news reporting (Lodish, 2011), others expressed their concern about what they regarded to be changing social taboos. 'The threshold for publishing gruesome images like those of Muammar Gaddafi's death is falling as the Internet and social media make many of the editorial decisions that used to be left to a small group of professional journalists', Tom Heneghan and Peter Apps (2011) of Reuters stated. Journalistic perceptions that public tolerance for such imagery is relaxing may well prove to be a self-fulfilling prophecy, of course, given the absence of agreed normative criteria to ascertain, let alone evaluate, change. Where to draw the line varied from one news organisation to the next as they pieced together the story, with hurried decisions evidently taken with reference to wider views about 'community standards', 'good taste' and 'ethical benchmarks'.

Former editor turned *Observer* columnist Peter Preston (2011) detected a new 'tone of vengeance' in much of the British coverage, which he attributed to the 'twin gods of modern journalism', namely 'the scoop' (debate having raged over who got the story first 'before Gaddafi's body was even cold') and the 'citizen-reporter-cum-camera-operator waving a mobile phone'. Factored together, they ensured this was 'a race beyond winning', in his view; 'It's all-embracing, all-consuming, utterly unavoidable; the defining taste of failure or success.' Editors cannot 'sit piously on the sidelines any longer', being effectively 'doomed to compete, because not doing so is a kind of censorship – and a shot in the foot, not the head'. *Newsweek*'s editors, when placing video footage on the magazine's Tumblr page, made a similar point about such pressures when they wrote: 'Warning: this is video of Muammar Gaddafi's corpse being kicked through the streets of Sirte. No way to whitewash that. We're posting it because many others have, and at this point, it's a video asset in the history books' (*Newsweek*, 2011).

In the days that followed, press commentators continued to mull over the wider implications for journalism. 'On balance', former newspaper editor Roy Greenslade (2011) maintained, 'I thought the publication of the Gaddafi pictures was justified, given the special circumstances surrounding the manner of his death, the context of his own tyranny and the widespread dissemination of them on the internet.' Columnist Suzanne Moore (2011), writing in London's *Mail on Sunday*, took issue with the 'full technicolour footage of a dying Gaddafi', making a distinction between what Libyan's may need to see after suffering terrible injustices under his brutal regime ('as Romanians needed to see Ceausescu's body or as Italians passed round photos of the corpses of Mussolini and his mistress'), and what 'we' in the West do not. 'The needle of our collective moral compass is spinning', she wrote; 'Gaddafi was bad, therefore all is permissible . . . Watch the compass spin its excuses: it's history; it's symbolism; it's new technology. My compass points downwards to grotesque gloating.' Meanwhile, she added, 'we watch death. Live. On every screen, on every page. Death, the final frontier? No, not any more. The barbarians are not at the gates. We have become them.'

This apparent disruption of a familiar politics of othering, whereby 'us' and 'them' dichotomies threatened to become destabilised, made apparent the ex-nomination (ostensible placing beyond words) of discomforting realities. In adopting a related line of critique, Jonathan Jones (2011) in the *Guardian* contended that to 'get upset by photographs of the dead Gaddafi is to pretend we did not know we went to war at all'. Moreover, he maintained, it is to 'fantasise that our own role is so just and proper and decent that it is not bloody at all'. In light of what he regards as the West's 'dangerous delusion' that war can be a decent, worthwhile endeavour, he poses the question:

> Why have the photographs and films of Gaddafi's end caused so much fuss and bother? Because they show us the reality of war that we are usually so good at ignoring. In 10 years of wars since 9/11 the worst pictures, the trophy images of the dead and grotesque scenes of road-side slaughter, have been kept away from the mainstream media, to be sought on the internet by those who wish to sup on horrors.
>
> But for once, with the death of Gaddafi, we have seen the face of war, washed in blood, bathed in cruelty. The horrible and haunting pictures of his last moments and his public exhibition simply show us, for once, what the wars of our time and all times look like. If we don't like what we see we must stop this foolish pretence that war, however 'just', can ever be anything but a brutal mess. (Jones, 2011)

There seemed to be little doubt that the very rawness of this footage was acutely unsettling to viewers otherwise habituated to routine, effectively sanitised renderings of the horrors of a warzone. Indeed, it arguably signalled a telling moment when the customary forms of journalistic mediation usually accompanying such imagery were dramatically transgressed.

Even for news organisations prepared to justify their use of such disturbing images on the basis that they were necessary facts integral to the truth of the story, characterising the precise nature of this type of combatant witnessing proved challenging. Several journalists and editors quoted in the coverage noted in passing that mobile telephones had effectively served as weapons in the hands of those surrounding Gaddafi from the moment he was pulled from the stormwater drain in Sirte. 'The Arab Spring has demonstrated the power and all but unstoppable reach of the citizen journalist, although it's debatable whether the term can easily be used for the people responsible for the filming of Gaddafi's death', Frank Krüger of South Africa's *Mail & Guardian* observed. 'Is it time for a new category', he wondered, 'the "fighter journalist"?' Precedents of form and practice were readily discernible, with examples of this type of combatant imagery traceable back to the earliest days of photography in warzones. Where digital imagery is concerned, the posting of execution videos on YouTube (Christensen, 2008; Kennedy, 2008, 2009; Moeller, 2009a; Snickars and Vonderau, 2009; Strangelove, 2010), or the harrowing documentation of torture in Abu Ghraib (Bennett et al., 2007; Hoskins and O'Loughlin, 2010; Matheson and Allan, 2009; Sontag, 2004), come immediately to mind as a profoundly disturbing case in point. As the Gaddafi controversy recedes in time, however, it would seem that ethical misgivings over the morality of using such graphic images remains as one of the most memorably contentious concerns.

One telling silence in the vast majority of commentaries, in my reading at least, was revealed by Eilis O'Hanlon writing in Ireland's *Sunday Independent*. In describing what she called the 'unexpected stirrings of sympathy' felt for a brutal dictator prompted by the imagery of his violent death, she proceeded to point out that 'it is impossible not to empathise in that moment with another scared and wounded human being, at least not without becoming less human in turn'. She then makes the simple, albeit disquieting point that these 'pictures forced us to put ourselves in the role of the victim and feel accordingly hunted, terrified, defiled'.

Making a difference

Throughout these pages, I have sought to delve into the reportage of real-world events with the aim of elucidating the basis for thinking through the imperative of witnessing precisely as it is taken up and re-inflected in wider discourses of journalism. In so doing, I have become increasingly aware of the extent to which prevalent conceptualisations of citizen journalism, in particular, risk reifying into place certain assumptions about the news media that look increasingly anachronistic in today's turbulent times. In some instances, citizen journalism is either disparaged as a passing fad, or reduced to simply the latest form of user-generated content in the long history of amateur involvement in news reporting. In others, citizen journalism is to be championed for its transformative potential, namely to democratise what was once considered the exclusive domain of the seasoned professional and, in so doing, rehabilitate a fading commitment to fourth-estate priorities. In the latter instance, however, the term is in danger of conceptual collapse under the sheer weight of the burden it is being asked to sustain.

Accordingly, the concept of 'citizen witnessing' as I have sought to develop it here is intended as a useful counterpoint to these more familiar positions, one which elaborates upon epistemic commitments that resist rigid categorisation on either side of the 'professional versus amateur' divide. Journalistic and citizen witnessing mutually imbricate in a relationship which, at its best, is one of respectful reciprocity. 'In an age of 24/7 rolling news, blogs and Twitter, we are on constant call wherever we are', the late war correspondent Marie Colvin (2010) observed, but 'the scene on the ground has remained remarkably the same for hundreds of years. Craters. Burnt houses. Mutilated bodies. Women weeping for children and husbands. Men for their wives, mothers, children.' Essentially, she added, 'someone has to go there and see what is happening', to 'bear witness'. She explained:

> You can't get that information without going to places where people are being shot at, and others are shooting at you. The real difficulty is having enough faith in humanity to believe that enough people, be they government, military or the man on the street, will care when your file reaches the printed page, the website or the TV screen. We do have that faith because we believe we do make a difference. (Colvin, 2010)

Colvin was convinced reporting from the frontline mattered, a view widely upheld in the outpouring of grief by her fellow journalists when she was killed in a rocket attack on Homs, Syria on 22 February 2012. 'Marie Colvin gave a voice to so many people's suffering, bore witness to so much injustice', CNN's Anderson Cooper tweeted as news of her death broke. In what proved to be Colvin's (2012) final dispatch from that city for the *Sunday Times*, she had documented the horrors wrought by Syrian military forces launching rockets, mortar shells and tank rounds at random, day after day. 'The scale of human tragedy in the city is immense', she wrote; 'The inhabitants are living in terror. Almost every family seems to have suffered the death or injury of a loved one.' She described the terrified people she encountered hiding in what was called 'the widows' basement', relaying their experiences in heart-rending quotations and vivid, poignant prose. Assisting those rescuing the wounded from bombed buildings was Abdel Majid, aged twenty, who, Colvin reported, had made a simple plea to her. '"Please tell the world they must help us," he said, shaking, with haunted eyes. "Just stop the bombing. Please, just stop the shelling"' (cited in Colvin, 2012).

Also making a critical difference were ordinary Syrians determined to take the place of international journalists prohibited from entering the country by Bashar Assad's regime. The day before Colvin was killed, the video blogger Rami al-Sayed (a.k.a. Syria Pioneer) succumbed to wounds suffered during a rocket attack in the Bab Amr district of Homs. 'Early this morning the bombardment of Homs was streamed live to the web by a citizen journalist', Ahmed Al Omran (2012) of NPR reported; 'But as the forces loyal to Bashar Assad continued their attack on the restive city, the stream went quiet and never came back again.' Together with this video stream, al-Sayed had posted more than 800 videos to his YouTube channel chronicling the assault on Homs over the previous eight months, many of which had been taken up and used by Western news organisations desperate to secure footage documenting the violence and its aftermath. Reading his messages to friends, it is apparent he believed he was witnessing genocide. 'Rami was killed because he was broadcasting real footage from

Bab Amr', Dr Mohammad al-Mohammad states in a YouTube video accompanying Omran's report, revealing to the camera the young man's wounds; 'Rami was killed because he was recording the truth.' It was this commitment to citizen witnessing that made his inclusion with professional correspondents poignantly appropriate in the news coverage to follow. 'Deaths of journalists are not special', an editorial leader published by the *Sydney Morning Herald* (2012) intoned following its reporting of the demise of Colvin, Ochlik and al-Sayed days before; 'All deaths in war are equally terrible, equally pitiable. But in bearing witness to the suffering of victims and the crimes of their oppressors, the message journalists send to the outside world is the one most feared by the powerful.' This is the reason why, the leader continued, 'increasingly they are targeting journalists and bloggers, the witnesses, the recorders and communicators of evidence of their inhumanity. Each death makes it only clearer why their work is of the first importance.'

In bringing this book's discussion to a close, we return to the question that initially framed our discussion – what does it mean to bear witness in a moment of crisis? – with a view to forging new avenues of exploration. My principal objective on these pages has been to discern and appraise the evidential basis for developing 'citizen witnessing' as a key concept for journalism, in part to contribute to ongoing efforts to think through with greater analytical specificity a host of issues clustered under 'citizen journalism' as a unifying thematic. In so doing, I have sought to prioritise the materiality of witnessing as a contingent process for examination, recognising that as a reportorial imperative it is routinely consolidated as a taken-for-granted feature of journalistic form, practice and epistemology. Indeed, an important dimension of the book's historical engagement has been to render problematic the relations of social authority underpinning the journalist's self-proclaimed status as a professional observer.

A central tenet of this performative ethos as it has evolved over the years revolves around the normative ideals it prefigures, not least the presumed capacity to uphold self-reflexively the codified strictures of dispassionate, objective informational relay for the benefit of distant publics. Questions of intentionality highlight varied inflections, with the journalist striving to bring to bear hard-won expertise based on training, experience and socialisation into professionally endorsed norms, values and protocols of procedure. These rules are all the easier to comprehend when they are broken, of course – hence our discussion in chapter 3 of Wilfred Burchett, sitting with his Baby Hermes typewriter in the shattered ruins of Hiroshima, striving to bear witness to the devastating effects of radiation sickness. Exceptions to the rules notwithstanding, the deliberative quality of the professional's methodical engagement is recurrently prized as a virtue in its own right, all the more so when set against the ad hoc, even accidental, nature of the ordinary citizen's sudden impulse to document and share a highly personal (and thereby unapologetically subjective) representation of what is transpiring around them. And yet, time and again, closer inspection of this presumed professional–amateur dichotomy has revealed a shifting continuum of emphases rather than stark polarities, where both 'sides' solicit definition in relation to the other.

In the course of examining the subtle, inchoate contours of the emergent ecology of citizen witnessing in online news reporting of crisis events, this book has necessarily adopted a relatively narrow remit for its mode of enquiry. Tracing the features of this ecology has proven challenging for a number of reasons, with one of the most formidable proving to be the salience of varied, contrasting discourses of digital technology – typically characterising mobile media as the preeminent drivers of citizen witnessing – in both journalistic and academic assessments. To advance a more nuanced perspective alert to lived experience, close investigation must take the place of broad assertions. Theorising technology as a singular agent removed from the contexts of its negotiation risks overstating its influence, as if each new device, resource or platform – the perceived impact of Twitter being the exemplar of this tendency – constitutes a sudden, prodigious departure from established conditions of visibility. That is to say, we need to avoid reaffirming the implicit premise that this ecology of citizen witnessing is punctuated by technology-driven revolutions. The appeal of this illusion of linearity, where one dramatic break-through follows another in a logical, rational sequence unfolding in the forward march of techno-progress, is difficult to resist. But resist it we must. The identification of technical innovations is crucial, yet equally noteworthy are the uneven ways in which these innovations are taken up, modified and recrafted to render them fit for purpose. Such a focus on the situated materiality of technology pinpoints the ways in which a citizen's precipitous decision to bear witness is shaped by the lived negotiation of its affordances and possibilities, as well as by its pressures and constraints.

The concept of citizen witnessing is a contested one, which is to acknowledge that it is socially and historically contingent in its inflection across diverse journalistic contexts. My effort to disentangle 'citizen' from 'witnessing', so as to rethink one in relation to the other, has similarly aimed to help establish a conceptual basis that is distinctive from more conventional approaches to citizen journalism. At stake, amongst other concerns, is the need to complicate some of the more pejorative dismissals of the individuals involved in newsgathering processes, particularly where it is alleged they are – virtually by definitional fiat – naive, untrustworthy or irresponsible due to personal motivations revolving around everything from reckless money-making to idle, frivolous spectatorship, or even gratuitous voyeurism, where crisis events are concerned. One need not believe that citizen witnesses are compelled by a singular desire to perform their civic duty to democracy to recognise the extent to which such contemptuous, folk devil-like stereotypes do so many of them a disservice. At the same time, my alignment of the word 'citizen' with 'witnessing' is intended to tease out some of the tacit tensions besetting journalism's investment in certain normative ideals, namely by calling for further consideration not only of the citizen as journalist but also the journalist as citizen.

Once again, familiar binaries buckle under the strain of keeping separate categories invoked, in the main, either for analytical convenience or for professional defensiveness. This book's exploration of the reportorial imperative of witnessing has sought to attend to its possibilities for reinvigorating civic engagement within democratic cultures as one way to overcome the limitations associated with these dichotomies. As important as I believe this is for heuristic purposes in journalism research, it is not the only reason. From one chapter to the next, these issues have been set against the backdrop of incidents around the globe where the nation-state's ideological appropriation of citizenship – from outright attacks on its legitimacy to the steady erosion of its protections, typically (and ironically) in the name of national security – has made journalism a site of struggle over one of the most vital of human rights, the right to bear witness.

Much work remains to further develop and operationalise citizen witnessing as a concept for journalism. It is my hope this book will serve to encourage efforts to elaborate upon its relevance, to enrich its explanatory potential, in ways that open up new opportunities for dialogue and debate about how best to improve the quality, depth and rigour of online news reporting in the public interest.

Notes

I 'Accidental Journalism'

1 Where news reporting of the Arab Spring is concerned, a number of well-respected journalists have posited this capacity to bear witness firmly within the realm of professional news reporting, for example BBC Radio 4's Justin Webb (2011). In arguing that 'good, old-fashioned reporting' of key developments performed by 'good, old-fashioned reporters' played a preeminent role, he insisted reporters are 'bearing witness to events in a way that cannot be replaced or seriously challenged by social media and "citizen journalists" or, indeed, by television pictures spewed out by an agency and voiced over in the comfort of a London edit suite' (2011: 2).

   Jon Leyne (2011), also working for the BBC to cover the uprisings, evidently concurs. In his words, 'for all the talk of the Twitter revolution, and the importance of social media, this has actually been a moment for the good old-fashioned foreign correspondent. Almost all the journalists who have broken the news have done it the traditional way, by being there long term, by making contacts and by knowing their subject.' Amongst the points to be explored in later chapters is precisely this tension between 'old-fashioned' newsgathering and recent innovations in citizen-led alternatives.

2 Anthony Shadid, a foreign correspondent for the *New York Times*, died from an acute asthma attack in Syria a week earlier. The paper's Executive Editor, Jill Abramson, wrote in an email to newsroom colleagues: 'Anthony died as he lived – determined to bear witness to the transformation sweeping the Middle East and to testify to the suffering of people caught between government oppression and opposition forces.' Former Executive Editor of the paper Bill Keller, similarly touched on the value of witnessing, posting on Twitter: 'Yes, a poet, but first and foremost an incomparable witness. Anthony Shadid, a New York Times Reporter, Dies in Syria' (both quotations were cited on the paper's blog, The Lede, on 17 February 2012).

3 Historical research by Margreta de Grazia (1992) into the use of quotation

marks in legal discourse, for example, reveals that they assumed their modern function – proclaiming that the words within quotes were accurately reproduced and correctly ascribed – by the end of the eighteenth century. Of particular import is the presupposition that words can be assignable, amounting to a conferral of ownership. 'A citizen or subject must be assumed to own words before being granted the right to keep them, even when it means withholding them from the legal process that seeks their disclosure', she writes; 'Ownership must also be assumed before written words are bracketed in proprietary markers' (1992: 554).

4 In searching for earlier uses of the term 'citizen witnessing', it soon becomes apparent that it seldom appears in discussions of journalism. In the handful of occurrences I have been able to identify, mainly in the blogosphere, it tends to be posited in contradistinction to citizen journalism. Typical in this regard is a short passage in a blog entry by Bill Doskoch (2007), which argues that video footage shot by 'a bystander with a digital camera' amounts to citizen witnessing, not journalism. 'Capturing one piece of information about an event is a building block of journalism', he writes, 'but taking a number of those blocks – some of which may be contradictory – and assembling them into a coherent, well-told story is where journalism starts.'

I have used the term in various places in my earlier work, including in *Online news: Journalism and the internet*, where I document how news organisations first began to refashion their online provisions to create spaces for ordinary citizens to bear witness about breaking news events (Allan, 2006). In *Digital war reporting*, my co-author Donald Matheson and I employ it when describing how news organisations seek 'to draw this burgeoning of citizen witness accounts within the news operation' in the reportage of crisis, such as violent conflicts and natural disasters (Matheson and Allan, 2009: 101).

Also worthy of note is Aryn Bartley's (2010) literary inflection of the term. In what proves to be a fascinating study, she explores 'citizen-witnessing narratives' in twentieth-century US literature, particularly the works of James Agee, John Howard Griffin and Grace Halsell, amongst others. More specifically, she theorises 'the ways citizen-witnessing narratives imagine the possibilities for the "good citizen" to act on her/his good will and to transform the workings of the professedly democratic state. Such texts model the ethical encounter – not as abstract and decontextualized – but as embodied in specific politically charged space' (2010: 14). On the notion of the 'good citizen' in this regard, see Michael Schudson (1998).

5 In this context, it is important to recognise the growing number of 'pro-am' (professional–amateur) collaborations concerned with 'real-time' newsgathering, such as the *Guardian*'s open source project, Storyful ('Storyful's team of professional journalists separate actionable news from the noise of the real-time web, 24/7') or MSNBC's BreakingNews.com. In the case of the latter, one of its editors states: 'Our goal is to empower the moment of

discovery', which is explained on the site's FAQ page as relying on a strategy whereby: 'Our editors scan wire services, live video feeds, RSS feeds, Twitter, YouTube and email alerts – using multiple screens at once! – to discover breaking news around the globe. News organizations send us tips by participating in our partner program, and their updates automatically appear in the "partner news" column. And you can help us discover breaking news reports by submitting links directly to our editors.'

Sites espousing an alternative ethos of crowdsourcing journalism include Ushahidi.com ('Ushahidi', the 'About us' page explains, means 'testimony' in Swahili, the site having been initially developed to map reports of violent incidents in Kenya – provided by citizen journalists – in the post-election crisis in 2008), as well as AllVoices.com ('Local to global news'), Demotix ('News by you'), GroundReport.com ('Democratize the media'), NowPublic.com ('Crowd Powered Media'), Spot.us ('Community-funded reporting'), amongst many others around the globe. Elsewhere, I have discussed citizen-led sites such as IndyMedia, OhmyNews and WikiNews in detail: see Allan (2006).

2 The Journalist as Professional Observer

1 'The conflict that is apparent in many Holocaust memoirs', Zoë Vania Waxman (2006) observes, 'is the attempt to bear witness to the Holocaust – while insisting on the uniqueness of the severity of the horror – at the same time ensuring that posterity *never forgets*, and therefore *never lets it happen again* by universalizing its importance' (2006: 182). She continues, describing how some Holocaust survivors, in assuming the identity of the witness, acquired a renewed sense of purpose. At the same time, she adds, 'their activities are inextricably mediated by the post-war comprehension or concept of the Holocaust and by the effects of testimony becoming a part of collective memory' (2006: 184). See also Bauman (1989), Frosh and Pinchevski (2009a), and Zelizer (1998).

2 In contrast with 'surveillance' (watching over), the term 'sousveillance' (watching from below) helps to capture further dimensions of these processes, notably the reverse tactics employed to monitor those in positions of authority 'by informal networks of regular people, equipped with little more than cellphone cameras, video blogs and the desire to remain vigilant against the excesses of the powers that be' (Hoffman, 2006; see also Bakir, 2010).

3 The emergence and consolidation of 'objectivity' in journalistic terms continues to attract considerable scholarly attention: see, for example, Donsbach (2010); Hartley (1992, 2010); Hampton (2010); Kaplan (2002, 2010); Mindich (1998); Schiller (1981); Schudson (1978, 2008).

4 'The Press is, for the purposes of democratic government, practically the sole education which the mass of the people at present has', F. H. Hayword and B. N. Langdon-Davies (1919) observe in their book *Democracy and the press*;

'Conscious of its power and responsibility it professes to make the effort to give the facts and to draw the inferences. The reader looks at the news and runs through the articles; if he [*sic*] is of an independent mind, he is critical about the articles and questions the inferences; it is the rarest thing in the world for him to question the facts. The result is an irresistible temptation for the newspaper controller to manipulate the facts so as to square them with the inferences he desires to draw' (1919: 4).

5 Lippmann further explored these themes in a co-authored study, 'A test of news', published in a special 42-page supplement to the *New Republic* in August 1920. Researched and written with Charles Merz, at the time Washington correspondent for the magazine, the study examined over 1,000 editions of the *New York Times* (from March 1917 to March 1920) with a view to ascertaining how it reported the Russian Revolution. Lippmann and Merz's (1920) analysis amounted to an indictment of the newspaper's coverage. In being 'nervously excited by exciting events', the *New York Times* had denied its readers access to the facts, and in so doing 'misled a whole nation'. Newspapers, they warned, should expect to come under increasingly intense supervision from their readers.

6 Relevant reviews here include Gruening (1922), Holcombe (1922) and Park (1922).

7 Reviews of Dewey's *The public and its problems* include Duffus (1927), Park (1929), Pepper (1928) and Smith (1929).

8 Indicative is Dewey's (1927) footnote in which he acknowledges an indebtedness to Lippmann 'for ideas involved in my entire discussion even when it reaches conclusions diverging from his' (1927: 116–17). Several journalism scholars have engaged with the 'Lippmann–Dewey debate' over the years, including Carl Bybee, James W. Carey, Daniel J. Czitrom, James Fallows, Hanno Hardt, Sue Curry Jansen, Robert W. McChesney, Jay Rosen, Michael Schudson and Mark Whipple. While I have focused here on certain features of this 'debate' in the 1920s, these contributions usefully inform a more sustained critique of its larger implications for journalism.

3 Bearing Witness, Making News

1 Similarly pertinent here was the previous day's edition of the *New York Times*, as it included a delayed report from Lawrence's colleague (and near-namesake) William L. Laurence. The front-page story, headlined 'US Atom Bomb Site Belies Tokyo Tales', reported on Laurence's visit to the 'atomic bomb range' in New Mexico where the 'first atomic explosion on earth' had taken place on 16 July 1945. In addition to listening to the 'expert testimony' of atomic scientists, members of a group of newspaper journalists and photographers witnessed for themselves the 'readings on radiation meters carried by a group of radiologists' on the test site. Such evidence, Laurence

reported in the account, provided 'the most effective answer today to Japanese propaganda that radiations were responsible for deaths even after the day of the explosion, Aug. 6, and that persons entering Hiroshima had contracted mysterious maladies due to persistent radioactivity' (*New York Times*, 12 September 1945). More specifically, it was the absence of radioactivity at the testing range, Laurence maintained, that allowed the US Army 'to give the lie to these [Japanese] claims' about lingering radiation in Hiroshima and Nagasaki.

Nowhere in this account is mention made of the fact that Laurence himself had been covertly working with the US War Department. Laurence was effectively on loan from the *New York Times*, at the request of General Groves, to be the Manhattan Project's official military spokesperson regarding pertinent events in the atomic bomb's development. For four months he wrote under conditions of strictest secrecy, which only began to be lifted the morning of 7 August, when news of the bombing of Hiroshima was announced. 'The world's greatest story was being broadcast', Laurence (1947) later recalled, 'and mine had been the honour, unique in the history of journalism, of preparing the War Department's official press releases for world-wide distribution. No greater honour could have come to any newspaperman, or anyone else for that matter' (1947: 187; see also Laurence 1946).

2 Life for the *hibakusha* in the years since the atomic attacks on Hiroshima and Nagasaki has been extremely difficult. Most have lived listless, broken lives, enduring medical symptoms that usually include chronic weakness and periods of intense lassitude (often making steady employment impossible). The lingering effects of radioactivity continue to this day, including in the bodies of those who were unborn in August 1945 but whose mothers were exposed to the after-effects. These people are prone to diseases and malformations (most notably leukaemia and other cancers, microcephaly, tuberculosis, liver cirrhosis and myopia, amongst many others) to a significantly higher extent than is prevalent in adjacent areas (see also Committee for the Compilation of Materials . . ., 1981; Lifton, 1967). Compounding the ongoing tragedy of these medical conditions was the stigmatisation of the *hibakusha* by those fearful of being somehow contaminated (literally or by association) in their presence. For years, the Japanese government refused to 'recognise' the afflicted, choosing instead to ignore their pleas for assistance, in part because it 'did not want to find itself saddled with anything like moral responsibility for heinous acts of the victorious United States' (Hersey, 1946: 92).

3 Further assessments of the strengths and limitations of citizen journalism, similarly directed toward generating public debate, include Beckett (2008), Gant (2007), Ghonim (2012), King (2010), Rosenberry and St John III (2010), Shirky (2008, 2010), Singer et al. (2011) and Turner (2010).

4 Reflecting on citizen camera witnessing ten years later, Friend (2011) writes: 'On Sept. 11, 2001, there was no such thing as a YouTube video.

Or a Facebook page. Or a Twitter feed. Cellphone cameras did not exist. Yet legions of people rushed to the site of the twin towers to document the attack and its aftermath. Their images, as much as those from stationary TV cameras or professional photographers, became our window onto the calamity. Meanwhile, countless others used their pagers, phones and PCs to enter firsthand reports of what things were like in Lower Manhattan. Thousands more, forwarding those accounts around the world, helped produce a people's chronicle of 9/11 that corresponds with – rivals, really – the record seen on television and in print.' What seemed so remarkable about citizen newsmaking that day, he adds, has become almost routine: 'Ten years after, we don't just expect a crowd-sourced profusion of digital images to accompany a significant event as it unfolds; for better or for worse, we demand it.'

5 'As best as anyone can figure, ABC affiliate WFAA in Dallas-Fort Worth obtained one of the first amateur videos of the falling space shuttle and had it on the air within 20 minutes', Brian Lambert (2003) reported. Soon after, 'Television coverage of the shuttle disaster followed what is now a familiar pattern. It moved steadily from indispensable, wide-ranging eyewitness reports and footage Saturday morning to near constant eulogizing (some good, much maudlin) and second-guessing punditry by Monday and Tuesday, interrupted only occasionally by fresh information.'

4 Witnessing Crises in a Digital Era

1 Sandy MacIntyre, Director of News for the AP Television News (APTN) agency, is quoted as stating: 'The growing number of people in the world who have their own cameras means that the very first thing we are going to look for is someone with a camera who was there and filmed it, because we cannot get there quicker than they did.' MacIntyre then added, 'all the pictures of waves hitting have been filmed by amateur cameramen', which meant APTN staff moved swiftly to identify citizens with pertinent imagery. 'We have been out actively seeking this stuff', he explained, 'with producers questioning every person they came across and staking out all the airports for people coming back from Colombo and Phuket.' In MacIntyre's estimation, at least ten clips of 'amateur footage' circulated amongst international broadcasters within the first five days following the catastrophe. 'Our guys in Colombo bumped into an English couple in their hotel and they showed them some great pictures', he said; 'This is how it has happened' (cited in the *Independent*, 3 January 2005).

2 Examples occurring around this time and shortly thereafter include citizen reporting of the French riots, the execution of Saddam Hussein (the audio-track of a prison guard's mobile-telephone recording being key) and a student's telephoned reports during the shootings at Virginia Tech University, amongst many others (see Allan, 2010c; Allan and Thorsen, 2009; Bakir, 2010; Beckett, 2008; Hanusch, 2010; Liu et al., 2009; Matheson and Allan,

2009; Russell, 2007; Sambrook, 2009; Wahl-Jorgensen and Hanitzsch, 2009; Wigley and Fontenot, 2009; Watson, 2011; Zelizer, 2012).

5 News, Civic Protest and Social Networking

1 Omar Amar cited by Channel 4 News (2011). This proved to be a salient point in the ensuing news coverage. 'The revolution has rippled beyond Tunisia, shaking other authoritarian Arab states, whose frustrated young people are often written off as complacent when faced with stifling bureaucracy and an impenetrable and intimidating security apparatus', Kareen Fahim (2011) observed in the *New York Times*; 'That assumption was badly shaken with Mr. Bouazizi's reaction to his slap, and now a picture of him, in a black jacket with a wry smile, has become the revolution's icon.' In the months since, however, doubts have arisen over the veracity of certain claims made about the events surrounding the famous 'martyr' credited with triggering the revolution. '[J]ust like the imperfections and flaws in Tunisia's subsequent "Jasmine" revolution, Mohamed Bouazizi's story is not quite the perfect metaphor that many have since written and talked about', the BBC's Wyre Davis (2011) contends; 'It seems that for some Tunisians, the 26-year-old martyr is no longer a political hero but a media creation, manufactured for the convenience of those – outsiders – who wax lyrical about the birth of the Arab Spring.'

Points of dispute concern whether Bouazizi was actually slapped by the police officer in question (she denies it), as well as the contention that it was a college student with the same name who posted online poetry and revolutionary song lyrics that served to inspire the people's revolutions. Still, few regard such disagreements as being significant, given the nature of the events that transpired in the aftermath.

2 Al Jazeera, self-described as 'the voice of the Arab street', distributed Flip video cameras to young Egyptians determined to engage in newsmaking, despite the risks for recipients. 'There simply are not enough journalists in the world to cover every event and so we have always relied on eyewitnesses; people who present us with facts, details of what has happened', explained Alan Fisher (2011), a senior correspondent for the network. In acknowledging that the term 'citizen reporters' often 'sits uncomfortably' with some of his colleagues, he contends that 'in its rawest form, the material provided is simply a commodity' that requires processing before it becomes 'real journalism' (2011: 156). At its best, however, their use of social media can help to fill 'the void, providing pictures and eye witness reports which allow organisations such as Al Jazeera to tell important stories which could have slipped by, ignored and unnoticed because access for traditional media was impossible' (2011: 157). Riyaad Minty, the network's head of social media, goes further, pointing out that it was the arrival of such imagery that alerted them that protests were underway. 'So not only did citizen journalism help Al Jazeera cover

the revolution', he concedes, 'it was actually the reason why Al Jazeera started reporting on Egypt in the first place' (cited in Mir, 2011).

3 Empirical studies of young people's mobile telephone use, particularly their generation of imagery, include Lillie (2011), Rantavuo (2008), Sarvas and Frohlich (2011) and Villi (2010); see also Buckingham and Willett (2009). *Guardian* journalist Paul Mason (2012) underscores how young people make the most of their status as a 'node' on a wider network, where mobile telephony is key. In 'the crush of every crowd we see arms holding cellphones in the air, like small flocks of ostriches, snapping scenes of repression or revolt, offering instant and indelible image-capture to a global audience', he writes; 'Cellphones provide the basic white sliced bread of insurrectionary communications: SMS.' It is SMS, he adds, that 'allows you to post to Twitter, or to microblogs, even if you don't have Internet access and can't read the results' (2012: 75). Similarly pertinent here is Alfred Hermida's (2012) description of Twitter as 'ambient journalism', that is: 'Ambient journalism posits that journalism itself has become omnipresent, like the air we breathe, due to the emergence and uptake of social awareness communication systems. Twitter is part of an ambient media system where users are able to dip in and out of flows of news and information from both established media and from each other' (2012: 673–4).

4 'Reading the riots', a *Guardian* – London School of Economics collaborative study, provides a number of important insights of value to this line of enquiry. Findings drawn from interviews with 270 people who took part in the disturbances in six cities reveal a range of perceptions regarding the factors behind the violence, with poverty being the most significant. 'Many said they were angry about perceived social and economic injustice, complaining about lack of jobs, benefits cuts and the closure of youth services', the study revealed; 'Just under half of those interviewed were students, and younger interviewees often expressed frustration over the increase in tuition fees and the scrapping of the education maintenance allowance' (Lewis et al., 2011).

A further dimension of the study examined a database of more than 2.6 million tweets (drawn from an assortment of riot-related hashtags, such as #EnglandRiots or #BirminghamRiots) in order to clarify the role of social media during the crisis. Contrary to many press reports, Twitter was seldom used by those directly involved, mainly because they considered the privacy afforded by the BlackBerry Messenger network to be vital. 'The internet and that is a bit too bait, so no one really broadcasts it on the internet', one Hackney rioter is quoted as stating; 'Like in Twitter there's like a hashtag innit, like if someone hashtags riots you can go to that certain page and see what everyone has been saying about the riots. Police could easily go to that page there and see who's been setting up or organising groups to come' (cited in Ball and Lewis, 2011).

A related analysis of how rumours circulated via Twitter – examples of which included: 'TIGER HAS BEEN LET OUT OF LONDON ZOO AND IS NOW LOOSE IN CAMDEN. NOT JOKING' and 'THEY'RE BURNING DOWN LONDON EYE!!!! THIS IS TOO MUCHH!!!!!!!!!!!' – similarly problematised claims made in the news coverage. Specifically, 'despite helping rumours spread at great speed, Twitter has an equal and opposite power to dispel them – often in the space of two or three hours, particularly if the counter-evidence is strong' (Richards and Lewis, 2011). A second phase of the study, involving interviews with police, court officials and judges, is underway.

5 'Coverage of Occupy has been mixed', Noam Chomsky (2012) later surmised; 'At first it was dismissive, making fun of people involved as if they were just silly kids playing games and so on. But coverage changed. In fact, one of the really remarkable and almost spectacular successes of the Occupy movement is that it has simply changed the entire framework of discussion of many issues. There were things that were sort of known, but in the margins, hidden, which are now right up front – such as the imagery of the 99% and 1%; and the dramatic facts of sharply rising inequality over the past roughly 30 years, with wealth being concentrated in actually a small fraction of 1% of the population.'

6 In February 2012, it was reported that the NYPD's Deputy Inspector Anthony Bologna was being sued by two protestors for his misuse of pepper spray. 'It is my hope that someday police will become the servants to the community that protect the rights of one and all', Horace Boothroyed III (2012) for Occupy Wall Street remarked on the blog Daily Kos at the time; 'Until then it is up to us to be citizen journalists and proactively use the courts and make these violations of enumerated rights . . . an actionable offense.' His advice was simple: 'do not forget to practice using the camera on your phone'. Particularly interesting to read in relation to these types of events is Ariella Azoulay's (2008) discussion of what she terms 'the civil contract of photography'.

6 WikiLeaks: Citizen as Journalist, Journalist as Citizen

1 On 31 August 2007, the *Guardian* become the first major news outlet to formally credit WikiLeaks by name. A news account written by Xan Rice (2007), headlined 'The Looting of Kenya', presented the findings of a 110-page 'secret report' commissioned by the Kenyan government. Alleged in the report was the 'breathtaking extent of corruption perpetrated by the family of the former Kenyan leader Daniel Arap Moi', with details that 'laid bare a web of shell companies, secret trusts and frontmen that his entourage used to funnel hundreds of millions of pounds into nearly 30 countries including Britain'. In the latter half of the *Guardian* account, Rice states that the report 'was obtained by the website WikiLeaks, which aims to help expose corruption', adding that it 'is believed to have been leaked by a senior government official upset about Mr Kibaki's failure to tackle corruption and by his alliance with Mr Moi before the presidential election in December'. Despite its central

role, no further mention is made of WikiLeaks in the item, nor did it figure in the related coverage of other Western media (beyond passing references from the AP and UPI news agencies). Brief mentions appeared in the African press – e.g. *Africa News* and the *Nation* (Kenya), respectively – which followed the *Guardian* in citing the website as a source. The site's self-declared intention to provide 'untraceable mass document leaking and participatory analysis' was noted, albeit without further comment.

2 The embargo period is a crucial element in the strategy, with Assange's remarks in an earlier interview explaining the rationale. 'It's counterintuitive', he said; 'You'd think the bigger and more important the document is, the more likely it will be reported on but that's absolutely not true.' In his view, it is all about supply and demand: 'Zero supply equals high demand, it has value. As soon as we release the material, the supply goes to infinity, so the perceived value goes to zero' (cited in Nystedt, 2009; see also Sreedharan et al., 2012). For further discussions of related strategies, see Assange (2011), Beckett with Ball (2012), Domscheit-Berg (2011), Leigh and Harding (2011), Sifry (2011) and the *New York Times* (2011). As one would expect, these accounts differ in places, revealing contradictions and inconsistencies, but together offer an array of invaluable insights.

3 Black continued: 'In my view, far from deserving condemnation for their courageous reporting, the *New York Times*, the *Washington Post*, and other newspapers should be commended for serving the purpose that the Founding Fathers saw so clearly. In revealing the workings of government that led to the Vietnam war, the newspapers nobly did precisely that which the Founders hoped and trusted they would do' (cited in *New York Times Co.* v. *United States*; see also Carey, 2011). In June 2011, with the federal government poised finally to release the Papers in their entirety, Ellsberg stated in an interview with the *New York Times* that there were 'still plenty of lessons to be drawn'. The Executive Branch, in his view, has been increasingly usurping the war-making powers of Congress. 'It seems to me that what the Pentagon Papers really demonstrated 40 years ago was the price of that practice', he stated; 'Which is that letting a small group of men in secret in the executive branch make these decisions – initiate them secretly, carry them out secretly and manipulate Congress, and lie to Congress and the public as to why they're doing it and what they're doing – is a recipe for, a guarantee of Vietnams and Iraqs and Libyas, and in general foolish, reckless, dangerous policies.' With respect to Bradley Manning, the alleged source of the WikiLeaks disclosures, he offered his praise. 'If he did what he's accused of, then he's my hero, because I've been waiting for somebody to do that for 40 years', he remarked; 'And no one has' (cited in Cooper and Roberts, 2011).

4 This was not the first time Assange resorted to this colourful turn of phrase. In an interview with Glenn Greenwald of Salon.com published several months earlier, he stated: 'so if you want to improve civilization, you have to

remove some of the basic constraints, which is the quality of information that civilization has at its disposal to make decisions. Of course, there's a personal psychology to it, that I enjoy crushing bastards, I like a good challenge, so do a lot of the other people involved in WikiLeaks. We like the challenge' (cited in Greenwald, 2010).

5 'I remember one of the things [Assange] said was that there was a problem when you put raw material on a Web site – each individual news organization says "Well we're not going to invest weeks trying to make sense of that, because for all we know, another media organization over the hill is already doing that. And two days before we're ready to go, they'll go, and all our effort will be wasted"', Davies added; 'He isn't just putting it out there for the sake of it. He's putting it out there because he wants the world to understand whatever the subject of the information is. And our operation has hugely increased that possibility' (cited in Hendler, 2010).

6 Silverman (2010) notes that Ben Smith of Politico.com offered further details about how the three news organisations approached the White House prior to publication: 'White House officials I talked to feel the *Times* was conscientious ... The administration was considerably less impressed with the *Guardian*'s outreach efforts – an administration official described their attempts to verify the reports through the White House and Pentagon as minimal. *Der Spiegel* reporters did a little better, requesting comments on a few of the reports, the person added.' Assange (2012), in an interview with Michael Hastings of *Rolling Stone* magazine, offered his take on the situation. With reference to Bill Keller, formerly of the *Times*, Assange stated: 'Keller also came out and said how pleased the White House was with them that they had not run WikiLeaks material the White House had asked them not to. It is one thing to do that, and it's another thing to proudly proclaim it. Why did Keller feel the need to tell the world how pleased the White House was with him? For the same reason he felt the need to describe how dirty my socks were. It is not to convey the facts – rather, it is to convey a political alignment. You heard this explicitly: Keller said, "Julian Assange may or may not be a journalist, but he's not my kind of journalist." My immediate reaction is, "Thank God I'm not Bill Keller's type of journalist"' (Assange, 2012).

7 See Anderson (1983) on the role of the press – or 'print-capitalism' – in the cultural projection of the nation as an 'imagined community'; and Zelizer (1993, 2010) on 'journalists as interpretive communities'.

7 'The Global Village of Images'

1 Concerns about an over-emphasis placed on speed are currently widespread, though few dispute they have long figured in journalistic assessments of foreign correspondence (see Allan and Zelizer, 2004; Cottle, 2009; Hoskins and O'Loughlin, 2010; Mirzoeff, 2005; Moeller, 2009a,b; Seib, 2010). 'As

a freelance journalist who spent 17 years overseas', Mary P. Nunan (2010) recalls, 'the US broadcast teams were by far the most egregious "parachute" journalists – dropping into a situation they knew virtually nothing about, covering it with the thinnest veneer of journalism, while relying on teams of local fixers and producers who do the actual legwork of journalism, before flying out again.'

2 An op-ed column by Roger Cohen (2011) of the *New York Times* illustrates this point – specifically, his claim that Tunisia represented 'perhaps the world's first revolution without a leader. Or rather, its leader was far away: Mark Zuckerberg, the founder of Facebook. Its vehicle was the youth of Tunisia, able to use Facebook for instant communication and so cyber-inspire their parents' (see also Kazamias, 2011).

3 The phrase 'Arab Spring' may well prove to be a 'mirage in the desert', Kate Smith and Ben McConville (2011) suggest. Adopting a similar line to Marsh (2011) above, they scrutinise the extent to which journalists elected to prioritise a 'simplified narrative which framed it as good vs. evil or tyranny vs. liberation rather than a more complicated idea about globalisation, demographic time bomb and the interconnectedness of the struggle over scarce and diminishing resources'. In their view, this latter narrative 'might ask too many questions about consumption in the West and its impact on others around the globe' (2011: 137). Considering it unlikely journalists were instructed to ignore the causes underlying events, they believe 'the rituals and self-censorship of newsroom cultures' warrant further attention in this regard.

4 In the view of John Mair (2011), a former current affairs producer, some correspondents 'suffered too much from "Rixos Hotel syndrome" named after the luxury hotel in Tripoli which the Gaddafi regime used to corral the foreign media for many months. There, the increasingly incredulous official spokesman Moussa Ibrahim "briefed" the assembled foreign media on how Gaddafi was winning the civil war right to and beyond the bitter end' (2011: 60; see also Mair and Keeble, 2011).

5 By this time, growing numbers of foreign correspondents were arriving in the city to document what was transpiring, including gruesome details of human carnage. Reflecting on questions of witnessing, Ruth Pollard (2011) of the *Sydney Morning Herald* related her experience at a warehouse on the outskirts of Tripoli that September. Once there, she found herself 'standing amid what was left of more than 50 people who had been killed, then burnt, by fleeing pro-Gaddafi soldiers'. She continues: 'The bodies – particularly the burnt ones – are not as confronting as you might think. It is the reaction of the living that lingers.' Two of the men accompanying her broke down in tears, weeping at the sight of so many bloated bodies on blood-soaked mattresses; 'To me it was the site of a massacre, evidence of crimes against humanity committed by retreating loyalist soldiers. To them it was something much more personal. After decades of Gaddafi rule, the cruelty he encouraged still shocked them.'

Driving back to Tripoli with them in silence, she thought about their respective perceptions: 'I knew I had crossed the line – I should have understood the cost to those witnessing such an atrocity, committed by their fellow citizens, on their own soil.' Left unspoken in this account is the obvious point that Pollard herself would seem to have become accustomed to encountering such horrific scenes when covering violent conflict. Still, 'despite the challenges', she concludes, 'it is a special privilege to bear witness to history'.

6 The importance of verification was underscored when scandal erupted over the blog 'A Gay Girl in Damascus' after it was revealed that the blogger in question, Amina Abdallah Araf al Omari, was actually a fictional character created by Tom MacMaster, a forty-year-old US citizen studying at Edinburgh University. Western media interest in the blog was understandable, Daniel Bennett (2011) points out in his analysis, namely because it was 'unusual and different, offering an alluring first-person glimpse into life in Damascus. Her blog personalised the potential for political and social change in Syria' (2011: 189). In other words, it was too good to be true, thereby offering a sober reminder of what can happen when face-to-face verification proves impossible.

References

Agence France-Presse (2008) Twitter, blogs provide riveting accounts of Mumbai attacks. 28 November.

Al Jazeera (2011a) Libya: The propaganda war. Al Jazeera Listening post. 12 March. www.aljazeera.com/programmes/listeningpost/2011/03/20113121012263363.html.

Al Jazeera (2011b) Images of revolution. Al Jazeera World. 19 October. www.aljazeera.com/programmes/aljazeeraworld/2011/10/2011101974451215541.html

Al Omran, A. (2012) Rami Al-Sayed, Syrian citizen journalist, is killed during attacks on Homs. National Public Radio, 21 February.

Allan, S. (2002) Reweaving the Internet: Online news of September 11. In B. Zelizer and S. Allan (eds.), *Journalism after September 11*. London and New York: Routledge, 55–74.

Allan, S. (2006) *Online news: Journalism and the Internet*. Maidenhead and New York: Open University Press.

Allan, S. (2007) Citizen journalism and the rise of 'mass self-communication': Reporting the London bombings. *Global Media Journal: Australian Edition*, 1(1), 1–20.

Allan, S. (2009) I-witnessing: Citizen journalism in times of crisis. Invited research lecture, Department of Media and Communications, London School of Economics and Political Science, 15 January.

Allan, S. (2010a) Journalism and its publics: The Lippmann–Dewey debate. In S. Allan (ed.), *The Routledge companion to news and journalism*. London and New York: Routledge, 60–70.

Allan, S. (2010b) Introduction: Recrafting news and journalism. In S. Allan (ed.), *The Routledge companion to news and journalism*, London and New York: Routledge, xxiii–xliv.

Allan, S. (2010c) Professionalism: Journalism without professional journalists?

References

In L. Steiner and C. Christians (eds.), *Key concepts in critical cultural studies*. Urbana: University of Illinois Press, 145–57.

Allan, S. (2012a) Civic voices: Social media and political protest. In P. Mihailidis (ed.), *News literacy: Global perspectives for the newsroom and the classroom*. New York: Peter Lang, 21–39.

Allan, S. (2012b) Journalism as interpretive performance: The case of WikiLeaks. In M. J. Broersma and C. Peters (eds.), *Rethinking journalism: Trust and participation in a transformed media landscape*. London and New York: Routledge, in press.

Allan, S. (2012c) Online news reporting of crisis events: Investigating the role of citizen witnessing. In E. Siapera and A. Veglis (eds.), *The handbook of global online journalism*. Oxford: Wiley-Blackwell, 331–52.

Allan, S. and Matheson, D. (2004) Online journalism in the information age. *Savoir, Travail et Société*, 2(3), 73–94.

Allan, S., Sonwalkar, P. and Carter, C. (2007) Bearing witness: Citizen journalism and human rights issues. *Globalisation, Societies and Education*, 5(3), 373–89.

Allan, S. and Thorsen, E. (eds.) (2009) *Citizen journalism: Global perspectives*. New York: Peter Lang.

Allan, S. and Thorsen, E. (2011) Journalism, public service and BBC News online. In G. Meikle and G. Redden (eds.), *News online: Transformation and continuity*. Basingstoke: Palgrave Macmillan, 20–37.

Allan, S. and Zelizer, B. (2004) Rules of engagement: Journalism and war. In S. Allan and B. Zelizer (eds.), *Reporting war: Journalism in wartime*. London and New York: Routledge, 3–22.

Allen, F. W. (1922) The social value of a code of ethics for journalists. *The ANNALS of the American Academy of Political and Social Science*, 101(1), 170–9.

Anderson, B. (1983) *Imagined communities: Reflections on the origin and spread of nationalism*. London: Verso.

Anderson, R. S. (2012) Remediating #Iranelection: Journalistic strategies for positioning citizen-made snapshots and text bites from the 2009 Iranian post-election conflict. *Journalism Practice*, 6(3), 317–36.

Angell, N. (1922) *The press and the organisation of society*. London: Labour Publishing Company.

Applegate, C. (2011) Tweeting the killing of bin Laden: How a little geekery and I (maybe) helped break a story, 4 May. Available at www.qwghlm.co.uk.

Arendt, H. (1990) *On revolution*. London: Penguin.

Ashuri, T. and Pinchevski, A. (2009) Witnessing as a field. In P. Frosh and A. Pinchevski (eds.), *Media witnessing: Testimony in the age of mass communication*. Basingstoke: Palgrave Macmillan, 133–57.

Assange, J. (2006) Conspiracy as governance. IQ.org, 3 December. http://estaticos.elmundo.es/documentos/2010/12/01/conspiracies.pdf.

References

Assange, J. (2010a) Defending the leaks: Q&A with WikiLeaks' Julian Assange. Time.com, 27 July.

Assange, J. (2010b) WikiLeaks founder Julian Assange on the 'war logs'. Spiegel Online, www.spiegel.de, 27 July.

Assange, J. (2010c) WikiLeaks founder Julian Assange: Transparent government tends to produce just government. Democracy Now, www.democracynow.org, 28 July.

Assange, J. (2010d) The truth will always win. *The Australian*, 7 December.

Assange, J. (2011) *Julian Assange: The unauthorised autobiography*. Edinburgh: Canongate.

Assange, J. (2012) Julian Assange: The *Rolling Stone* interview, conducted by M. Hastings. *Rolling Stone*. 2 February.

Associated Press (1991) Man beaten by police gets released from jail. *The Register-Guard*. 7 March.

Atal, M. R. (2011) How information travels. Instant Cappuccino, www.maharafi-atal.com, 4 May.

Atton, C. (2010) Alternative journalism: Ideology and practice. In S. Allan (ed.), *The Routledge companion to news and journalism*. London and New York: Routledge, 169–78.

Azoulay, A. (2008) *The civil contract of photography*. New York: Zone Books.

Bahador, B. and Tng, S. (2010) The changing role of the citizen in conflict reporting. *Pacific Journalism Review*, 16(2), 178–94.

Bakir, V. (2010) *Sousveillance, media and strategic political communication*. London: Continuum.

Balaji, M. (2011) Racializing pity: The Haiti earthquake and the plight of 'Others'. *Critical Studies in Media Communication*, 28(1), 50–67.

Ball, J. and Lewis, P. (2011) Twitter and the riots: How the news spread. *The Guardian*, 7 December.

Barkho, L. (2010) *News from the BBC, CNN, and Al-Jazeera: How the three broadcasters cover the middle east*. Creskill, NJ: Hampton.

Barnhurst, K. G. and Nerone, J. (1999) The president is dead: American news photography and the new long journalism. In B. Brennan and H. Hardt (eds.), *Picturing the past: Media, history & photography*. Urbana and Chicago: University of Illinois Press, 60–92.

Barron, D. (2011) Graphic Gadhafi images highlight changed news era. *Houston Chronicle*, 20 October.

Bartley, A. (2010) Encountering democracy: The citizen-witness in twentieth-century US literature. Unpublished Ph.D. thesis, Michigan State University.

Bartter, M. A. (1988) *The way to ground zero: The atomic bomb in American science fiction*. New York: Greenwood Press.

Bauman, Z. (1989) *Modernity and the Holocaust*. Cambridge: Polity Press.

Baxter, S. (2011) Colonel Gaddafi, the trophy corpse. *The New Statesman*, 21 October.

References

BBC Monitoring (2011) New media emerge in 'liberated' Libya. 25 February. www.bbc.co.uk/news/world-middle-east-12579451.

Beaumont, C. (2008) Mumbai attacks: Twitter and Flickr used to break news. *The Telegraph*, 27 November.

Beaumont, P. (2011a) The truth about Twitter, Facebook and the uprisings in the Arab world. *The Guardian*, 25 February.

Beaumont, P. (2011b) Reporting Libya: Freelance coverage, full-time dangers. *The Guardian*, 13 November.

Beckett, C. (2008) *SuperMedia: Saving journalism so it can save the world.* Oxford: Blackwell.

Beckett, C. with Ball, J. (2012) *WikiLeaks: News in the networked era.* Cambridge: Polity Press.

Bell, M. (1997) TV news: How far should we go? *British Journalism Review*, 8(1), 7–16.

Bennett, D. (2011) A 'gay girl in Damascus', the mirage of the 'authentic voice' and the future of journalism. In J. Mair and R. L. Keeble (eds.), *Mirage in the desert? Reporting the 'Arab Spring'.* Bury St Edmunds: Abramis, 187–95.

Bennett, L.W., Lawrence, R. G., and Livingston, S. (2007) *When the press fails: Political power and the news media from Iraq to Katrina.* Chicago: University of Chicago Press.

Bird, K. and Lifschultz, L. (eds.) (1998) *Hiroshima's shadows.* Stony Creek, CT: Pamphleteer's Press.

Black, S. (2008) Twitter fills the Myanmar/China media vacuum. 19 May, www.crikey.com.au.

Boaden, H. (2008) The role of citizen journalism in modern democracy. Keynote speech at the e-Democracy conference, RIBA, London, 13 November.

Boczkowski, P. J. (2010) *News at work: Imitation in the age of information abundance.* Chicago: University of Chicago Press.

Boltanski, L. (1999) *Distant suffering: Morality, media and politics.* Cambridge: Cambridge University Press.

Boothroyed III, H. (2012) NYPD Tony Bologna is sued by his victims. Daily Kos blog, 13 February.

Bostwick, C. F. (2003) Enhanced Columbia picture aids probe. *The Daily News of Los Angeles*, 8 February.

Boudreau, J. (2011) Occupy Wall Street, brought to you by social media. *San José Mercury News*, 4 November.

Boyer, P. (1985) *By the bomb's early light: American thought and culture at the dawn of the atomic age.* New York: Pantheon Books.

Brabant, M. (2008) Rebellion deeply embedded in Greece. BBC News Online, 9 December.

Bradley, T. (1992) Reaction. *The Los Angeles Times*, 30 April.

Breslin, S. (2011) Why we love the porn of war. Forbes.com, 20 October.

References

Bruns, A. (2005) *Gatewatching: Collaborative online news production.* New York: Peter Lang.

Buckingham, D. and Willett, R. (eds.) (2009) *Video cultures: Media technology and everyday creativity.* Basingstoke: Palgrave Macmillan.

Burchett, W. (1945) The atomic plague. *The Daily Express,* 5 September.

Burchett, W. (1983) *Shadows of Hiroshima.* London: Verso.

Burke, P. (2001) *Eyewitnessing: The uses of images as historical evidence.* Ithaca, NY: Cornell University Press.

Busari, S. (2008) Tweeting the terror: How social media reacted to Mumbai. CNN, 27 November.

Butler, J. (2009) *Frames of war: When is life grievable?* London: Verso.

Campbell, D. (2007) Geopolitics and visuality: Sighting the Darfur conflict. *Political Geography,* 26, 357–82.

Carey, J. W. (1969) The communications revolution and the professional communicator. Reprinted in E. S. Munson and C. A. Warren (eds.), *James Carey: A critical reader.* Minneapolis: University of Minnesota Press, 128–43.

Carey, J.W. (2011) American journalism on, before, and after September 11. In B. Zelizer and S. Allan (eds.), *Journalism after September 11.* London and New York: Routledge, 85–103.

Carr, D. (2010) WikiLeaks taps power of the press. *The New York Times,* 12 December.

Carter, C. and Allan, S. (2005) Hearing their voices: Young people, citizenship and online news. In A. Williams and C. Thurlow (eds.), *Talking adolescence: Perspectives on communication in the teenage years.* New York: Peter Lang, 73–90.

Carvin, A. (2011) Interview with J. Weiner, The art of the RT: NPR's Andy Carvin tweets the Libyan revolution. Vanity Fair.com, 24 February.

Castells, M. (2000) *The rise of the network society,* 2nd edn. Oxford: Blackwell.

Castells, M. (2007) Communication, power and counter-power in the network society. *International Journal of Communication,* 1(1): 238–66.

Castells, M. (2009) Of walls and flows: An interview with Manuel Castells. *Occupied London: An anarchist journal of theory and action.* Available at www.occupiedlondon.org/castells/.

Castells, M. (2011) *Communication power.* Oxford: Oxford University Press.

Caulfield, B. and Karmali, N. (2008) Mumbai: Twitter's moment. Forbes.com, 28 November.

Chalfen, R. (2002) Snapshots 'r' us: The evidentiary problematic of home media. *Visual Studies,* 17(2), 141–9.

Channel 4 News (2011a) Arab revolt: Social media and the people's revolution. Channel4.com, 25 February.

Channel 4 News (2011b) Journalist witnesses Syrian authorities torturing activists. Channel4.com, 25 October.

References

Chivers, C. J., et al., (2010) View is bleaker than official portrayal of war in Afghanistan. *The New York Times*, 25 July.

Chomsky, N. (2012) What next for Occupy? Interview with M. Kamil and I. Escuela for InterOccupy. *The Guardian*, 30 April.

Chouliaraki, L. (2006) *The spectatorship of suffering*. London: Sage.

Chouliaraki, L. (2010a) Journalism and the visual politics of war and conflict. In S. Allan (ed.), *The Routledge companion to news and journalism*. London and New York: Routledge, 520–32.

Chouliaraki, L. (2010b) Ordinary witnessing in post-television news: Towards a new moral imagination. *Critical Discourse Studies*, 7(4), 305–19.

Christensen, C. (2008) Uploading dissonance: YouTube and the US occupation of Iraq. *Media, War & Conflict* 1(2), 155–75.

Clarke, K. (2011) Punish the feral rioters, but address our social deficit too. *The Guardian*, 5 September.

CNN transcript (1991) *Crossfire*. Cable News Network, 6 March.

Cohen, N. and Stelter, B. (2010) Iraq video brings notice to a web site. *The New York Times*, 6 April.

Cohen, R. (2009a) A journalist's 'actual responsibility'. *The New York Times*, 5 July.

Cohen, R. (2009b) New tweets, old needs. *The New York Times*, 10 September.

Cohen, R. (2011) Facebook and Arab dignity. *The New York Times*, 24 January.

Cohen, S. (2001) *States of denial: Knowing about atrocities and suffering*. Cambridge: Polity Press.

Coker, M. and Dagher, S. (2011) Gadhafi forces seek to widen grip. *The Wall Street Journal*, 5 March.

Colvin, M. (2010) Our mission is to report these horrors of war with accuracy and without prejudice. Speech delivered at memorial service, St Bride's Church, London, 10 November. Available at www.stbrides.com/news/archives/2010/11/truth_at_all_costs.html#.

Colvin, M. (2012) Final dispatch from Homs, the battered city. *The Sunday Times*, 19 February.

Committee for the Compilation of Materials on Damage Caused by the Atomic Bombs in Hiroshima and Nagasaki (1981) *Hiroshima and Nagasaki: The physical, medical, and social effects of the atomic bombs*. London: Hutchinson.

Cooper, A. (2010) In the midst of looting chaos. AC360° Anchor blog, 18 January.

Cooper, M. and Roberts, S. (2011) After 40 years, the complete Pentagon Papers. *The New York Times*, 7 June.

Cottle, S. (2009) *Global crisis reporting: Journalism in the global age*. Maidenhead: Open University Press.

Cottle, S. (2011) Media and the Arab uprisings 2011: Research notes. *Journalism: Theory, Practice & Criticism*, 12(5), 647–59.

References

Cottle, S. (2013) Journalists witnessing disasters: From the calculus of death to the injunction to care. Special issue of *Journalism Practice*, forthcoming.

Cottle, S. and Lester, L. (eds.) (2011) *Transnational protests and the media*. New York: Peter Lang.

Couldry, N. (2012) *Media, society, world: Social theory and digital media practice*. Cambridge: Polity Press.

Dahlgren, P. (ed.) (2007) *Young citizens and new media*. London: Routledge.

Dahlgren, P. (2009) *Media and political engagement*. Cambridge: Cambridge University Press.

Darroch, V. (2000) The six million words a day man: the anonymous communicator. *Scotland on Sunday*, 13 August.

Davidson, R. (2003) It's a real kick in the teeth, just when we need it least. *The Sunday Herald*, 2 February.

Davies, N. (2008) *Flat earth news*. London: Chatto and Windus.

Davies, N. (2010) Afghanistan war logs: Story behind biggest leak in intelligence history. *The Guardian*, 25 July.

Davies, N. and Leigh, D. (2010) Afghanistan war logs: Massive leak of secret files exposes truth of occupation. *The Guardian*, 25 July.

Davies, W. (2011) Covering the 'Arab Spring' has been dangerous, exciting and unpredictable. In J. Mair and R. L. Keeble (eds.), *Mirage in the desert? Reporting the 'Arab Spring'*. Bury St Edmunds: Abramis, 48–55.

Davis, W. (2011) Doubt over Tunisian 'martyr' who triggered revolution. BBC News, 17 June.

De Grazia, M. (1992) Sanctioning voice: Quotation marks, the abolition of torture, and the Fifth Amendment. *Cardozo Arts & Entertainment Law Journal*, 10(2), 545–66.

Deggans, E. (2011) How the Rodney King video paved the way for today's citizen journalism. CNN.com, 5 March.

Denmon, D. (2011) 'Luck' led journalist to exclusive on JFK assassination film. WFAA, KENS5.com, 21 November. Available at www.kens5.com/video/featured-videos/134254893.html.

Desmond, R.W. (1984) *Tides of war: World news reporting, 1931–1945*. Iowa City: University of Iowa Press.

Deutsch, L. (2001) 10 years later, LAPD struggling. Associated Press, 2 March.

Dewey, J. (1922) Review of *Public opinion. The New Republic*, 3 May, 286–8.

Dewey, J. (1925) Practical democracy. *The New Republic*, 2 December, 52–4.

Dewey, J. (1927) *The public and its problems*. Athens, OH: Swallow Press.

Dolnick, S. (2008) Bloggers provide raw view of Mumbai attacks. Associated Press, 30 November.

Domingo, D. and Paterson, C. (eds.) (2011) *Making online news*. New York: Peter Lang.

Domscheit-Berg, D. (2011) *Inside WikiLeaks: My time with Julian Assange at the world's most dangerous website*. London: Jonathan Cape.

References

Donsbach, W. (2010) Journalists and the profession identities. In S. Allan (ed.), *The Routledge companion to news and journalism*. London and New York: Routledge, 38–48.

Doskoch, B. (2007) Actually, Mathew, it's citizen witnessing. Media, BPS, Film, Minutaie blog, 15 November. Available at www.billdoskoch.ca.

Duffus, R. L. (1927) Dewey on democracy. *The New York Times*, 23 October, 15.

Duffy, J. (2000) The amateurs capturing history. BBC News Online, 28 July.

Economist, The (2008) Rioters of the world unite. *The Economist*, 18 December.

Economist, The (2011) #Occupytheweb democracy in America blog. *The Economist*, 11 October.

Eddo-Lodge, R. (2011) Twitter didn't fuel the Tottenham riot. Guardian Unlimited, 8 August.

Ellis, J. (2000) *Seeing things: Television in the age of uncertainty*. London: I. B. Tauris.

Ellis, J. (2012) *Documentary: Witness and self-revelation*. London: Routledge.

Ellsberg, D. (2011) Why the Pentagon Papers matter now. *The Guardian*, 13 June.

Emerson, B. (1991) Video boom has spawned a new breed of citizen news-hounds. *The Atlanta Journal and Constitution*, 24 April, Section C, 1.

Evans, B. (1959) Improvisation in jazz. Liner notes for Miles Davis, *Kind of blue*. Produced by Irving Townsend, Columbia Records, CL 1355.

Fahim, K. (2011) Slap to a man's pride set off tumult in Tunisia. *The New York Times*, 21 January.

Farley, J. (2011) Observations of a jailed journalist. *Metro Focus*, 27 September.

Feis, H. (1966) *The atomic bomb and the end of World War II*. Princeton, NJ: Princeton University Press.

Fenton, N. (ed.) (2010) *New media, old news: Journalism and democracy in the digital age*. London: Sage.

Fisher, A. (2011) The 'Arab Spring', social media, and Al Jazeera. In J. Mair and R. L. Keeble (eds.), *Mirage in the desert? Reporting the 'Arab Spring'*. Bury St Edmunds: Abramis, 149–59.

Foley, J. (2011) Like battlefield tourists, Libyan rebels film the fight. The Global Post.com, 5 October.

Foucault, M. (1977) *Discipline and punish: The birth of the prison*. London: Penguin.

Foucault, M. (1980) Truth and power. In C. Gordon (ed.), *Power/Knowledge: Selected interview and other writings 1972–1977*. Brighton: Harvester Press, 109–33.

Fowler-Watt, K. (forthcoming) The storytellers tell their stories: The journalist as educator. Unpublished Ph.D. thesis, University of Southampton.

Fox News (2010) Administration calls war document leak illegal, harmful amid calls for probe. FoxNews.com, 26 July.

References

Friend, C. and Singer, J. B. (eds.) (2007) *Online journalism ethics*. New York: Armonk.

Friend, D. (2007) *Watching the world change: The stories behind the images of 9/11*. London: I. B. Tauris.

Friend, D. (2011) Seeing 9/11 through a digital prism. *The Wall Street Journal*, 29 August.

Frisch, A. (2004) *The invention of the eyewitness: Witnessing & testimony in early modern France*. Chapel Hill, NC: UNC Department of Romance Languages.

Frosh, P. (2006) Telling presences: Witnessing, mass media, and the imagined lives of strangers. *Critical Studies in Media Communication*, 23(4), 265–84.

Frosh, P. and Pinchevski, A. (2009a) Introduction: Why media witnessing? Why now? In P. Frosh and A. Pinchevski (eds.), *Media witnessing: Testimony in the age of mass communication*. Basingstoke: Palgrave Macmillan, 1–19.

Frosh, P. and Pinchevski, A. (eds.) (2009b) *Media witnessing: Testimony in the age of mass communication*. Basingstoke: Palgrave Macmillan.

Gallagher, I. and Farrell, S. (2011) Riot blaze: North London in flames as police cars, bus and shops burn over police shooting of 'Gangster'. *The Daily Mail*, 6 August.

Gant, S. (2007) *We're all journalists now: The transformation of the press and reshaping of the law in the internet age*. New York: Free Press.

Gayle, D. (2011) 'I killed Gaddafi', claims Libyan rebel as most graphic video yet of dictator being beaten emerges. *The Daily Mail*, 25 October.

Gebauer, M., et al. (2010) Explosive leaks provide image of war from those fighting it. *Der Spiegel*, 25 July.

Gemenis, R. (2008) Greece in turmoil: Riots and politics. OpenDemocracy, 10 December.

Gerodimos, R. and Ward, J. (2007) Rethinking online youth civic engagement: Reflections on web content analysis. In B. D. Loader (ed.), *Young citizens in the digital age*. London: Routledge, 114–26.

Ghanavizi, N. (2011) Political protest and the Persian blogosphere. In S. Cottle and L. Lester (eds.), *Transnational protests and the media*. New York: Peter Lang, 255–67.

Ghonim, W. (2012) *Revolution 2.0: The power of the people is greater than the people in power*. London: Fourth Estate.

Gillmor, D. (2006a) The decline (and maybe demise) of the professional photojournalist. CitMedia.org, 4 December.

Gillmor, D. (2006b) *We the media: Grassroots journalism by the people, for the people*. Sebastopol, CA: O'Reilly Media.

Gillmor, D. (2011) Rodney King and the rise of the citizen photojournalist. MediaActive.com, 2 March.

References

Gimbel, S. E. (2005) Q&A: How has Katrina affected online journalism? Conference news, Online News Association, 28 October. http://conference. journalists.org/2005conference/archives/2005/10/qa_how_has_katr.php.

Goldstein, M. (2006) The other beating. *The Los Angeles Times*, 19 February.

Gombrich, E. H. (1982) *The image and the eye*. London: Phaidon.

Gowing, N. (2009) Real-time media is changing our world. *The Guardian*, 11 May.

Green, J. (2010) *The eyes of the people: Democracy in an age of suspicion*. Oxford: Oxford University Press.

Greenslade, R. (2010) 'Data journalism' scores a massive hit with Wikileaks revelations. Greenslade Blog, www.guardian.co.uk, 26 July.

Greenslade, R. (2011) Why *Daily Record* was censured by PCC for using picture of a dead man. *The Guardian*, 25 October.

Greenwald, G. (2010) The war on WikiLeaks and why it matters. Salon.com, 27 March.

Greer, C. and McLaughlin, E. (2010) We predict a riot? Public order policing, new media environments and the rise of the citizen journalist. *British Journal of Criminology*, 50(6), 1041–59.

Greer, C. and McLaughlin, E. (2011) 'This is not justice': Ian Tomlinson, institutional failure and the press politics of outrage. *British Journal of Criminology*, 52(2), 274–93.

Gruening, E. (1922) Review of *Public opinion*. *The Nation*, 26 July, 97–8.

Guedes Bailey, O. and Cammaerts, B., Carpentier, N. (2008) *Understanding alternative media*. Maidenhead: Open University Press.

Gunter, J. (2011) 'Wherever there was news, we went': Libya's 'A-Team' fixers on getting the story out. Journalism.co.uk, 17 November.

Guynn, J. (2008) SoCal earthquake has everyone a-Twitter. *The Los Angeles Times*, 29 July.

Haberman, C. (2011) A new generation of dissenters. City Room blog, The New York Times, 10 October.

Habermas, J. (1989) *The structural transformation of the public sphere*. Cambridge: Polity Press.

Halleck, D. (1998) Perpetual shadows: Representing the atomic age. *Wide Angle*, 20(2), 70–6.

Halliday, J. (2011a) Libya calls western journalists 'al-Qaida collaborators'. *The Guardian*, 24 February.

Halliday, J. (2011b) London riots: Sky, ITN and CNN reporters attacked. *The Guardian*, 9 August.

Halliday, J. (2011c) Gaddafi death video: BBC defends use of 'shocking' images. *The Guardian*, 21 October.

Hammond, P. (ed.) (1997) *Cultural difference, media memories: Anglo-American images of Japan*. London: Cassell.

Hampton, M. (2004) *Visions of the press in Britain, 1850–1950*. Urbana: University of Illinois Press.

Hampton, M. (2010) The Fourth Estate ideal in journalism history. In S. Allan (ed.), *The Routledge companion to news and journalism*. London and New York: Routledge, 3–12.

Hänska-Ahy, M. T. and Shapour, R. (2012) Who's reporting the protests? Converging practices of citizen journalists and two BBC World Service newsrooms, from Iran's election protests to the Arab uprisings. *Journalism Studies*, 13, in press.

Hanusch, F. (2010) *Representing death in the news: Journalism, media and mortality*. London: Palgrave.

Hariman, R. and Lucaites, J. L. (2007) *No caption needed: Iconic photographs, public culture, and liberal democracy*. Chicago: University of Chicago Press.

Hartley, J. (1992) *The politics of pictures: The creation of the public in the age of popular media*. London and New York: Routledge.

Hartley, J. (2010) Journalism, history and the politics of popular culture. In S. Allan (ed.), *The Routledge companion to news and journalism*. London and New York: Routlege, 13–24.

Hassan, R. (1999) Globalization: Information technology and culture in the space economy of late capitalism. *Information, Communication and Society* 2(3), 300–17.

Hastings, D. (1991a) Without videotape, TV officials say beating would not have stood out. Associated Press, 6 March.

Hastings, D. (1991b) Man who shot beating video trying to cope with national attention. Associated Press, 27 March.

Haven, P. (2008) Greek-inspired protests spread across Europe. Associated Press Worldstream, 12 December.

Hayword, F. H. and Langdon-Davies, B. N. (1919) *Democracy and the press*. Manchester: National Labour Press.

Heath, A. (2008) Mumbai attacks: A defining moment for citizen journalism? Demotix.com, 28 November.

Hendler, C. (2010) The story behind the publication of WikiLeaks's Afghanistan logs. *Columbia Journalism Review*, 28 July.

Heneghan, T. and Apps, P. (2011) Is gruesome no longer taboo? Reuters.com, 21 October.

Hennessy-Fiske, M. (2011) Reporter recalls Kennedy assassination, interview with Zapruder. *Los Angeles Times*, 22 November.

Hermida, A. (2012) Tweet the news: Social media streams and the practice of journalism. In S. Allan (ed.), *The Routledge companion to news and journalism*, revised edn. London and New York: Routledge, 671–82.

Herrmann, S. (2008) Mumbai, Twitter and live updates. BBC News Online, 4 December.

Hersey, J. (1946/1989) *Hiroshima*. New York: Vintage Books.

References

Hesford, W. S. (2004) Documenting violations: Rhetorical witnessing and the spectacle of distant suffering. *Biography*, 27(1), 104–44.

Hobbs, R. (2010) Digital and media literacy: A plan of action. A White Paper on the Digital and Media Literacy Recommendations of the Knight Commission on the Information Needs of Communities in a Democracy. Washington DC: The Aspen Institute.

Hockaday, M. (2011) The challenges of reporting Gaddafi's death. The Editors blog, BBC News, 21 October.

Hocking, W. E. (1929) Review of *The public and its problems*. *Journal of Philosophy*, 26(12), 329–35.

Hoffman, J. (2006) Sousveillance. *The New York Times*, 10 December.

Hogan, M. J. (ed.) (1996) *Hiroshima in history and memory*. Cambridge: Cambridge University Press.

Holcombe, A. N. (1922) Review of *Public opinion*. *American Political Science Review*, 16(3), 500–1.

Holehouse, M. and Millward, D. (2011) How technology fuelled Britain's first 21st century riot. *The Telegraph*, 8 August.

Hope, T. (2012) War on the streets. *Photo Professional*, 64(February), 24–8. Available at www.16beavergroup.org/mtarchive/archives/002849print.html.

Hoskins, A. and O'Loughlin, B. (2010) *War and media: The emergence of diffused war*. Cambridge: Polity Press.

Hu, J. (2001) Home videos star in online attack coverage. CNET News, 12 October.

Huffington, A. (2009) Bearing witness 2.0: You can't spin 10,000 tweets and camera phone uploads. *The Huffington Post*, 13 July.

Human Rights Watch (2009) 'We are afraid to even look for them': Enforced disappearances in the wake of Xinjiang's protests. HRW, October. Available at www.hrw.org.

Human Rights Watch (2010) Libya: Stop blocking independent web sites. HRW, www.hrw.org, 3 February.

Huxford, J. (2004) Surveillance, witnessing and spectatorship: The news and the 'war of images'. *Proceedings of the Media Ecology Association*, 5, 1–21.

Ibrahim, Y. (2010) The non-stop 'capture': The politics of looking in postmodernity. *The Poster*, 1(2), 167–85.

Independent, The (2005) Immediacy of amateur coverage comes into its own. 3 January.

Inglis, F. (2002) *People's witness: The journalist in modern politics*. New Haven and London: Yale University Press.

International Press Institute (2012) Deadly trends for journalists in 2011. IPI, 4 January.

Ito, M. (2010) Lessons for the future from the first post-Pokémon generation. *Nieman Reports*, 64(2), 18–20.

References

Jacobs, R. N. (2000) *Race, media, and the crisis of civil society: From Watts to Rodney King*. Cambridge: Cambridge University Press.

Jacobs, S. P. (2010) New York Times strikes back at WikiLeaks founder. TheDailyBeast.com, 28 July.

Jarvis, J. (2008) In Mumbai, witnesses are writing the news. *The Guardian*, 1 December.

Jawad, R. (2011a) 'Tripoli witness' recounts life in hiding. BBC News, 26 August.

Jawad, R. (2011b) BBC's 'Tripoli witness' comes out of hiding. Interview transcript, National Public Radio, 31 August. Available at www.npr.org.

Johnston, R. J. (1963) Movie amateur filmed attack: Sequence is sold to magazine. *New York Times*, 24 November, 5.

Jones, J. (2010) Statement of National Security Advisor General James Jones on Wikileaks. Office of the Press Secretary, 25 July. Available at www.whitehouse.gov/the-press-office/statement-national-security-advisor-general-james-jones-wikileaks.

Jones, J. (2011) The west wrings its hands over dead Gaddafi photos, but war is always hell. *The Guardian*, 25 October.

Jurkowitz, M. (2003) Again on TV, riveting scenes and gathering of grief. *The Boston Globe*, 2 February.

Kahney, L. (2001) Who said the Web fell apart? Wired News, 12 September.

Kalter, L. (2011) Five websites where citizen journalists are documenting riots in London. International Journalists' Network, IJNet.org, 8 August.

Kaplan, R. (2002) *Politics and the American press: The rise of objectivity, 1865–1920*. Cambridge: Cambridge University Press.

Kaplan, R. (2010) The origins of objectivity in American journalism. In S. Allan (ed.), *The Routledge companion to news and journalism*. London and New York: Routledge, 25–37.

Karim, K. H. (2011) Covering Muslims: Journalism as cultural practice. In B. Zelizer and S. Allan (eds.), *Journalism after September 11*, 2nd edn. London and New York: Routledge, 131–46.

Kazamias, A. (2011) Covering the 'Arab Spring': Oriental revolutionaries in the mainstream Western media. In J. Mair and R. L. Keeble (eds.), *Mirage in the desert? Reporting the 'Arab Spring'*. Bury St Edmunds: Abramis, 139–46.

Keane, J. (2003) *Global civil society?* Cambridge: Cambridge University Press.

Keen, A. (2007) *The cult of the amateur: How today's Internet is killing our culture and assaulting our economy*. London: Nicholas Braeley.

Keller, B. (2010) The war logs articles. *The New York Times*, 25 July.

Kellner, D. (2002) New media and new literacies: Reconstructing education for the new millennium. In L. A. Lievrouw and S. Livingstone (eds.), *Handbook of new media*. London: Sage, 90–104.

Kemp, S. and Turner, M. (2011) London riots: Journalists under attack share stories from the front lines. *Hollywood Reporter*, 10 August.

References

Kennedy, L. (2008) Securing vision: Photography and US foreign policy. *Media, Culture & Society*, 30(3), 279–94.

Kennedy, L. (2009) Soldier photography: Visualizing the war in Iraq. *Review of International Studies*, 35, 817–33.

Khan, S. (2008) Twitter cause a little controversy after Mumbai attacks – What about Pakistan? Green & White, http://greenwhite.org, 27 November.

Khatchadourian, R. (2010) No secrets: Julian Assange's mission for total transparency. *The New Yorker*, 7 June.

Khiabany, G. and Sreberny, A. (2009) The Iranian story: What citizens? What journalism? In S. Allan and E. Thorsen (eds.), *Citizen journalism: Global perspectives*. New York: Peter Lang, 121–32.

King, E. (2010) *Free for all: The internet's transformation of journalism*. Evanston, IL: Northwestern University Press.

Kirkpatrick, D. D. (2011) Qaddafi brutalizes foes, armed or defenceless. *The New York Times*, 4 March.

Kirkpatrick, D. D. and Sanger, D. E. (2011) A Tunisian–Egyptian link that shook Arab history. *The New York Times*, 13 February.

Kitch, C. (2009) Tears and trauma in the news. In B. Zelizer (ed.), *The changing faces of journalism*. New York: Routledge, 29–39.

Komninos, M. and Vamvakas, V. (2011) December 2008 revolt media (Greece). In J. Downing (ed.), *Encyclopedia of social movement media*. London: Sage, 159–62.

Krüger, F. (2011) Dying all over the front pages. *Mail & Guardian* (South Africa), 28 October.

Kurasawa, F. (2009) A message in a bottle: Bearing witness as a mode of transnational practice. *Theory, Culture & Society*, 26(1), 92–111.

Kurtz, H. (1991) Video vigilante seeks reward. *The Washington Post*, 4 June, B1.

Kurtz, H. (2010) Air leaks from the WikiLeaks balloon. *The Washington Post*, 28 July.

Lam, A. (2008) Letter from Athens. *New America Media*, 16 December.

Lambert, B. (2003) Media column. *Saint Paul Pioneer Press*, 5 February.

Lasica, J. D. (2003) Blogs and journalism need each other. *Nieman Reports*, Fall, 57(3), 70–4.

Lasica, J. D. (2005) Citizens' media gets richer. *OJR: The Online Journalism Review*, 7 September.

Lasswell, H. D. (1925) Review of *The phantom public*. *American Journal of Sociology*, 31(1), 533–5.

Laurence, W. L. (1946) *Men and atoms*. London: Hodder and Stoughton.

Laurence, W. L. (1947) *Dawn over zero: The story of the atomic bomb*. London: Museum Press.

Lawrence, W. H. (1945) No radioactivity in Hiroshima ruin. *The New York Times*, 13 September.

References

Leavis, F. R. and Thompson, D. (1933) *Culture and environment*. London: Chatto and Windus.

Lee, J. (2000) Point, shoot and coin it. *The Times*, 4 August.

Lee, M. (2008) Blogs feed information frenzy on Mumbai attacks. Reuters, 27 November.

Leigh, D. and Harding, L. (2011) *WikiLeaks: Inside Julian Assange's war on secrecy*. London: Guardian Books.

Levey, N. N. and Martinez, J. (2010) WikiLeaks reflects new model for muck-raking. *Pittsburgh Post-Gazette*, 27 July.

Lewis, J., Inthorn, S. and Wahl-Jorgensen, K. (2005) *Citizens or consumers? What the media tell us about political participation*. Maidenhead: Open University Press.

Lewis, P. (2011) Riots: The week that shook Britain. *The Guardian*, 13 August.

Lewis, P., Newburn, T., Nall, J. and Taylor, M. (2011) English rioters warn of more to come. *The Guardian*, 5 December.

Leyne, J. (2011) The reverberating echo chamber: Beyond the spectacle. In J. Mair and R. L. Keeble (eds.), *Mirage in the desert? Reporting the 'Arab Spring'*. Bury St Edmunds: Abramis, 40–3.

Lieberman, J. (2010) Lieberman condemns leak of Afghan war materials, 26 July. Available at http://lieberman.senate.gov/index.cfm/news-events/news/2010/7/lieberman-condemns-leak-of-afghan-war-materials.

Lievrouw, L. A. and Livingstone, S. (eds.) (2002) *Handbook of new media*. London: Sage.

Life (1963) Split-second sequence as the bullets struck. *Life*, 29 November.

Lifton, R. J. (1967) *Death in life: The survivors of Hiroshima*. London: Weidenfeld and Nicolson.

Lifton, R. J. and Mitchell, G. (1995) *Hiroshima in America*. New York: Avon.

Lillie, J. (2011) Nokia's MMS: A cultural analysis of mobile picture messaging. *New Media & Society*, 14(1), 80–97.

Lippmann, W. (1920) *Liberty and the news*. New York: Harcourt, Brace and Howe.

Lippmann, W. (1922) *Public opinion*. New York: Free Press.

Lippmann, W. (1925) *The phantom public*. New York: Harcourt Brace.

Lippmann, W. and Merz, C. (1920) A test of the news. A Supplement to *The New Republic*, 4 August, 1–42.

Lister, M., Dovey, J., Giddings, S., Grant, I. and Kelly, K. (2008) *New media: A critical introduction*, 2nd edn. London and New York: Routledge.

Liu, S., Palen, L., Sutton, J., Hughes, A. L. and Vieweg, S. (2009) Citizen photojournalism during crisis events. In S. Allan and E. Thorsen (eds.), *Citizen journalism: Global perspectives*. New York: Peter Lang, 43–63.

Loader, B. D. (ed.) (2007) *Young citizens in the digital age*. London: Routledge.

Lodish, E. (2011) Gaddafi's end: How cell phones became weapons of choice. GlobalPost.com, 21 October.

References

Lotan, G. (2011) Breaking Bin Laden: Visualizing the power of a single tweet. blog.socialflow.com, 6 May.

Loyd, A. (2012) The cosmos has made a terrible mistake. *The Times*, 23 February.

Maclear, K. (1999) *Beclouded visions: Hiroshima–Nagasaki and the art of witness*. Albany: State University of New York Press.

Madrigal, A. (2010) Wikileaks may have just changed the media, too. *The Atlantic*, 25 July.

Mahr, K. (2009) Neda Agha-Soltan. *Time*, 8 December.

Mair, J. (2011) Behind the Sky scoop: The Libyan revolution and British TV news. In J. Mair and R. L. Keeble (eds.), *Mirage in the desert? Reporting the 'Arab Spring'*. Bury St Edmunds: Abramis, 59–64.

Mair, J. and Keeble, R. L. (eds.) (2011) *Mirage in the desert? Reporting the 'Arab Spring'*. Bury St Edmunds: Abramis.

Markham, T. (2011) Hunched over their laptops: Phenomenological perspectives on citizen journalism. *Review of Contemporary Philosophy*, 10, 150–64.

Marsh, K. (2011) The 'Arab Spring' did not take place. In J. Mair and R. L. Keeble (eds.), *Mirage in the desert? Reporting the 'Arab Spring'*. Bury St Edmunds: Abramis, 109–20.

Mason, P. (2012) *Why it's kicking off everywhere: The new global revolutions*. London: Verso.

Matheson, D. (2003) Scowling at their notebooks: How British journalists understand their writing. *Journalism*, 4, 2, 165–83.

Matheson, D. and Allan, S. (2009) *Digital war reporting*. Cambridge: Polity Press.

Matheson, D. and Allan, S. (2010) Social networks and the reporting of conflict. In R. L. Keeble, J. Tulloch and F. Zollmann (eds.), *Peace journalism, war and conflict resolution*. New York: Peter Lang, 173–92.

McAthy, R. (2011) 'It's gone viral': How a student's riot liveblog brought a million views in a day. Journalism.co.uk, 10 August.

McAthy, R. and Gunter, J. (2010) Wikileaks editor Julian Assange says there is 'more to come' after Afghanistan leak. Journalism.co.uk, 26 July.

McChesney, R.W. and Pickard, V. (eds.) (2011) *Will the last reporter please turn out the lights? The collapse of journalism and what can be done to fix it*. New York: The New Press.

McDermott, A. (2001) Amateur video plays prominent role in society. CNN transcript, *CNN Saturday Morning News* with M. O'Brien as CNN Anchor, 3 March.

McIntyre, J. (2010) WikiLeaks: Whistleblowers or info-terrorists? LineOf Departure.com, 27 July.

McNair, B. (2011) Managing the online news revolution: The UK experience. In G. Meikle and G. Redden (eds.), *News online: Transformations and Continuities*. London: Palgrave MacMillan, 38–52.

References

Meikle, G. and Redden, G. (eds.) (2011) *News online: Transformations and continuities*. London: Palgrave Macmillan.

Mellor, N. (2011) 'Why do they hate us?' Seeking answers in the pan-Arab news coverage of 9/11. In B. Zelizer and S. Allan (eds.), *Journalism after September 11*, 2nd edn. London and New York: Routledge, 147–66.

Messenger-Davies, M. (2010) *Children, media and culture*. Maidenhead: Open University Press.

Mihailidis, P. (2009) *Media literacy: Empowering youth worldwide*. Washington, DC: Center for International Media Assistance.

Mihailidis, P. (ed.) (2012) *Global perspectives for the newsroom and the classroom*. New York: Peter Lang.

Mindich, D. T. Z. (1998) *Just the facts: How 'objectivity' came to define American journalism*. New York: NYU Press.

Mir, M. (2011) Was Al Jazeera English's coverage of the 2011 Egyptian revolution 'campaigning journalism'? In J. Mair and R. L. Keeble (eds.), *Mirage in the desert? Reporting the 'Arab Spring'*. Bury St Edmunds: Abramis, 160–71.

Mirzoeff, N. (2005) *Watching Babylon: The war in Iraq and global visual culture*. New York and London: Routledge.

Mirzoeff, N. (2011) *Right to look: A counterhistory of visuality*. Durham, NC: Duke University Press.

Mitchell, A. (2010) Revealing the digital news experience: For young and old. *Nieman Reports*, 64(2), 27–9.

Mitchell, D. (2011) No, Twitter hgasn't replaced CNN. blogs.sfweekly.com, 3 May.

Mitchell, W. J. T. (2011) *Cloning terror: The war of images, 9/11 to the present*. Chicago: University of Chicago Press.

Moeller, S. D. (1999) *Compassion fatigue: How the media sell disease, famine, war, and death*. New York: Routledge.

Moeller, S. D. (2009a) *Packaging terrorism: Co-opting the news for politics and profit*. Malden, MA: Wiley-Blackwell.

Moeller, S. D. (2009b) *Media literacy: Citizen journalists*. Washington, DC: Center for International Media Assistance.

Moore, S. (2011) Yes, he had it coming, but did we really need to gloat like barbarians? *Mail on Sunday* (London), 23 October.

Morozov, E. (2008) The alternative's alternative. OpenDemocracy, 29 December.

Morozov, E. (2011) *The net delusion: How not to liberate the world*. London: Allen Lane.

Mortensen, M. (2011) When citizen photojournalism sets the news agenda: Neda Agha Soltan as a Web 2.0 icon of post-election unrest in Iran. *Global Media and Communication*, 7(4), 4–16.

Mortensen, M. (2012) The eyewitness in the age of digital transformation. In K. Andén-Papadopoulos and M. Pantti (eds.), *Amateur images and global news*. Bristol: Intellect, 61–76.

References

Moses, A. (2008) Mumbai attacks reported live on Twitter, Flickr. *The Sydney Morning Herald*, 27 November.

Mulhmann, G. (2008) *A political history of journalism*. Cambridge: Polity Press.

Mulhmann, G. (2010) *Journalism for democracy*. Cambridge: Polity Press.

Myers, S. (2010) How WikiLeaks is changing the news power structure. www. poynter.org, 27 July.

Myers, S. (2011a) How citizen journalism has changed since George Holliday's Rodney King video. www.poynter.org, 3 March.

Myers, S. (2011b) How 4 people & their social network turned an unwitting witness to bin Laden's death into a citizen journalist. www.poynter.org, 5 May.

Myers, S. (2011c) Why the man who tweeted Osama bin Laden raid is a citizen journalist. www.poynter.org, 5 May.

Neuman, J. (1996) *Lights, camera, war: Is media technology driving international politics?* New York: St Martin's Press.

New York Times, The (1920) Press agents and public opinion, 5 September, 3.

New York Times, The (1998) The Zapruder film. Editorial leader, *The New York Times*, 23 June.

New York Times, The (2011) *Open secrets: WikiLeaks, war and American diplomacy.* E-book.

New York Times Co. v. United States. Certiorari to the United States Court of Appeals for the Second Circuit. No. 1873. Argued: 26 June 1971 – Decided: 30 June 1971; Mr Justice Black, with whom Mr Justice Douglas joins, concurring. www.law.cornell.edu/supct/html/historics/USSC_CR_0403_0713_ZC.html.

Newman, K. (1999) *Millennium movies: End of the world cinema.* London: Titan Books.

Newsweek (2011) Tumblr post, 20 October. Available at http://newsweek. tumblr.com/post/11694030747/warning-this-is-video-of-muammar-gaddafis-corpse.

Nip, J. (2009) Citizen journalism in China: The case of the Wenchuan earthquake. In S. Allan and E. Thorsen (eds.), *Citizen journalism: Global perspectives.* New York: Peter Lang, 95–106.

Nunan, M. P. (2010) Compassion, self-congratulation and cynicism: Haiti and broadcast news, 16 January. Available at http://trueslant.com/.

Nystedt, D. (2009) Wikileaks plans to make the web a leakier place. ComputerWorld.com, 9 October.

O'Carroll, L. (2011) London riots: Photographers targeted by looters. Guardian Unlimited, 9 August.

O'Carroll, T. (2011) Cameras, livestreaming and activism at Occupy Wall Street. Video for Change blog, 8 November.

O'Connell, P. L. (2001) Online diary: Taking refuge on the Internet, a quilt of tales and solace. *The New York Times*, 20 September.

O'Hanlon, E. (2011) Seeing death as it happens brings cruel realities of war to the fore. *Sunday Independent* (Ireland), 30 October.

References

O'Neill, M. (2011) How YouTube is aiding the Libyan revolution. *Social Times*, 26 February.

Obama, B. (2011) Transcript: Obama announces the death of Osama bin Laden. Available at http://articles.cnn.com, 2 May.

Oborne, P. (2011) The moral decay of our society is as bad at the top as the bottom. *The Telegraph*, 11 August.

Oliver, K. (2001) *Witnessing: Beyond recognition*. Minneapolis: University of Minnesota Press.

Ostrow, J. (2003) With images hard to grasp, TV still conveyed tragedy. *The Denver Post*, 2 February.

Pantti, M. and Bakker, P. (2009) Misfortunes, memories and sunsets: Non-professional images in Dutch news media. *International Journal of Cultural Studies*, 12(5), 471–89.

Papacharissi, Z. A. (2010) *A private sphere: Democracy in a digital age*. Cambridge: Polity Press.

Park, R. E. (1922) Review of *Public opinion*. *American Journal of Sociology*, 28(2), 232–4.

Park, R. E. (1929) Review, *The public and its problems*. *The American Journal of Sociology*, 34(6), 1192–4.

Pasternack, A. (2010) The strange history of the Zapruder film. MotherBoard, 22 November. Available at http://motherboard.vice.com.

Peat, D. (2010) Cellphone cameras making everyone a walking newsroom. *Toronto Sun*, 1 February.

Pepper, D. (2008) India's media blasted for sensational Mumbai coverage. *Christian Science Monitor*, 24 December.

Pepper, S. C. (1928) Review, *The public and its problems*. *International Journal of Ethics*, 38(4), 478–80.

Perlmutter, D. D. (1999) *Visions of war: Picturing warfare from the stone age to the cyber age*. New York: St Martin's Griffin.

Peters, J. D. (2001) Witnessing. *Media, Culture & Society*, 23(6), 707–23.

Peters, J. D. (2009) An afterword: Torchlight red on sweaty faces. In P. Frosh and A. Pinchevski (eds.), *Media witnessing: Testimony in the age of mass communication*. Basingstoke: Palgrave Macmillan, 42–8.

Pew Research Center's Internet & American Life Project (2011) Social networking sites and our lives. Available at http://pewinternet.org/Reports/2011/Technology-and-social-networks.aspx.

Pfanner, E. (2011) Cameron exploring crackdown on social media after riots. *The New York Times*, 11 August.

Politkovskaya, A. (2006) A condemned woman. *The Guardian*, 14 October.

Pollard, R. (2011) Bearing witness to the horror and the hope of a nation reborn. *The Sydney Morning Herald*, 10 September.

Poniewozik, J. (2011) Did you need to see Gaddafi's corpse? *Time*, 20 October.

References

Poole, O. (2011) The good guys were for once saved. The bad guys beaten. In J. Mair and R. L. Keeble (eds.), *Mirage in the desert? Reporting the 'Arab Spring'*. Bury St Edmunds: Abramis, 18–35.

Poulsen, K. and Zetter, K. (2010) US intelligence analyst arrested in Wikileaks video probe. Wired.com, 6 June.

Powaski, R. E. (1987) *March to Armageddon: The United States and the nuclear arms race, 1939 to the present*. New York: Oxford University Press.

Power, N. (2011) There is a context to London's riots that can't be ignored. *The Guardian*, 8 August.

Preston, P. (2011) Boundaries are crossed as grim images of Gaddafi flood the media. *The Observer*, 23 October.

Pulitzer, J. (1904) The School of Journalism in Columbia University, 2006 facsimile reproduction: *The School of Journalism*. Seattle: Inkling Books.

Radio Free Asia (2009) Media strategy in Xinjiang. RFA, 16 July.

Rantavuo, H. (2008) *Connecting photos: A qualitative study of cameraphone photo use*. Helsinki: University of Art and Design Helsinki.

Reading, A. (2009) Mobile witnessing: Ethics and the camera phone in the 'war on terror'. *Globalizations*, 6(1), 61–76.

Rees, J. (2000) Snapshots that froze history. *Sunday Business*, 30 July.

Rentschler, C. (2004) Witnessing: US citizenship and the vicarious experience of suffering. *Media, Culture & Society*, 26(2), 296–304.

Rentschler, C. (2009) From danger to trauma: Affective labor and the journalistic discourse of witnessing. In P. Frosh and A. Pinchevski (eds.), *Media witnessing: Testimony in the age of mass communication*. Basingstoke: Palgrave Macmillan, 158–81.

Reporters Sans Frontières (2009) Concern about harsh crackdown following Xinjiang rioting. RSF press release, 8 July.

Reuters (2008) Protestors rule the web in internet backwater Greece. *Reuters Global News Journal*, 18 December.

Rhodes, R. (1986) *The making of the atomic bomb*. New York: Touchstone / Simon and Schuster.

Rice, X. (2007) The looting of Kenya. *The Guardian*, 31 August.

Richards, B. (2010) News and the emotional public sphere. In S. Allan (ed.), *The Routledge companion to news and journalism*. London and New York: Routledge, 301–11.

Richards, J. and Lewis, P. (2011) How Twitter was used to spread – and knock down – rumours during the riots. *The Guardian*, 7 December.

Riegert, K., Hellman, M., Robertson, A. and Mral, B. (2010) *Transnational and national media in global crisis: The Indian Ocean tsunami*. Creskill, NJ: Hampton.

Robinson, S. (2009) 'If you had been with us': Mainstream press and citizen journalists jockey for authority over the collective memory of Hurricane Katrina. *New Media and Society*, 11(5), 795–814.

References

Robinson, S. and DeShano, C. (2011) Citizen journalists and their third places; What makes people exchange information online (or not). *Journalism Studies* 12(5): 642–57.

Rockow, L. (1926) Review of *The phantom public*. *The Nation*, 19 May, 556–7.

Rodríguez, C. (2011) *Citizens' media against armed conflict: Disrupting violence in Colombia*. Minneapolis: University of Minnesota Press.

Rosen, J. (2006) The people formerly known as the audience. Pressthink.org, 27 June.

Rosen, J. (2010a) The Afghanistan war logs released by Wikileaks, the world's first stateless news organization. Pressthink.org, 26 July.

Rosen, L. (2010b) Understanding the iGeneration: Before the next mini-generation arrives. *Nieman Reports*, 64(2), 24–6.

Rosenberry, J. and St. John III, B. (eds.) (2010) *Public journalism 2.0: The promise and reality of a citizen-engaged press*. New York and London: Routledge.

Rosoff, M. (2011) Twitter just had its CNN moment. *Business Insider*, 2 May.

Rubin, S. (1991) The home video news amateurs' tapes get on TV. *The San Franciso Chronicle*, 3 April, B3.

Russell, A. (2007) Digital communication networks and the journalistic field: the 2005 French riots. *Critical Studies in Media Communication* 24(4): 285–302.

RWB (2011) Countries under surveillance: Libya. Reporters Without Borders http://en.rsf.org/surveillance-libya,39717.html.

S, A. (2008) Eye witness from Thessaloniki. OpenDemocracy, 12 December.

Said, E. (1977) *Orientalism*. London: Penguin.

Said, E. (1990) Islam through Western eyes. *The Nation*, 26 April.

Said, E. (1997) *Covering Islam: How the media and the experts determine how we see the rest of the world*, 2nd edn. London: Vintage.

Sambrook, R. (2009) Citizen journalism. In J. Owen and H. Purdey (eds.), *International news reporting*. Oxford: Wiley-Blackwell, 220–42.

Sandels, A. (2011) LIBYA: Amateur video footage purportedly depicts battle scenes in Zawiyais. *The Los Angeles Times*, 24 February. Available at http://latimesblogs.latimes.com.

Sarvas, R. and Frohlich, D. M. (2011) *From snapshots to social media – The changing picture of domestic photography*. London: Springer.

Schechter, D. (2005) Helicopter journalism. Mediachannel.org, 5 January.

Schiller, D. (1981) *Objectivity and the news*. Philadelphia: University of Pennsylvania Press.

Schmidt, T. S. (2007) A Wiki for whistle-blowers. *Time*, 22 January.

Schudson, M. (1978) *Discovering the news: A social history of American newspapers*. New York: Basic Books.

References

Schudson, M. (1998) *The good citizen: A history of American civic life*. New York: Free Press.

Schudson, M. (2008) *Why democracies need an unlovable press*. Cambridge: Polity Press.

Sefton-Green, J. (eds.) (1998) *Digital diversions: Youth culture in the age of multimedia*. London: UCL Press.

Seib, P. (2010). News and foreign policy: Defining influence, balancing power. In S. Allan (ed.), *The Routledge companion to news and journalism*. London and New York: Routledge, 533–41.

Shalett, S. (1945) First atomic bomb dropped on Japan. *The New York Times*, 7 August.

Shanbhag, A. (2008) Mumbai blasts: Taj burning: More pics from terrorist killing. 26 November. Available at http://arunshanbhag.com/tag/taj-burning/.

Shirky, C. (2008) *Here comes everybody: The power of organizing without organizations*. New York: Allen Lane.

Shirky, C. (2010) *Cognitive surplus: Creativity and generosity in a connected age*. New York: Allen Lane.

Shukri, M. (2011) How social media gets information to Libyan population. BBC News Online, 22 February.

Siegel, J. (2011) Witnessing war: Blogs from soldiers in Iraq and Afghanistan. Media@LSE Electronic M.Sc. Dissertation Series. London: LSE.

Sifry, M. L. (2011) *WikiLeaks and the age of transparency*. Berkeley, CA: Counterpoint.

Silverman, C. (2010) How WikiLeaks outsourced the burden of verification. *Columbia Journalism Review*, 30 July.

Silverstone, R. (2006) *Media and morality*. Cambridge: Polity Press.

Sinclair, U. (1920) *The brass check: A study of American journalism*. Pasadena, CA.

Singer, J. B., Hermida, A., Domingo, D., et al. (2011) *Participatory journalism: Guarding the open gates at online newspapers*. Malden, MA: Wiley-Blackwell.

Smith, K. and McConville, B. (2011) How the media marginalised the economic roots of the 'Arab Spring'. In J. Mair and R. L. Keeble (eds.), *Mirage in the desert? Reporting the 'Arab Spring'*. Bury St Edmunds: Abramis, 128–38.

Smith, T.V. (1929) Review of *The public and its problems*. *The Philosophical Review*, 38(2), 177–80.

Smith-Spark, L. (2011) Graphic images capture Gadhafi's final moments. CNN, 20 October.

Snickars, P. and Vonderau, P. (eds.) (2009) *The YouTube reader*. Stockholm: National Library of Sweden.

Snow, J. (2005) Nothing beats the reporter on the spot. *The Guardian*, 21 November.

Snow, J. (2011) The golden age of journalism. *Port Magazine*, March.

References

Sontag, S. (1977) *On photography*. London: Penguin.

Sontag, S. (2003) *Regarding the pain of others*. London: Penguin.

Sontag, S. (2004) *Regarding the torture of others*. *New York Times Magazine*, 23 May.

Sonwalkar, P. (2009) Byte by byte: Journalism's growing potential to reflect the idea of India. *Journalism: Theory, Practice and Criticism*, 10(3), 374–6.

Sreedharan, C., Thorsen, E. and Allan, S. (2012) WikiLeaks and the changing forms of information politics in the network society. In E. Downey and M. A. Jones (eds.), *Public service, governance and Web 2.0 technologies: Future trends in social media*. Hershey PA: IGI Global, 167–80.

Stack, G. (2009) 'Twitter revolution' Moldovan activist goes into hiding. *The Guardian*, 15 April.

Stanley, A. (2010) Broadcast coverage: Compassion and self-congratulation. *The New York Times*, 16 January.

Stelter, B. (2011) How the Bin Laden announcement leaked out. Media Decoder Blog, *The New York Times*, 1 May.

Stelter, B. and Cohen, N. (2008) Citizen journalists provided glimpses of Mumbai attacks. *The New York Times*, 29 November.

Stirland, S. L. (2008) As TV networks focus on Mumbai landmarks, local captures ground shots on Flickr. Wired.com, 27 November.

Stolley, R. B. (1998) Zapruder Rewound. *Life*, 21(10), September.

Strangelove, M. (2010) *Watching YouTube: Extraordinary videos by ordinary people*. Toronto: University of Toronto Press.

Stray, J. (2010) Is this the future of journalism? *Foreign Policy*, 7 April.

Strom, S. (2010) Pentagon sees a threat from online muckrakers. *The New York Times*, 17 March.

Strunsky, S. (1925) Government by the people. *The New York Times*, 25 October, BR1.

Stuffco, J. (2008) Mumbai crisis put 'citizen journalists' in spotlight. CTV.ca, 28 November.

Sturken, M. (2007) *Tourists of history: Memory, kitsch, and consumerism from Oklahoma City to ground zero*. Durham and London: Duke University Press.

Sweeney, C.W. with Antonucci, J. A. and Antonucci, M. K. (1997) *War's end: An eyewitness account of America's last atomic mission*. New York: Avon Books.

Sydney Morning Herald (2012) Editorial: The death of a witness. 24 February, 12.

Tait, R. and Weaver, M. (2009) How Neda Agha-Soltan became the face of Iran's struggle. *The Guardian*, 22 June.

Tait, S. (2011) Bearing witness, journalism and moral responsibility. *Media, Culture & Society*, 33(8), 1220–35.

Taubert, E. (2012) So, you're still using the phrase citizen-journalism. Dailycrowdsource.com, 14 May.

References

Tester, K. (2001) *Compassion, morality and the media.* Buckingham: Open University Press.

Thiessen, M. (2010) WikiLeaks must be stopped. *The Washington Post,* 3 August.

Thurman, N. (2008) Forums for citizen journalists? Adoption of user generated content initiatives by online news media. *New Media & Society,* 10(1), 139–57.

Thussu, D. (2009) Turning terrorism into a soap opera. *British Journalism Review,* 20(1), 13–18.

Topol. S. A. (2011) This is how you start a war: Libya's frantic flight for the future. *Gentleman's Quarterly,* June. www.gq-magazine.co.uk.

Townend, J. (2009) Difficult to get western media attention on Kenyan killings and disappearances, says WikiLeaks editor. Journalism.co.uk, 5 June.

Trice, M. (2011) Frontline history is not war porn. Partisans.org, 21 October.

Tsimas, P. (2008) Transcript of speech to Global Forum for Media Development, posted by Andrew Lam on 'Chez Andrew'. New America Media blog, 10 December.

Tumber, H. (2010) Journalists and war crimes. In S. Allan (ed.), *The Routledge companion to news and journalism.* London and New York: Routledge, 533–41.

Turkle, S. (2011) *Alone together: Why we expect more from technology and less from each other.* New York: Basic Books.

Turner, G. (2010) *Ordinary people and the media.* London: Sage.

Vågnes, Ø. (2011) *Zaprudered: The Kennedy assassination in visual culture.* Austin, TX: University of Austin Press.

Vande Berg, L. R. (1995) Living room pilgrimages: Television's cyclical commemoration of the assassination anniversary of John F. Kennedy. *Communication Monographs,* 62, 47–64.

Villi, M. (2010) *Visual mobile communication: Camera phone photo messages as ritual communication and mediated presence.* Aalto: Aalto University School of Art and Design.

Vis, F. (2009) Wikinews reporting of Hurricane Katrina. In S. Allan and E. Thorsen (eds.), *Citizen journalism: Global perspectives.* New York: Peter Lang, 65–74.

Wahl-Jorgensen, K. and Hanitzsch, T. (eds.) (2009) *Handbook of journalism studies,* London and New York: Routledge.

Wallace, S. (2009) Watchdog or witness? The emerging forms and practices of videojournalism. *Journalism,* 10, 5, 684–701.

Warnick, B. (2002) *Critical literacy in a digital era.* Mahwah, NJ: Lawrence Erlbaum.

Washbrook, C. (2011) Online journalist Mohammed Nabbous killed in Libya. The SpyReport, 20 March. Available at www.mediaspy.org.

Watson, H. (2011) Preconditions for citizen journalism: A sociological assessment. Sociological Research Online, 16(3) 6.

References

Waxman, Z.V. (2006) *Writing the Holocaust: Identity, testimony, representation.* Oxford: Oxford University Press.

Weart, S. R. (1988). *Nuclear fear: A history of images.* Cambridge, MA, and London: Harvard University Press.

Webb, J. (2011) Why the job of the journalist remains so vital today. In J. Mair and R. L. Keeble (eds.), *Mirage in the desert? Reporting the 'Arab Spring'.* Bury St Edmunds: Abramis, 1–3.

Weber, M. (1919) Politics as a vocation. In D. Owen and T. B. Strong (eds.) (2004) *The vocation lectures*, trans. by R. Livingstone. Indianapolis, IN: Hackett, 32–94.

Weine, S. (2006) *Testimony after catastrophe.* Evanston, IL: Northwestern University Press.

Weller, G. (2006) *First into Nagasaki.* New York: Three Rivers Press.

Wigley, S. and Fontenot, M. (2009) Where media turn during crises: A look at information subsidies and the Virginia Tech shootings. *Electronic News*, 3(2), 94–108.

Willey, M. W. (1926) Review of *The phantom public*. *Social Forces*, 4(4), 854–8.

Williams, J. (2012) When journalism comes under fire. BBC News Online, The Editors blog, 21 February.

Williams, R. (1963) *Culture and society, 1780–1950.* Harmondsworth: Penguin.

Wines, M. (2009) In latest upheaval, China applies new strategies to control flow of information. *The New York Times*, 6 July.

Witherow, J. (2012) Letter to staff. *The Times*, 22 February.

Wolfe, A. (2008) Twitter in controversial spotlight amid Mumbai attacks. *Information Week*, 29 November.

Wolff, M. (2010) Can WikiLeaks save journalism? Newser.com, 27 July.

Woodward, R. B. (2003) The 40th anniversary of a 26-second reel. *The New York Times*, 16 November.

Wrone, D. R. (2003) *The Zapruder film: Reframing Kennedy's assassination.* Lawrence: University Press of Kansas.

Zelizer, B. (1992) Covering the body: The Kennedy assassination, the media, and the shaping of collective memory. Chicago, IL: University of Chicago Press.

Zelizer, B (1993) Journalists as interpretive communities. *Critical Studies in Mass Communication,* 10(3), 219–37.

Zelizer, B. (1998) *Remembering to forget: Holocaust memory through the camera's eye.* Chicago: University of Chicago Press.

Zelizer, B. (2002a) Photography, journalism, trauma. In B. Zelizer and S. Allan (eds.), *Journalism after September 11.* London and New York: Routledge, 48–68.

Zelizer, B. (2002b) Finding aids to the past: Bearing personal witness to traumatic public events. *Media, Culture & Society*, 24, 697–714.

Zelizer, B. (2005) Journalism through the camera's eye. In S. Allan (ed.), *Journalism: Critical issues.* Maidenhead: Open University Press, 167–76.

References

Zelizer, B. (2007) On 'having been there': 'Eyewitnessing' as a journalistic key word. *Critical Studies in Media Communication*, 24(5), 408–28.

Zelizer, B. (2010) *About to die: How news images move the public.* New York: Oxford University Press.

Zelizer, B. (2012) Journalists as interpretive communities, revisited. In S. Allan (ed.), *The Routledge companion to news and journalism*, revised edn. London and New York: Routledge, 181–90.

Zelizer, B. and Allan, S. (eds.) (2011) *Journalism after September 11*, 2nd edn. London and New York: Routledge.

Index

Index

247

Index

Index

Index

Index

Weller, George 66–7
whistle blower 24, 152–6, 164,
    166–8, 172–5
WikiLeaks 24, 152–73, 182, 215–17
Wikinews 209
Wikipedia 114, 117, 154–5
Wikis 9, 94, 123, 154, 155
Wired 110, 161
witness-ambassador 37–8

You Witness News 109
Your News (BBC) 109
YouTube 68, 109, 114, 121, 131,
    133, 135, 136, 141, 148, 157,
    181, 186, 190, 191, 200, 202,
    203, 209, 211

Zapruder, Abraham 22, 59, 67,
    68–75, 82, 84–5